The Restoration of Messianic Hope

The Restoration of Messianic Hope

The Resurrection of Jesus in the Literary Context of Matthew's Prologue

BRIAN MAIN

◥PICKWICK *Publications* • Eugene, Oregon

THE RESTORATION OF MESSIANIC HOPE
The Resurrection of Jesus in the Literary Context of Matthew's Prologue

Copyright © 2025 Brian Main. All rights reserved. Except for brief quotations in critical publications or reviews, no part of this book may be reproduced in any manner without prior written permission from the publisher. Write: Permissions, Wipf and Stock Publishers, 199 W. 8th Ave., Suite 3, Eugene, OR 97401.

Pickwick Publications
An Imprint of Wipf and Stock Publishers
199 W. 8th Ave., Suite 3
Eugene, OR 97401

www.wipfandstock.com

PAPERBACK ISBN: 979-8-3852-3687-9
HARDCOVER ISBN: 979-8-3852-3688-6
EBOOK ISBN: 979-8-3852-3689-3

Cataloguing-in-Publication data:

Names: Main, Brian, author.

Title: The restoration of messianic hope : the resurrection of Jesus in the literary context of Matthew's prologue / Brian Main.

Description: Eugene, OR: Pickwick Publications, 2025. | Includes bibliographical references.

Identifiers: ISBN 979-8-3852-3687-9 (paperback). | ISBN 979-8-3852-3688-6 (hardcover). | ISBN 979-8-3852-3689-3 (ebook).

Subjects: LCSH: Bible—Matthew—Criticism, interpretation, etc. | Jesus Christ—Resurrection.

Classification: BS2575.2 M35 2025 (print). | BS2575.2 (epub).

VERSION NUMBER 06/19/25

Unless otherwise indicated, all Scripture quotations are the author's own translations.

To Beth

Your love, faith, and patience have been constant reminders of the hope we share because of Jesus' resurrection.

Contents

Preface | ix

Acknowledgments | xi

Abbreviations of Ancient Sources | xiii

1. The Methodology of Narrative Criticism | 1
2. Verbal and Conceptual Similarities Between Matthew's Prologue and Resurrection Narrative | 34
3. Characterization Part One: Introduction and Jesus the Messiah | 58
4. Characterization Part Two: Other Characters in Matthew's Prologue and Resurrection Narrative | 86
5. Settings | 122
6. Plot | 152
7. Point of View | 176
8. Conclusions | 191

Bibliography | 199

Preface

This book is a slightly revised and updated version of the PhD dissertation I completed at The Catholic University of America. It is the fruit, however, of more than a season of academic inquiry. It began during my time as a student at Covenant Theological Seminary, when a friend asked, with maybe a frustrated tone, why evangelical preaching of the gospel made so little of Jesus' resurrection. My response probably left him even more frustrated, since I did not understand why the resurrection should deserve more attention.

Although I had quickly dismissed my friend's question that day, his question never left me. Years later, when I was reading the Book of Acts, his question prompted me to pay special attention to the content of the apostles' evangelistic preaching. I was struck by their consistent emphasis on and explanation of the resurrection of Jesus—an emphasis that outweighed even his crucifixion. I saw this emphasis, but I did not yet understand it. Why did the apostles give so much more attention to Jesus' resurrection than I would give it?

During my years as a PhD student, when I taught Sunday school, I would point out the apostles' emphasis on Jesus' resurrection, but I could not explain the reason for that emphasis. When it came time to choose a dissertation topic, therefore, I was eager to devote more attention to Jesus' resurrection.

If Jesus' resurrection was central to the apostles' understanding of the gospel in Acts, I reasoned, then the four canonical Gospels should help us to understand why it was central. Matthew's Gospel, since I had preached through it and completed a doctoral seminar on it, was an ideal place to start. During that same season, I was introduced to narrative criticism, a methodology that provided a means for investigating the ways in which aspects of a Gospel narrative influence its audience's understanding of it.

To keep my research within a reasonable scope, my supervisor suggested that I limit my study to Matthew's prologue (1:1—4:11) and resurrection narrative (28:1–20).

What follows is a narrative-critical study of Matthew's prologue and resurrection narrative. Chapter 1 introduces narrative criticism as a methodology and discusses the ways it was previously applied to Matthew's resurrection narrative. Chapter 2 discusses a number of verbal and conceptual similarities between Matthew's prologue and resurrection narrative and the possible effects of those similarities. Chapters 3 through 7 analyze these portions of Matthew by giving attention to four important literary features—characterization, setting, plot, and point of view. These chapters include discussions of the ways these literary features may affect the audience. Finally, chapter 8 presents my conclusion regarding the significance of Jesus' resurrection in light Matthew's prologue. It is a conclusion that I hope will help move Jesus' resurrection back toward the center of the church's understanding and preaching of the gospel.

Brian Main
February 2025

Acknowledgments

This project would not have been possible without the encouragement, support, prayers, and advice of many others. Through them, I have experienced God's grace and provision in unexpected and humbling ways.

First, I want to thank my parents and parents-in-law, who never questioned the wisdom of pursuing doctoral studies even though it put more physical distance between us. Thank you for a lifetime of unselfish love.

I am grateful to pastors who have shepherded our family well into and through this project. John Thompson, Tim Loyola, Steve King, Tom Oostdyk, Greg O'Dell, Josh Ratliff (and others!), thank you for investing in us and for walking through hardship with us while modeling resurrection hope.

More professors than I could name have taught me how to carefully interpret the Bible. From Covenant Theological Seminary, I especially want to thank David Chapman, Dan Doriani, and Jack Collins, who taught me the biblical languages and helped me to read the Gospels carefully. I also want to thank David Turner of Grand Rapids Theological Seminary, who helped me more than he knows to grow as a scholar. In addition, I must thank Keith Darrell, the seminary friend whose question about the resurrection started this journey.

My experience as a PhD student at The Catholic University of America was made joyful through friendships with and encouragement from Adam Tune, Maria Rodriguez, Katherine Brown, Sung Cho, and Ms. Willie Joyner. I am deeply grateful to my supervisor, Ian Boxall, who taught me with excellence and shepherded me with kindness. I want to thank my dissertation readers, John Paul Heil and Bradley Gregory, whose advice and insights helped me to learn more and to produce a better study.

The members of two churches have been a particular blessing to us. To those who were members of Walnut Creek Community Church/Cross Point Bible Fellowship in Ohio, thank you for tolerating long sermons through Matthew while encouraging the potential that you saw in me. I miss you. And to the members of our current church family, Cherrydale Baptist Church, thank you for embracing us and loving us well through our greatest challenges.

Finally, thank you to my children, Megan, Joe, and Kate, for patiently enduring having a dad in school for so many years. I always loved you more than school, and I rejoice in my times with you. And to Beth, my patient and loving wife, to whom this book is dedicated. Thank you for being the person through whom I experience God's grace most profoundly. It is a great privilege to walk with you in the hope of the resurrection.

Abbreviations of Ancient Sources

1 En.	First Enoch
1QH	Thanksgiving Hymns (a Qumran text)
1QIsa	The Great Isaiah Scroll (a Qumran text)
1QSb	Rule of the Blessings (a Qumran text)
2 Bar.	Second Baruch (Syrian Apocalypse)
2 En.	Second Enoch
4 Ezra	Fourth Ezra
4QFlor	Florilegium, also Midrash on Eschatologya (a Qumran text)
4Q161	a Qumran text
4Q174	a Qumran text
4Q252	Commentary on Genesis A (a Qumran text)
Ant.	*Antiquities of the Jews* (Josephus)
Did.	Didache
Jub.	Jubilees
J.W.	*The Jewish War* (Josephus)
LAE	Life of Adam and Eve
LXX	Septuagint (Greek translation of the Hebrew Bible)
MT	Masoretic Text
NT	New Testament
OT	Old Testament
Pss. Sol.	Psalms of Solomon

Q	Quelle (Source)
Sir	Sirach
Tob	Tobit
T. Levi	Testament of Levi
T. Sim.	Testament of Simeon
T. 12 Patr.	Testament of the Twelve Patriarchs
Wis	Wisdom of Solomon

1

The Methodology of Narrative Criticism

INTRODUCTION

The resurrection of Jesus is integral to the conclusions of all four canonical Gospels, is prominent in the apostles' preaching in Acts (e.g., 2:24–32; 13:32–37; 17:31), and is mentioned in the majority of the Pauline epistles, as well as in Hebrews, 1 Peter, and Revelation. According to Paul, the resurrection of Jesus is so important that "if Christ has not been raised, then our preaching is in vain, and your faith is in vain" (1 Cor 15:14). Nevertheless, modern scholars and preachers tend to identify Jesus' crucifixion as the purpose or climax of his ministry,[1] giving the impression that his resurrection is of less significance than his crucifixion.[2] As noted by Barth and Fletcher, "Western theological thought, while affirming that 'on the third day he rose again from the dead,' has nonetheless given

---

1. See, for example, Kingsbury, *Matthew as Story*, 92. See also Caneday, "Christ's Baptism," 76, and Goodacre, "Scripturalization," 36–37. See Hunsberger for an explanation and critique of the relative neglect of the resurrection in contemporary understandings of the gospel ("Recovering," 253–65).

2. Some suggest that this is the case not only in Catholic and Protestant, but also in Orthodox, traditions (see Gaffin, "Redemption and Resurrection," 17). While the Orthodox Church claims that the resurrection is at the center of its life and worship (see Poe, *The Gospel*, 177), a modern example like the St. Athanasius Orthodox Academy's *Orthodox Study Bible*, when commenting on Jesus' resurrection in Matthew 28, does not seem to emphasize the resurrection any more than Catholic or Protestant works do [*Orthodox Study Bible* (1323–27)].

relatively more weight to the crucifixion as the primary expression of the Christ event."[3]

This study assumes that contemporary teaching and preaching should place a value on Jesus' resurrection that is consistent with its value in the NT. For this to happen, the significance of his resurrection must be better understood and explained, as that of his crucifixion has been.[4] One promising approach to arrive at a better understanding of Jesus' resurrection is to perform a narrative-critical analysis of a resurrection narrative in light of its relationship to the whole of the Gospel in which it is found. Such an approach could show how the resurrection narrative fits into, and provides a fitting conclusion to, that Gospel's narrative. In this study, such an approach will be applied to the Gospel of Matthew with the goal of understanding the significance of Jesus' resurrection in that Gospel—and perhaps in the overall theology of the NT.

This first chapter prepares for a narrative-critical analysis of Matthew's prologue (1:1—4:11) and its effect on its implied audience's understanding of the significance of Jesus' resurrection. We have chosen to study Matthew's prologue both because of the verbal and conceptual parallels between it and Matthew's resurrection narrative (i.e., Matthew 28) and because of the "primacy effect" that it has on the implied audience's understanding of the rest of the narrative.[5] In this chapter, the origins of NT narrative criticism will be described and its key principles and terms defined. Criticisms of the application of narrative criticism to NT narrative works will then be discussed. Narrative criticism's relationship to redaction and composition criticism will be described. Previous contributions of narrative criticism to the understanding of Matthew's resurrection narrative will be discussed and compared to conclusions produced by other methodologies. Finally, the use of narrative criticism in this study will be described.

---

3. Barth and Fletcher, *Acquittal*, v.

4. Contemporary emphasis on the crucifixion of Jesus may result from efforts since the time of the Reformation to understand and explain that event, even if not all have explained it in the same way.

5. For the purpose of this study, Matthew's prologue will be defined as 1:1—4:11, all of which indisputably precedes the public ministry of Jesus.

The Origins of Narrative Criticism as a Methodological Approach to the NT

In the 1980s, narrative criticism emerged as a methodology for biblical studies. Narrative criticism is an approach to interpreting biblical narratives using literary categories while giving attention to a work's final form and its literary unity.[6] This approach was first applied to the NT when NT scholar David Rhoads collaborated with English scholar Donald Michie to analyze Mark's Gospel from a literary perspective.[7] Shortly after the publication of Rhoads and Michie's book, narrative criticism was applied to other NT narrative works,[8] securing its place among other methodologies available for the study of NT.

Powell explains the emergence of narrative criticism in light of separate developments in the fields of biblical studies and literary theory. Some biblical scholars, contending that historical-critical methods failed to appreciate the literary qualities of biblical works, expressed a desire for a more literary approach,[9] especially to the Gospels.[10] For example, Beardslee, a historical critic, stated that form criticism ought to consider a text's literary meaning and its impact on readers while giving attention to the larger form of a Gospel.[11] Frei, who worked primarily in the field of hermeneutics, argued that historical critics' focus on questions of the Gospels' factuality led them to ignore their realistic narrative shape and that shape's interpretive significance.[12] The meaning of the Bible had come to be viewed as the meaning of the events narrated in it, rather than of the words used to narrate them.[13] As historical critics employed redaction criticism, the evangelists came to be viewed more as authors

---

6. Powell, *What Is Narrative Criticism?*, 7.

7. Rhoads and Michie, *Mark as Story*.

8. Edwards, *Matthew's Story of Jesus*; Kingsbury, *Matthew as Story*; Culpepper, *Anatomy*; Tannehill, *Narrative Unity*.

9. Historical critics did employ the term "literary criticism" prior to the rise of narrative criticism. For them, however, literary criticism referred to pursuits such as form and source criticism, which considered literary features in the attempt to answer historical questions. The more recent use of the term refers to the consideration of other types of literary features (see below) and an initial focus on the "story world" of the text rather than on the history behind the text. See Beardslee for an example of the use of literary criticism in both of these ways (*Literary Criticism*, iii–iv).

10. Powell, *What Is Narrative Criticism?*, 1–3.

11. Beardslee, *Literary Criticism*, 12–13.

12. Frei, *Eclipse*, 150.

13. Frei, *Eclipse*, 268.

who worked "freely and creatively with their material."[14] As a result, Perrin, who employed historical (especially redaction) criticism, concluded that the authorial character of the evangelists required the use of literary criticism in Gospel research.[15] Since the Gospels came to be viewed, at least by some, as both history *and* literature, Petersen concluded that the text "must be comprehended in its own terms before we can ask of what it is evidence."[16] He attempted to show that literary criticism was a necessary stage in historical-critical investigation.[17] Culpepper, a narrative critic of John's Gospel, claimed that literary (i.e., narrative) criticism and historical criticism, since they produce different types of data, must be in dialogue with one another.[18]

By the late 1970s, historical critics were calling for a more literary approach to the Gospels, but a defined literary approach was not yet available to biblical scholars. Concepts developed by secular literary critics, however, would form the basis of a literary approach to biblical literature. Chatman is foremost among the secular literary critics whose work influenced NT narrative criticism.[19] His focus was not on developing a method of interpretation, but on developing a theory of narrative that could be applied to narratives of all forms.[20]

Under the influence of French structuralism, Chatman came to view narrative as consisting of two parts—story and discourse.[21] The story is the "what" of the narrative, while the discourse is the "way" the

---

14. Perrin, "Evangelist as Author," 8.

15. Perrin points out that "literary criticism" must include "every aspect of the work of the evangelists as authors," an approach that differs from the typical use of "literary criticism" in Biblical studies to refer to the consideration of "sources and literary relationships" (i.e., source criticism; "Evangelist as Author," 9–10). Cf. Powell, *What Is Narrative Criticism?*, 3. Perrin's view of the author is similar to that of Thompson (*Matthew's Advice*, 12–13), who championed composition criticism as a developed form of redaction criticism. What Perrin called for, however, was a more literary approach, while Thompson's was still mainly historical.

16. Petersen, *Literary Criticism*, 20.

17. Petersen, *Literary Criticism*, 21, 91–92.

18. Culpepper, *Anatomy*, 5.

19. See Rhoads and Michie, *Mark as Story*, 2 n 3, and Kingsbury, *Matthew as Story*, 1.

20. Chatman, *Story and Discourse*, 18–22.

21. Fowler criticizes Powell for minimizing "the debt that narrative criticism owes to structuralism" ("What Is Enough?" 172). Powell is clear, though, that narrative criticism's use of different concepts and its emphasis on surface meaning, rather than on meaning found in a text's deep structure, allow it to avoid some of the criticisms aimed at structuralism (*What is Narrative Criticism?*, 14).

story is told.[22] The elements of the story include events, characters, and settings—the raw data used to construct the narrative. Powell includes plot ("the interaction of these elements") under story,[23] but Chatman is more accurate when he says, "The events in a story are turned into a plot by its discourse."[24] Either way, the implied author has chosen which events to include or emphasize in the narrative, as well as how to arrange and logically connect them, so that plot is properly thought of as "story-as-discoursed."[25]

The discourse is the way in which the narrative is communicated. It includes concepts like point of view and narrator. Some NT narrative critics consider literary or rhetorical devices—such as irony, symbolism, inclusion (inclusio), and chiasm—part of discourse.[26] The discourse is the means by which the implied author brings about the desired effect of the narrative on the implied audience. It produces an aesthetic effect which transcends the mere communication of information. Chatman's model distinguishes story from discourse to facilitate their analysis, but since all stories are presented by means of discourse the two do not exist separately.

Chatman's approach has been criticized for its heavy dependence on fiction despite its claim to include both fiction and film, with some questioning whether it can be appropriately applied to other forms of narrative.[27] He has also been criticized for failing to demonstrate the relationship between his notion of the implied reader and the experience of real readers.[28] Chatman later acknowledged that he was engaged in an ongoing discussion regarding the nature of narrative and that the discussion had not yet reached its conclusion.[29] The field of narrative theory, or narratology, has continued to evolve since Chatman's *Story and*

---

22. Chatman, *Story and Discourse*, 9.
23. Powell, *What Is Narrative Criticism?*, 23.
24. Chatman, *Story and Discourse*, 43.
25. Chatman, *Story and Discourse*, 43.
26. Powell, *What Is Narrative Criticism?*, 23–34.
27. Tomasulo, review of *Story and Discourse*, 71.
28. Fowler, "Who Is 'the Reader'?," 13. This study will use the term "implied audience" to reflect the view that most original recipients of Matthew's Gospel heard it read publicly and did not read it privately (cf. Rhoads and Dewey, "Performance Criticism," 15–16). In some places, when the work of others is being discussed, the term "implied reader" will be used.
29. Chatman, *Coming to Terms*, 2.

Discourse.[30] Nevertheless, it is Chatman's use of certain literary categories (i.e., plot, character, setting, and point of view),[31] his distinction between story and discourse,[32] and his model of narrative communication that have been adopted into the methodology of narrative criticism as it has been applied to the NT.[33]

An additional feature of narrative criticism is derived from the New Criticism. The New Criticism focused on the text as an end in itself and rejected any interest in the author's intent.[34] Although this approach has fallen out of favor with both secular and biblical critics, its focus on the text in its final form as "an organic whole, a unity that needs to be examined on its own terms" remains important to narrative criticism.[35] Because narrative criticism and the New Criticism shared an interest in the final form of the text, the more recent discrediting of the New Criticism has led some to object to narrative criticism as a legitimate methodology.[36] Many narrative critics, however, are interested in authorial intent

---

30. For a fairly recent collection of essays on the development and state of narrative theory, see Phelan and Rabinowitz, *Companion to Narrative Theory*. Monika Fludernik's essay in this collection, "Histories of Narrative Theory," discusses some more recent developments in narrative theory, including the integration of narratology with psychoanalysis, feminist studies, cultural studies, and postcolonial studies. These developments also include the application of narrative theory to information and media technology, to conversation analysis, and to media and genres beyond film and fiction, as well as the consideration of the relationship of narrative to cognition and to rhetoric and ethics. Another development, noted in Korthals Altes, *Ethos*, 95, is a shift of focus from developing a theory of narrative that accounts for all narrative to the interpretation of individual works.

31. Rhoads and Michie, *Mark as Story*, 2; Kingsbury, *Matthew as Story*, 3, 30.

32. Kingsbury, *Matthew as Story*, 2–3.

33. Powell, *What Is Narrative Criticism?*, 19; Kingsbury, *Matthew as Story*, 37–40.

34. Powell, *What Is Narrative Criticism?*, 4; Resseguie, *Narrative Criticism*, 22–23. Chatman did not explicitly reject interest in authorial intent. He did, however, prefer to speak of "textual intent" (cf. implied author) rather than of any real author's intent (*Coming to Terms*, 77–81).

35. Resseguie (*Narrative Criticism*, 21–22) explains that the New Criticism was discredited by both biblical and secular literary critics for rejecting the relevance of author, readers, and background information for the interpretation of a text, as well as for its refusal to consider race, gender, politics, or sexuality. Narrative criticism does consider the reader/audience, albeit the implied reader/audience. Certain applications of narrative criticism also seek to understand the author's intent. In addition, narrative criticism does consider background information to be necessary for understanding the text, even while giving interpretive priority to the text's story world.

36. As an example of such an objection to narrative criticism, see Fowler, "What Is Enough?," 172–73.

and find that analysis of the text as a unified whole helps to discern that intent.[37]

As narrative criticism developed, it came to be applied in author-, text-, or reader-oriented ways.[38] Since all three orientations seek to understand the response of the implied audience by means of a literary analysis of the narrative, they are all properly viewed as approaches to narrative criticism. Although they have the same exegetical approach, they differ in their hermeneutical approach;[39] each attempts to make different use of the results of narrative-critical analysis.

A text-oriented approach to narrative criticism focuses on the implied audience's expected response, assigning a normative status to this response.[40] The meaning of the text is found in this expected response. This approach considers the real author's intention to be the domain of redaction criticism rather than of narrative criticism.[41] A text-oriented approach reflects narrative criticism's original and purest form, as it retains the New Criticism's refusal to consider authorial intent, the historical circumstances of a narrative's composition, or its effect on contemporary, real readers.[42]

A reader-oriented approach to narrative criticism focuses on understanding the responses of real readers.[43] The expected response of the implied audience, though not required of real readers, serves as a guide for evaluating their responses and helps the interpreter to understand the factors that lead to unexpected responses.[44] A reader-oriented approach to narrative criticism resembles reader-response criticism and is nearly identical to some examples of it. It differs, though, from reader-response criticism in its effort to identify the implied audience's response, which is not always present in reader-response criticism.[45]

37. Powell, "Reading Strategy," 26.
38. Powell, "Reading Strategy," 43.
39. Powell, "Reading Strategy," 22–23.
40. Powell, "Reading Strategy," 33.
41. Edwards, *Narrative Portrait*, 8. Edwards strongly advocates for a text-oriented approach as the only proper form of narrative criticism.
42. Edwards, *Narrative Portrait*, 6–7.
43. Powell, *Chasing the Eastern Star*, 7–8. Powell outlines and demonstrates his own reader-oriented application of narrative criticism in this book. Cf. Howell, *Inclusive Story*, 42–43, 51, who finds an important role for real readers in producing meaning, although they are constrained by the author's conventions.
44. Powell, *Chasing the Eastern Star*, 8–9.
45. Powell, "Reading Strategy," 39–40.

An author-centered approach to narrative criticism views the expected response of the implied audience as reflecting the intent of the historical author.[46] In *Mark as Story*, Rhoads and Michie indicated that their analysis of the implied reader's (i.e., audience's) response allowed them to speculate about the response of a first-century reader.[47] Since the response of the original audience is assumed to correspond to the author's intention,[48] the expected response of the implied audience can lead to conclusions about the historical author.[49] An author-centered approach to narrative criticism is able to provide what historical critics like Perrin and Peterson had called for—a literary approach to the NT that contributes to historical discussions.

Narrative-Critical Studies of Matthew's Gospel

Richard Edwards's *Matthew's Story of Jesus*, published in 1985, was the first narrative-critical monograph on Matthew.[50] Edwards's work was the last in a series of four works which considered the Gospels from a literary perspective.[51] Although the first three in the series do not employ narrative criticism, Edwards's came after *Mark as Story*, allowing him to use the newly developed methodology; discussions about the application of narrative criticism to Matthew had begun a few years earlier.[52] Jack Dean Kingsbury's narrative-critical study, *Matthew as Story*, was published the following year.[53] Although Edwards negatively reviewed Kingsbury's book as a form of redaction criticism rather than of literary (narrative)

---

46. Powell, "Reading Strategy," 39–40.

47. Rhoads and Michie, *Mark as Story*, 140. Cf. Carter, who defines the authorial audience as "an ideal audience though it approximates an actual audience" (*Matthew: Storyteller, Interpreter, Evangelist*, 4).

48. Merenlahti and Hakola, who argue that the Gospels are non-fictional narratives, in which "narrative structures are more transparent to the aims and purposes of the author than in non-fictional [sic] narratives. Instead of a yawning gulf, there is continuity between elements of 'reality' and elements of the narrative world" ("Reconceiving," 37–38).

49. Carter, *Matthew: Storyteller, Interpreter, Evangelist*, 4–5.

50. Edwards, *Matthew's Story of Jesus*.

51. The other three works in the series are Kelber, *Mark's Story of Jesus*; Edwards, *Luke's Story of Jesus*; and Kysar, *John's Story of Jesus*.

52. For example, Anderson, "Point of View"; Anderson, "Implied Reader"; Kingsbury, "Figure of Jesus."

53. Kingsbury, *Matthew as Story*.

criticism,[54] Kingsbury is recognized as the most important early practitioner of Matthean narrative criticism.

Prior to the publication of *Matthew as Story*, some of Kingsbury's students had written dissertations that applied narrative criticism to Matthew.[55] Kingsbury's influence through his students, along with his stature as a well-known redaction critic prior to his foray into narrative criticism, likely explain why his influence has been greater than Edwards'. One of Kingsbury's students, Mark Allan Powell, has become a leading voice in narrative criticism. Powell has helped to clarify the methodology of narrative criticism and defend its merits. He has applied narrative criticism to Matthew in various works,[56] and has engaged in a form of reader-response criticism that benefits from narrative criticism.[57]

In the forty years since the publication of *Matthew as Story*, other scholars have applied narrative criticism to Matthew. Some more notable contributors to this field have been David Garland, Margaret Davies, and Augustine Stock, who wrote narrative-critical commentaries on Matthew.[58] John Paul Heil has made a significant contribution to Matthean narrative criticism with a monograph on Matthew's passion and resurrection narrative and several articles on Matthew.[59] Heil also co-authored with Warren Carter an audience-oriented study of Jesus' parables in Matthew.[60] In that work, they employ "audience-oriented criticism" as a subcategory of narrative criticism. They emphasize the response of the "authorial audience," which is similar to the implied audience, but may be reconstructed using information from outside the text as well as information within it.[61] This attention to the authorial audience's response allows their approach to contribute to discussions about historical events.

---

54. Edwards, review of *Matthew as Story*, 505–6.

55. Bauer, "Structure"; Witherup, "Cross of Jesus." Others would complete narrative-critical dissertations soon after, including Powell, "Religious Leaders"; and Reeves, "Resurrection Narrative."

56. Powell, *Methods for Matthew*; Bauer and Powell, *Treasures*.

57. Powell, *Chasing the Eastern Star*.

58. Garland, *Reading Matthew*; M. Davies, *Matthew*; Stock, *Method and Message*.

59. Heil, *Death and Resurrection*; "Blood of Jesus"; "Roles of the Women"; "Narrative Structure"; "Ezekiel 34"; "Double Meaning."

60. Carter and Heil, *Matthew's Parables*.

61. Carter and Heil, *Matthew's Parables*, 11, 210–11.

Principles Used in NT Narrative Criticism

Narrative criticism, as explained by NT narrative critics, incorporates several principles:[62]

1. Narrative criticism focuses on the final form of the text.

   For narrative critics, any development of the text prior to its final form is irrelevant to understanding the narrative as the implied author presents it. This does not mean that narrative critics have no interest in the possibility of such development or in the incorporation of previously existing source material. It means that narrative criticism is applied to a text in its final form while at least temporarily bracketing out questions about the text's development.

2. Narrative criticism emphasizes the unity of the text as a whole.

   Narrative critics seek to understand the way the entire story works, rather than to analyze distinct units that may have been incorporated from other sources. Narrative critics assume that the text in its final form is expected to be read or heard as a coherent, unified story. This assumption allows for minor gaps or inconsistencies within that story. Narrative critics seek to resolve such gaps by harmonizing the information in the text rather than breaking the narrative into separate parts with differing interests or theologies.[63]

3. Narrative criticism analyzes a narrative in terms of its literary features.

   While narrative critics consider the literary features of a narrative (see chart below), they do not all give attention to the same features. They also sometimes use different terminology to refer to the same features. The chart below compares the literary features analyzed by prominent narrative critics.

---

62. These principles are derived primarily from Powell (*What is Narrative Criticism?*) and Resseguie (*Narrative Criticism*), whose works address narrative criticism as a methodology (rather than being examples of the methodology) and come after the initial attempts (by Rhoads and Michie, Kingsbury, Culpepper, and Tannehill) to apply narrative-critical principles to specific writings.

63. Although he is a critic of narrative criticism, Ashton describes "instinctively seeking a patterned arrangement" as a legitimate, synchronic approach to reading the Gospels (*Studying John*, 148). See also Rhoads et al., *Mark as Story*, 3rd ed., 5.

	Rhoads/ Michie, Mark as Story	Kingsbury, Matthew as Story	Culpepper, Anatomy of the Fourth Gospel	Powell, What is Narrative Criticism?	Resseguie, Narrative Criticism of the NT
Plot/Events	X	X	X	X	X
Character(ization)	X	X	X	X	X
Setting	X	X		X	X
Point of View	X	X	X	X	X
Rhetoric	X				X
Narrator	X	X	X	X	X
Style	X				

The literary features most commonly analyzed by narrative critics will be further defined below.

4. Narrative criticism distinguishes between real and textually-implied author and audience, between implied audience and narratee, and between implied author and narrator.

Chatman's model of narrative communication, which strongly influenced narrative criticism, can be depicted as follows:[64]

Real author → Implied author → (Narrator) → (Narratee) → Implied reader → Real reader

In this model, the real author and real reader are considered to be outside of the narrative text. The model was developed to account for all possible narrative communication. Since a real author can be a group rather than an individual, and since even a single author is a complex person who cannot be fully known by a reader, the concept of an implied author is used. The implied author, who is implied by the text itself, may or may not be like the real author.[65] The implied author can only speak through the narrator. A narrator is not always necessary, as in some dramas or films, and was therefore placed in parentheses by Chatman.

The narrator is the creation of the implied author whose "voice" is "heard" by the implied audience. Although Edwards refers to the narrator's "artistry," narrative critics typically follow Chatman, ascribing artistic choices to the implied author and viewing the narrator more as a

64. Chatman, *Story and Discourse*, 151.
65. Chatman, *Story and Discourse*, 148–49.

character defined by the text.⁶⁶ The narrator cannot possess intentions or make choices, but the implied author can.⁶⁷ In theory, a narrator may be unreliable or may have a value system or point of view that is in conflict with the implied author's, making the distinction between the two necessary.⁶⁸ In biblical texts, however, narrative critics see the narrator as reliable, sharing the values and point of view of the implied author, making this distinction inconsequential.⁶⁹

Narrative critics sometimes discuss the characteristics of the narrator. For example, Kingsbury describes Matthew's narrator as reliable, omnipresent, speaking in the third person, directing helpful commentary to the reader, and having a vantage point between the resurrection and the parousia.⁷⁰ The implied author uses the narrator to guide the implied audience to adopt his or her point of view, providing "the standards of morality and belief that govern the story."⁷¹

Like the narrator, the narratee is not required and is therefore placed in parentheses. The implied reader (or implied audience) is distinct from the narratee, since a narratee (e.g., Theophilus in Luke and Acts) is often not present. Because real readers can come from any possible background, culture, or period of history, they can be very different from the audience implied by the text and are therefore distinct in Chatman's model.⁷²

5. The goal of narrative criticism is to understand the text itself, especially its effect on the audience implied by the text.⁷³

Narrative critics at least temporarily bracket out historical questions in order to enter into and understand the "story world" of the text.⁷⁴

---

66. Edwards, *Matthew's Story of Jesus*, 93.
67. Chatman, *Coming to Terms*, 85.
68. Chatman, *Story and Discourse*, 148–49.
69. Chatman, *Story and Discourse*, 26; Kingsbury, *Matthew as Story*, 31.
70. Kingsbury, *Matthew as Story*, 31–33.
71. Skinner, "Telling the Story," 10–11.
72. Chatman, *Story and Discourse*, 149–50.
73. Powell, *What Is Narrative Criticism?*, 19–21. Resseguie does not state that this is *the* goal of narrative criticism, but he does state that it is "important to the understanding of a text" (*Narrative Criticism*, 30).
74. Powell, *What Is Narrative Criticism?*, 7–8; Rhoads and Michie, *Mark as Story*, 1, 62. See also Kingsbury, who writes, "When one reads Matthew, one temporarily takes leave of one's familiar world of reality and enters into another world that is autonomous in its own right. This world, which possesses its own time and space, is peopled by

They seek to understand not just the meaning of the words, but the narrative's effect on the audience.[75] Since real readers encounter the text in any number of ways, resulting in diverse interpretations, narrative critics seek to understand the effect on the audience implied by the text rather than on real readers. This distinguishes narrative criticism from reader-response criticism, in which the subjective responses of real readers determine the meaning.[76]

The distinction between the implied audience and any real reader allows narrative critics to base their analyses on the text itself and to maintain an element of objectivity in their conclusions. Iser described the implied reader as including both the prestructuring of potential meaning and the actualization of that meaning (apparently by real readers) that can vary throughout history, so that the definition of a text's implied reader can change over time.[77] For narrative critics, however, the implied audience does not change with time, but is "an imaginary person who is to be envisaged . . . as responding to the text at every point with whatever emotion, understanding, or knowledge the text ideally calls for," or "that imaginary person in whom the intention of the text is to be thought of as always reaching its fulfillment."[78] For this reason, some prefer the term "ideal reader" to "implied reader" or "implied audience."[79]

Narrative critics differ over whether this implied audience should be thought of as encountering the text for the first time or multiple times.[80] This study assumes that the implied author's unique arrangement and presentation of the narrative is best experienced by an audience that is not already familiar with its arrangement and presentation. As Edwards writes, "reading is a cumulative process,"[81] meaning that the effect of a narrative comes about as it is experienced from beginning to end. It is reasonable to expect a first-time audience—one that does not already

---

characters and marked by events that, in varying degrees, are extolled or decried in accordance with this world's own system of values" (*Matthew as Story*, 2).

75. Iser, *Act of Reading*, 4–5.
76. Powell, *What Is Narrative Criticism?*, 16–18.
77. Iser, *Implied Reader*, xii.
78. Kingsbury, *Matthew as Story*, 38.
79. For example, Rhoads et al., *Mark as Story*, 3rd ed., 7.
80. Edwards explains his approach as examining "the narrative from the point of view of a reader who begins at the beginning," suggesting a first-time reader (*Matthew's Story of Jesus*, 9). Powell prefers to think of the implied reader as having read the narrative more than once (*What is Narrative Criticism?* 20).
81. Edwards, *Matthew's Story of Jesus*, 9.

know what comes next—to experience the affective response intended by the (implied) author and produced by the narrative's particular "sequence of information and its relation to earlier portions of the story."[82] Although those who experience Matthew's narrative multiple times will certainly gain a greater understanding of it than will a first-time hearer, because narrative criticism is focused on the narrative's effect on the implied audience—and because that effect is partly affective—our approach will assume a first-time audience while paying close attention to the narrative's sequence.

The implied audience, then, encounters Matthew's narrative for the first time while possessing the prior knowledge necessary to understand the narrative and respond to it in an expected way. Following Powell, we view this prior knowledge as including: "basic linguistic and literary competence;" basic knowledge of the geography, history, and social customs referred to in the narrative; and knowledge of the Old Testament and of oral traditions about Jesus.[83] This background knowledge prevents the implied audience from being distracted or confused by questions about its content. Since the original audience of Matthew is likely to have heard portions of the narrative before in one form or another (i.e., Mark's Gospel or oral traditions), the implied audience should not be thought of as coming to the text in total naïveté.[84] Its first-time encounter with a new way of narrating familiar events will bring about the expected response. The response of the implied audience may be inferred to be similar to that of a sympathetic real audience in the first century.[85] For those whose approach to narrative criticism is author-centered, the implied audience's response is understood to be consistent with the author's intent.[86]

---

82. Edwards, *Matthew's Story of Jesus*, 9.

83. Powell, *Chasing the Eastern Star*, 84, 91–93, 98–100, 104–5.

84. As Turner says, this approach fits a view of the Gospels "as theologically interpreted history, written for the edification of Christian communities" (*Matthew*, 8).

85. Turner, *Matthew*, 140.

86. Powell, *What Is Narrative Criticism?*, 28.

Definitions of Literary Features Analyzed by Narrative Critics

In this section, the literary features most commonly analyzed by narrative critics will be defined. These features are characters, settings, plot, and point of view.

Characters

Characters are the individuals or groups who perform, are affected by, or respond to the events that make up the plot.[87] The implied audience receives information about a character when the implied author has the narrator *show* or *tell* what a character is like.[88] The narrator *shows* what a character is like by narrating his or her actions or responses to events (e.g., Jesus' anger and compassion toward groups at the Temple, Matt 21:12–14) or through the words of other characters (e.g., Jesus explaining John the Baptist, 11:10–11). A narrator *tells* what a character is like by means of direct commentary to the reader (e.g., Joseph was "a righteous man," 1:19), which, if the narrator is omniscient, can include the character's thoughts or motivations. Although characterization by means of telling is more precise because it is explicit, most characterization in NT narrative comes by means of showing, leaving it to the audience to evaluate characters correctly.[89]

Narrative critics typically follow secular literary critics in classifying characters as round (complex) or flat (simple), and dynamic (changing) or static (unchanging),[90] although such categories appear to produce fewer helpful insights than do considerations of a character's relationship to the narrative's plot. Narrative critics also consider a character's degree of agreement with the narrative's normative point of view, which is typically the point of view of Jesus and God.[91]

---

87. Powell, *What Is Narrative Criticism?*, 51.
88. Powell, *What Is Narrative Criticism?*, 52–53.
89. Powell, *What Is Narrative Criticism?*, 52.
90. Powell, *What Is Narrative Criticism?*, 54–55. Moore suggests that roundness of character has unfairly been equated with full, human individualism ("No Humans or Animals," 82–87).
91. Powell, *What Is Narrative Criticism?*, 55; Resseguie, *Narrative Criticism*, 169. The point of view of Jesus may not always be identical in every aspect to that of God, as Matt 24:36 suggests. Although Jesus, during his earthly life, may be presented as having less knowledge than the Father, they would consistently share the same evaluative point

Settings

Settings are the spaces in which characters exist and events take place. Narrative critics consider spatial, temporal, and social settings.[92] Settings are sometimes incidental and do not, therefore, affect the interpretation of the narrative. They may also be symbolic, provide structure for the story, reveal characters, determine conflict, or contribute to the mood of the narrative.[93]

Since the settings of the events in the Gospels and Acts may be derived from historical events or from traditional reports of events, the author may not have felt the freedom to choose or invent a setting the way an author of fiction might.[94] It is no surprise, then, that narrative critics often derive fewer valuable insights from analysis of setting than from analysis of other literary features. Nevertheless, there are cases in which setting is significant. For example, Jesus performed several significant acts on mountains (Matt 4:8; 5:1ff; 17:1ff; 28:16ff), a setting which has been interpreted as identifying him as the new Moses.[95] Jesus' entry into Jerusalem on a donkey and a colt (21:7–10) had a significance in Jerusalem that it would not have had elsewhere. In addition to place, setting can also refer to time. Whether or not Jesus' trial at night constituted a violation of Jewish law (26:57–75),[96] the nighttime setting of Jesus' arrest did reveal the Jewish leaders' fear of arresting him publicly (cf. 26:3–5).

Plot

The plot consists of events that have been selected and arranged in a particular way by the implied author. Aristotle described plot as the

---

of view (see below).

92. Powell, *What Is Narrative Criticism?*, 70–75.

93. Powell, *What Is Narrative Criticism?*, 70–75.

94. Comparison of Synoptic Gospel parallels suggests that authors may have enjoyed some freedom regarding the narrative setting of an event (e.g., the different settings of similar sayings in Matthew's Sermon on the Mount in Matthew 5–7 and Luke's Sermon on the Plain in Luke 6:20–49). It is unlikely, however, that Gospel author-redactors felt the same degree of freedom that an author of a purely fictional narrative would have felt.

95. Allison, *New Moses*, 170; Rogers, "Great Commission," 383–98; and W. D. Davies and Allison, *Saint Matthew*, 1:423–24.

96. See Morris, who raises this as a potential violation of the law, but he also discusses other ways of understanding the events of that night (*Matthew*, 679).

"arrangement of incidents" that suggests a chronological or causal relationship between them.[97] Narrative critics sometimes see a hierarchy among events, designating events essential to the plot as *kernel events*, and those that could be removed without disturbing the plot's logic as *satellite events*.[98] For example, Matt 16:13–28, where Jesus affirmed Peter's confession that he is the Christ (v. 16), first predicted his passion and resurrection (v. 21), and called his disciples to imitate his self-denial and suffering (v. 24), is a kernel event since it is essential to the plot. On the other hand, Jesus' parables regarding his return in Matthew 25 are satellite events, since their removal would not disrupt the logical flow of the narrative. Matera employed this distinction between kernel and satellite events in his effort to determine the structure of Matthew.[99]

The early narrative-critical work on Matthew by Kingsbury and Edwards focused primarily on plot.[100] The results of their work illustrate the ways that plot analysis can affect interpretation. Referring to Jesus' Great Commission (28:18–20), Edwards writes, "The reader is thus encouraged to remain active while seeking to understand the message of the Son/teacher who died to save others and was raised to carry out the Father's will."[101] He draws the notions of Jesus' death "to save others" and "the Father's will" from earlier sections of the plot, since they do not appear in the pericope on which he is commenting. Kingsbury concludes, regarding Jesus' resurrection, that God shows that Jesus was right when he said, much earlier in 16:25, that whoever loses his life will find it.[102] Kingsbury also draws on earlier elements of the plot when he concludes that, after Jesus' resurrection, the disciples understand his call to them to be a call to "suffering discipleship, or to servanthood," a motif not present in the resurrection narrative.[103]

---

97. Chatman, *Story and Discourse*, 43–46; Powell, *What Is Narrative Criticism?*, 36–41.
98. Chatman, *Story and Discourse*, 53–54; Powell, *What Is Narrative Criticism?*, 36.
99. Matera, "Plot," 233–53.
100. Kingsbury, *Mathew as Story*, vii; Edwards, *Matthew's Story of Jesus*, 9.
101. Edwards, *Matthew's Story of Jesus*, 94–95.
102. Kingsbury, *Matthew as Story*, 90–91.
103. Kingsbury, *Matthew as Story*, 92.

Point of View

Point of view can refer to one's physical perspective, including spatial and temporal points of view. For example, the spatial point of view of the implied author of Matthew is that of an eyewitness to the events narrated. The implied author's temporal point of view is between the resurrection of Jesus and his parousia. Point of view can also refer to one's mental perspective (the situation from which one thinks about a subject), resulting in a psychological point of view.

Point of view can also refer to one's worldview, giving rise to the term "evaluative (or ideological) point of view." Kingsbury concludes that Jesus' evaluative point of view in Matthew, which is appropriated by the disciples, is one of suffering discipleship, or servanthood.[104] A character's evaluative point of view may be different from that of the implied author, God, or Jesus. For example, the evaluative point of view of Caiaphas was that Jesus was a blasphemer (Matt 26:65). Phraseological point of view, referring to speech, is closely related to evaluative point of view, assuming that speech of characters is consistent with their beliefs, since most reliable information about characters' beliefs is found in their speech.[105] In the Gospels and Acts, the normative point of view is always that of Jesus and God, which the reliable narrator shares.[106] This is the point of view toward which the narrator guides the implied audience.[107]

Narrative Criticism's Goal

Narrative critics typically give attention to the literary features discussed in this section. Their focus on these features is the result of the influence of literary critics who, at the time, were not concerned with the interpretation of narratives, but with explaining how narratives work. It was left to NT narrative critics to determine how these literary features should lead to interpretive results. Since the stated goal of narrative criticism is to understand the effect of a narrative on the implied audience, which must be inferred or reconstructed from the text, some degree of subjectivity

---

104. Kingsbury, *Matthew as Story*, 92.

105. Kingsbury, *Matthew as Story*, 33–37.

106. Jesus represents, and even makes known, God's evaluative point of view regarding people and actions (e.g., Matthew 23), even though he may do so with limited knowledge (cf. Matt 24:36) during his earthly ministry.

107. Powell, *What Is Narrative Criticism?*, 23–25.

is unavoidable. After all, it is difficult to conclude with certainty what the implied audience's expected response is. This is especially true when conclusions arise from the interpreter's own reading experience or when the interpreter is unable to argue, on the basis of the text, that a particular response is the expected one.

In theory, narrative criticism seeks to establish objective results on the basis of observable features in the text. For example, Pennington observes that "the main point of a passage is usually found in the climax and resolution and/or the following action/interpretation."[108] It is striking, however, that many conclusions reached by narrative-critical studies are not explained in terms of the relationships of those conclusions to the literary features described above. This is despite the fact that these studies devote significant space to the discussion of these features. As a result, it is difficult to know exactly how a narrative-critical approach has contributed to these conclusions. Such results reflect the subjectivity of reader-response criticism more than the objectivity that narrative criticism seems to promise.[109] One understands why Resseguie, explaining the usefulness of narrative criticism, does not promise definitive results that cannot be obtained through other methodologies, but rather, more conservatively, "close readings" and a "fresh and new" view of a narrative.[110]

Powell observes that secular scholars moved decisively from a text-oriented to a reader-oriented interpretive approach around the time that NT narrative critics were seeking to move their colleagues from an author-oriented to a text-oriented approach.[111] Many NT scholars followed the example of their secular counterparts by developing an interest in reader-response criticism, in which the responses of real readers, which could be described with greater certainty, became the focus. Perhaps some moved from an author-oriented, historical approach directly to a reader-oriented approach—bypassing text-oriented narrative criticism—because some narrative-critical studies produced conclusions that were no different from the conclusions produced by other methodologies. For example, Edwards could argue that Kingsbury was still doing redaction criticism because his narrative-critical conclusions matched the results

---

108. Pennington, *Reading the Gospels*, 176.

109. Powell describes narrative criticism as more text-centered and, therefore, more objective, than a reader-centered, pragmatic, approach (*What Is Narrative Criticism?*, 20).

110. Resseguie, *Narrative Criticism*, 39, 254.

111. Powell, "Reading Strategy," 21–22.

of redaction-critical work he had previously done.[112] Nevertheless, some narrative critics have employed this methodology to produce fresh conclusions and to relate these conclusions to objective considerations in the text. An example is John Paul Heil, in *The Death and Resurrection of Jesus Christ*, who focuses on structural patterns in the narrative and on anticipations of Jesus' death and resurrection in the text.[113]

OBJECTIONS TO NARRATIVE CRITICISM

Several scholars have voiced objections to narrative criticism. Those objections have come from the perspectives of historical, literary, and reader-response criticism.

Objections from a Historical-Critical Perspective

John Ashton objected to the application of narrative criticism to the study of John's Gospel, and his objections are relevant to its application to NT narrative in general. He points out that narrative criticism has adopted its concepts from literary criticism despite those concepts having been developed through the consideration of more complex, fictional works.[114] He concludes that narrative criticism's results are of little value because it is unable to consider the Gospels other than as fiction.[115] He also argues against narrative criticism's treatment of a text as having literary integrity on the basis of its transmission as a single text unless other factors, such as consistent style and tone, support the claim of its integrity.[116] He adds that narrative criticism arbitrarily dismisses older, historical questions that were addressed by historical-critical approaches.[117] Ashton argues that narrative criticism can do nothing more than show us how our understanding has resulted from "our first, quasi-instinctive response."[118]

In reply, it should be noted that Chatman had not limited his study of narrative to complex literature or fiction. Although he does not mention

---

112. Edwards, review of *Matthew as Story*, 505–6.
113. Heil, *Death and Resurrection*, xi.
114. Ashton, *Studying John*, 158, 165.
115. Ashton, *Studying John*, 164.
116. Ashton, *Studying John*, 143, 165.
117. Ashton, *Studying John*, 143.
118. Ashton, *Studying John*, 160.

NT narrative in *Story and Discourse* or *Coming to Terms*, his mention of the Pentateuch in the latter suggests that his model is applicable to biblical narrative.[119] Chatman aimed to develop a theory of narrative that accounts for all forms of narrative, written or unwritten, and even for those as simple as a comic strip.[120] As narrative works, the Gospels and Acts are within the range of literary forms for which Chatman sought to account in developing his model.

As for the assumption of literary integrity, a text that was handed down as a single text (i.e., with no indication that it is to be read as a collection of disparate texts) calls for it to be read as a single, unified text. Although Ashton wrote about John's Gospel, for which a claim of literary integrity is more controversial than for Matthew's, his demand that evidence support that claim is relevant to Matthew.[121] Narrative criticism's claim of literary integrity, along with any conclusions based on such a claim, can and should be strengthened by the evidence of its integrity.[122] As explained above, narrative criticism's dismissal of historical questions may be only temporary, making the claim that narrative critics simply dismiss such questions an inaccurate one. Most narrative critics are interested in historical questions.[123] They are convinced, however, that a text's claims about historical events are not fully understood apart from the overall context (i.e., the entire composition) in which those claims are found. Therefore, "Questions about history and setting may . . . operate alongside the use of literary tools."[124]

While some narrative-critical conclusions are indeed subjective and difficult to defend, Ashton's objections do not nullify the potential value of narrative-critical conclusions that are based on objective considerations in the text. Ashton's claim that narrative criticism merely helps one to appreciate one's own "quasi-instinctive response" assumes that all "instinctive" responses are consistent with the results of narrative-critical analysis. Many contemporary readers, however, have a "quasi-instinctive

119. Chatman, *Coming to Terms*, 90–92.
120. Chatman, *Story and Discourse*, 24.
121. Ashton, *Studying John*, 147.
122. In the present study, the identification of numerous verbal and conceptual links between Matthew's prologue and its resurrection narrative will demonstrate that (at least) these two portions of this Gospel are intended to be read as the beginning and the end of a single, unified story.
123. See, for example, Rhoads and Michie, who consider the effect of Mark's story on a first-century reader (*Mark as Story*, 140–42).
124. Thiselton, *New Horizons*, 484.

response" that differs from that of the implied audience. Real readers typically encounter these texts in parts (i.e., portions of the overall composition) and in a community in which they are taught how to understand them. Narrative criticism can help a reader to set aside certain presuppositions and experience a narrative in a way that more closely resembles the experience of its implied audience. This experience may result in a different, nuanced, or more complete understanding than their "quasi-instinctive" one. In fact, narrative criticism provides parameters and criteria for this "new" experience of a potentially familiar text.[125]

Objections from a Literary-Critical Perspective

A different kind of objection to narrative criticism of the Gospels comes from Stephen Moore.[126] He objects that secular literary critics do not support narrative critics' assumption that a text must be read as a unit and on its own terms.[127] He adds that narrative-critical discussions may produce an understanding of the text with a greater degree of unity than that text itself possesses, thereby neglecting certain features of the narrative.[128] Moore also criticizes narrative critics' practice of separating form and content despite claiming that they are inseparable.[129]

Moore's objection to the assumption that a narrative must be read as a unit and on its own terms is similar to Ashton's objection to the assumption of a text's literary integrity, although these objections have different bases. The response to Ashton will not be repeated, but it should be a sufficient response to Moore on this point. Moore's claim that narrative criticism, especially when focused on plot, can neglect other features of the text is a potential, rather than inherent, problem with narrative criticism. If narrative criticism is practiced carefully and with discipline, this neglect is avoidable. Even if a narrative contains multiple plot lines, the most prominent plot line that emerges through narrative-critical analysis

---

125. This is why Resseguie (*Narrative Criticism*, 31) and Longman (*Literary Approaches*, 151) are correct to include "defamiliarization" of texts among the benefits of literary or narrative criticism.

126. Moore, *Literary Criticism*.

127. Moore, *Literary Criticism*, 12.

128. Moore, *Literary Criticism*, 23–24. Cf. his page 39 where he suggests that point of view is typically given little consideration.

129. Moore, *Literary Criticism*, 64–66.

deserves to be noticed and considered, even if it is not the only aspect to consider when interpreting a text.

Moore's objection that narrative critics abstract content from form is a challenging one, although he does not explain how one ought to discuss content without abstracting it. One must remember that, since literary critics like Chatman did not use their theories to interpret specific texts, narrative critics were still seeking to establish the most appropriate and useful approaches for their new methodology. Their failure to arrive at a clearly defined approach does not necessarily invalidate their conclusions.

Objections from the Perspective of Reader-Response Criticism

Robert Fowler, a reader-response critic who has written on Mark's Gospel, argues that narrative criticism wrongly seeks to discern a single plot in the Gospels, when ancient literature could have multiple plots and was more concerned with the rhetorical power of language than with content.[130] He claims that narrative criticism, because it separates story world and real world, is "politically naïve and ethically disengaged."[131] He also sees no difference between narrative critics' efforts to discern the response of the implied audience and the effort of historical critics to discern authorial intent and the response of the original audience. Fowler also objects that narrative criticism encourages uncritical reading by avoiding historical criticism's skepticism.[132] In addition, Powell implies that some (unnamed) reader-response critics consider the notion of an ideal implied reader to be unrealistic and not reflective of any real reader.[133]

Fowler's objection that narrative criticism ignores the presence of multiple plot lines is similar to Moore's objection that plot-focused narrative criticism ignores other features of the text. The response to Moore is a sufficient response to Fowler at this point and will not be repeated. As for the narrative critic's separation of story world and real world, it was noted above that this need only be a temporary separation. Therefore, the claim that narrative criticism has no ability to address real ethical

130. Fowler, "What Is Enough?," 173.
131. Fowler, "What Is Enough?," 173.
132. Fowler, "What Is Enough?," 173.
133. Powell, *What Is Narrative Criticism?*, 20. Powell's response to this criticism is found below.

issues is not valid. Although some narrative critics may not view their conclusions as reflective of actual historical events, many, especially those who use an author-oriented approach, do address historical and real-world matters. Narrative criticism does not discourage critical reading, although it does seek to hear the message of the story before engaging in critique or evaluating historical claims. Finally, Fowler's assessment of the concept of implied audience fails to appreciate that this concept provides for an additional, and potentially valuable, means of discerning the author's intent and the response of the original audience. In many cases, conclusions regarding the implied audience's expected response resemble the conclusions of historical critics about the real author or audience. Narrative criticism, however, also has the potential to produce additional and valid insights and should not be written off as redundant.

Powell defends the use of the concept of the implied reader, acknowledging that reading perfectly as the implied reader is unattainable, but arguing that it remains valuable as a way to set interpretive criteria on the basis of the text.[134] One may add that a focus on elements within the text that suggest a particular response from the implied audience may identify responses different from those that emerge from consideration of the historical context alone.

The discussion above shows that some objections to narrative criticism are inaccurate, at least regarding the actual practice of many narrative critics who are interested in historical questions and who apply their narrative-critical conclusions to historical questions. Other objections do not invalidate narrative criticism as a useful approach to interpreting the Gospels and Acts, because they object to potential, rather than inherent, problems. A careful and disciplined use of narrative criticism has the potential to avoid such problems. These criticisms do remind narrative critics of the importance of using objective data to support (1) any claim of a work's integrity and (2) any conclusions that result from their analysis. The present study will heed this reminder by using verbal and conceptual connections to argue for the unity of Matthew's prologue and resurrection narrative (see chapter 2). It will also base conclusions regarding the significance of Jesus' resurrection on observable features of Matthew's narrative.

---

134. Powell, *What Is Narrative Criticism?*, 21.

The Relationship of Narrative Criticism to Other Holistic Approaches

Narrative criticism bears similarities to redaction criticism and composition criticism, which were recognized methodologies prior to the emergence of narrative criticism. Redaction criticism arose out of—and in response to—form criticism. Form criticism sought to determine the *Sitz im Leben* of the various parts of the gospel tradition and viewed the evangelists merely as editors or compilers of those traditions. Redaction criticism views the evangelists as authors "who have worked creatively with the gospel materials at their disposal."[135] Therefore, a comparison of the author-editor's finished work (normally Matthew or Luke) with his source material (usually Mark or a reconstructed Q) provides insight into the theology of the community in which the final form was produced.[136] This is especially possible when there are consistent patterns in the redactional changes identified.

While redaction criticism focuses on comparisons with parallel passages, composition criticism focuses on the work as a whole, "viewed rigorously and persistently in its entirety."[137] Like redaction criticism, the interest of composition criticism is in the theology of the evangelist (or of his community).[138] That theology, however, is derived from the overall content of the work, rather than from what is unique to that work in comparison to its sources.[139] It is "concerned with the evangelist's selection and redaction of existing material, his composition of new material and his arrangement of redacted or freshly created material into new units and patterns."[140] Composition criticism's attention to literary and narrative features of texts helped to pave the way for the developments found in NT narrative criticism.[141]

---

135. Kingsbury, *Matthew*, 15–16.

136. This is the typical view of redaction criticism (cf. R. F. Collins, *Introduction*, 198, 212). See, however, Bauckham, who argues in *All Christians* that the Gospels were originally intended to be circulated among all the churches at the time.

137. Moore, *Literary Criticism*, 4.

138. Moore, *Literary Criticism*, 7.

139. R. F. Collins defines redaction criticism as including composition criticism, assigning the term "emendation criticism" to what is typically referred to as redaction criticism (*Introduction*, 206). Most scholars, however, distinguish these two methodologies.

140. Thompson, "Reflections," 366. See also Thompson, *Matthew's Advice*, 12–13.

141. Senior, "Directions," 6.

An author-oriented approach to narrative criticism considers the expected response of the implied audience to reflect the intentions of the historical author.[142] So an author-oriented approach to narrative criticism shares with redaction and composition criticism an interest in the theology or purpose of the real, historical author. Narrative criticism, like composition criticism, differs from redaction criticism, as normally practiced, by focusing on the overall composition of the work, rather than on those aspects unique to it.[143] Narrative criticism differs from both redaction and composition criticism in how it seeks to understand the author's intention. Author-oriented narrative criticism seeks to understand the author's intentions through (1) analysis of the narrative's literary features and (2) the effect of the narrative on the implied audience. Redaction and composition critics do not explicitly consider such features. Instead, they seek to understand the author's intentions directly through the text, rather than indirectly through the implied audience, bypassing consideration of the aesthetic or rhetorical effects of a narrative that was of such interest to literary critics in the first place. The author-centered approach to narrative criticism has the potential to complement historical criticism by providing an alternative means of identifying authorial intent.[144]

Although narrative criticism may be distinguished from redaction criticism and composition criticism, it may be used to pursue similar interests. Thiselton argues that we "should not drive too sharp a wedge" between the concerns of narrative criticism and those of redaction and composition criticism.[145] Since biblical narrative is directed literature "which embodies truth-claims about ideas," a literary approach may produce answers to the kinds of theological questions that redaction and composition criticism are designed to answer.[146] This similarity in interest is most evident when the narrative-critical approach is author-centered.

---

142. Powell, "Reading Strategy," 43. The view of Moore (*Literary Criticism*, 7) and Matera ("Plot," 234) that literary (narrative) criticism is not interested in theology assumes a text-oriented approach rather than the author-centered approach that Powell describes.

143. Powell, *What Is Narrative Criticism?*, 7.

144. Powell, "Reading Strategy," 30–31.

145. Thiselton, *New Horizons*, 484.

146. Thiselton, *New Horizons*, 484.

Contributions of Narrative Criticism to Understanding Jesus' Resurrection in Matthew

The contributions of narrative criticism to the understanding of Jesus' resurrection in Matthew are best understood against the background of conclusions reached using other methodologies. To evaluate these contributions, fifty-five commentaries and monographs on Matthew were examined for (1) their methodological approach, (2) their interpretation of the significance of Jesus' resurrection in Matthew 28, and (3) references to Matthew's prologue (1:1—4:11) in their discussions of Jesus' resurrection. Of these fifty-five, thirteen claim (explicitly, or implicitly through terminology like "implied reader") to employ a narrative-critical methodology,[147] twenty-nine claim to use some other methodology (historical-critical, redaction-critical, theological, etc.),[148] and thirteen, while employing some other methodology, evidence some degree of narrative-critical consideration, normally by stating that the narrative is considered as a literary whole.[149]

In the works that employed a methodology other than narrative criticism, the predominant interpretations of Jesus' resurrection are (1) the vindication of Jesus' teaching or identity,[150] (2) his exaltation,

---

147. Edwards, *Matthew's Story of Jesus*; Kingsbury, *Matthew as Story*; Heil, *Death and Resurrection*; M. Davies, *Matthew*; Garland, *Reading Matthew*; Reeves, *Resurrection Narrative*; Stock, *Method and Message*; Pregeant, *Matthew*; Cabrido, *Shepherd of Israel*; Turner, *Matthew*; J. K. Brown, *Matthew*; R. Reeves, *Matthew*; Moloney, *Shape*.

148. Lange, *Matthew*; Lagrange, *Matthieu*; Argyle, *Matthew*; Jones, *Matthew*; Bonnard, *Matthieu*; Filson, *Matthew*; Kingsbury, *Matthew* (Proclamation Commentaries); Meier, *Vision of Matthew*; Schweizer, *Matthäus*; Osborne, *Resurrection Narrative*; Schniewind, *Matthäus*; Patte, *Matthew*; W. D. Davies and Allison, *Saint Matthew*; Faculty of Theology, University of Navarre, *Navarre Bible*; Gnilka, *Das Matthäusevangelium*; Bruner, *Matthew 13-28*; Harrington, *Matthew*; Mounce, *Matthew*; Hagner, *Matthew 1-13*; Hare, *Matthew*; Gundry, *Matthew*; Hagner, *Matthew 14-28*; Keener, *Matthew*; Wright, *Matthew for Everyone*; Bruner, *Matthew 1-12*; Wilkins, *Matthew*; Luz, *Matthew 21-28*; Hauerwas, *Matthew*; Luz, *Matthew 1-7*; Woodley, *Matthew: God With Us*; Evans, *Matthew*; Case-Winters, *Matthew*.

149. Hill, *Matthew*; Léon-Dufour, *Matthieu*; Beare, *Matthew*; Ellis, *Matthew*; Meier, *Vision of Matthew*; Morris, *Matthew*; Senior, *Matthew*; France, *Matthew*; Mitch and Sri, *Matthew*; Osborne, *Matthew*; Talbert, *Matthew*; Allen, *Matthew*; Boxall, *Discovering Matthew*.

150. Bruner, *Matthew 13-28*, 789; Case-Winters, *Matthew*, 338; W. D. Davies and Allison, *Saint Matthew*, 3:673; Gundry, *Matthew*, 585; Hagner, *Matthew 14-28*, 874-75; Hare, *Matthew*, 327; Hauerwas, *Matthew*, 245; Lange, *Matthew*, 548; Luz, *Matthew 21-28*, 597; Patte, *Matthew*, 400; Wilkins, *Matthew*, 939; Wright, *Matthew for Everyone*, 200.

enthronement, or authority (usually with reference to Dan 7:14),[151] (3) a sign that the eschatological age or kingdom of heaven is now present,[152] and (4) that Jesus would continually be with his followers.[153] Among the works with methodological approaches implying some degree of consideration of literary features, the two most common interpretations are the same as those above with no claim of a literary or narrative-critical approach—(1) the vindication of Jesus,[154] and (2) his exaltation or authority (also referring often to Dan 7:14).[155]

Among the works that claim to employ a narrative-critical methodology, the most common interpretations of Jesus' resurrection are the same as the most common found elsewhere—(1) vindication,[156] and (2) authority.[157] In addition, there is a tendency within this group of works to emphasize (3) the way in which Jesus' death and resurrection serve as a model of discipleship or servanthood for the disciples and readers,[158]

---

151. Bonnard, *Matthieu*, 416–18; Case-Winters, *Matthew*, 341; W. D. Davies and Allison, *Saint Matthew*, 3:673; Evans, *Matthew*, 483; Filson, *Matthew*, 302; Gnilka, *Das Matthäusevangelium*, 507; Gundry, *Matthew*, 595; Hagner, *Matthew 14–28*, 875; Hare, *Matthew*, 329; Harrington, *Matthew*, 414–16; Hauerwas, *Matthew*, 245; Jones, *Matthew*, 321; Lagrange, *Matthieu*, 544; Lange, *Matthew*, 541; Luz, *Matthew 21–28*, 623–24; Meier, *Vision of Matthew*, 361; Mounce, *Matthew*, 267–68; Osborne, *Resurrection Narratives*, 97; Patte, *Matthew*, 400; Schniewind, *Matthäus*, 276; Schweizer, *Matthäus*, 348; Wilkins, *Matthew*, 933.

152. Case-Winters, *Matthew*, 341; Hagner, *Matthew 14–28*, 874–75; Harrington, *Matthew*, 412; Hauerwas, *Matthew*, 245; Jones, *Matthew*, 321, Kingsbury, *Matthew* (Proclamation Commentaries), 27; Schniewind, *Matthäus*, 279; Schweizer, *Matthäus*, 346–47; Woodley, *Matthew*, 261; Wright, *Matthew for Everyone*, 200.

153. Filson, *Matthew*, 40; Kingsbury, *Matthew*, 27; Wilkins, *Matthew*, 946; Woodley, *Matthew*, 262.

154. Boxall, *Discovering Matthew*, 167; Léon-Dufour, *Matthieu*, 157; Mitch and Sri, *Matthew*, 365; Osborne, *Matthew*, 1070; Senior, *Matthew*, 171; Talbert, *Matthew*, 316.

155. Boxall, *Discovering Matthew*, 173; Ellis, *Matthew*, 98; France, *Matthew*, 1112; Hill, *Matthew*, 361; Meier, *Vision of Matthew*, 212–13; Mitch and Sri, *Matthew*, 367; Morris, *Matthew*, 739; Talbert, *Matthew*, 316.

156. J. K. Brown, *Matthew*, 319; Cabrido, *Shepherd of Israel*, 38; M. Davies, *Matthew*, 203; Edwards, *Matthew's Story of Jesus*, 38; Heil, *Death and Resurrection*, 9; Kingsbury, *Matthew as Story*, 90–91; Pregeant, *Matthew*, 190; Reeves, *Resurrection Narrative*, 61; Turner, *Matthew*, 679.

157. J. K. Brown, *Matthew*, 318; M. Davies, *Matthew*, 204; Garland, *Reading Matthew*, 265–66; Kingsbury, *Matthew as Story*, 91–92; Reeves, *Resurrection Narrative*, 90; Turner, *Matthew*, 682; R. Reeves, *Matthew*, 567.

158. M. Davies, *Matthew*, 204; Heil, *Death and Resurrection*, 9; Kingsbury, *Matthew as Story*, 92; Reeves, *Resurrection Narrative*, 61; Turner, *Matthew*, 683; Stock, *Method and Message*, 435.

and (4) that the resurrection will lead to Jesus' return to rule or judge.[159] In all three groups of works, significant attention is paid to references or allusions to the OT and to the historical backgrounds of Matthew's resurrection narrative. Conclusions regarding the significance of Jesus' resurrection are typically based on these backgrounds (e.g., the frequent reference to Dan 7:14), *rather than* on the information explicitly included in Matthew's narrative. Such background information is essential for a complete understanding of Jesus' resurrection. Nevertheless, dependence on such information can lead to neglect—even among narrative critics—of information within Matthew's story world that could shed additional light on the resurrection. Our approach will be to focus on the information found in Matthew's narrative and its effect on the implied audience's understanding of Jesus' resurrection.

Jack Dean Kingsbury

Three studies will illustrate previous contributions of narrative criticism to the understanding of Jesus' resurrection in Matthew. The first is Jack Dean Kingsbury's *Matthew as Story*.[160] Kingsbury presents the following conclusions about Jesus' resurrection as a result of its place in Matthew's overall narrative: (1) God vindicates Jesus as in the right in spite of the accusations against him by the Jewish leaders; (2) in light of Jesus' teaching that "whoever loses his life will find it" (16:25; cf. 10:39) and the loss of his own life, "God certifies the truth of Jesus' words and the efficacy of his trust" in God;[161] (3) the disciples perceive that Jesus is indeed the Son of God and that his central purpose was his death on the cross and the resulting salvation from sins;[162] (4) Jesus' resurrection, along with his future glorious return to carry out the final judgment, is proof of God's vindication of Jesus;[163] and (5) the disciples therefore perceive that Jesus' "suffering sonship is their call to suffering discipleship, or to servanthood."[164] Kingsbury's work reflects some of the contributions of a narrative-critical approach. While emphasizing vindication like other

159. M. Davies, *Matthew*, 204; Kingsbury, *Matthew as Story*, 93; Turner, *Matthew*, 683.
160. Kingsbury, *Matthew as Story*.
161. Kingsbury, *Matthew as Story*, 91.
162. Kingsbury, *Matthew as Story*, 92.
163. Kingsbury, *Matthew as Story*, 93.
164. Kingsbury, *Matthew as Story*, 92.

scholars do, Kingsbury clarifies the nature of that vindication. It contrasts with the Jewish leaders' accusations and confirms a particular teaching of Jesus found earlier in the Gospel (16:25). His approach also demonstrates greater sensitivity to the theme, found earlier in the Gospel, of Jesus' future return (24:29–31; 25:31–46).[165] Finally, his approach leads to conclusions about the effect of this narrative on the disciples and, therefore, on the implied audience which adopts their evaluative point of view.[166]

Keith Howard Reeves

One of Kingsbury's students, Keith Howard Reeves, provides a literary-critical analysis of Matthew's resurrection narrative.[167] He makes the following observations about the resurrection of Jesus: (1) "God vindicates the character of Jesus by raising him from the dead on the third day, as Jesus predicted."[168] (2) Matthew presents the women and the guards as examples of faithful and hostile witnesses.[169] (3) Matthew chooses to direct the audience's attention to the appearance and commission in Galilee.[170] (4) The audience would understand the resurrection to mean that Jesus' authority is from God.[171]

Reeves repeats the view that the resurrection "vindicates" Jesus but does not clarify the meaning of this vindication the way Kingsbury does. It is, therefore, left unclear whether his literary approach contributes to this part of his interpretation. In seeking to appreciate the response expected of the implied audience, Reeves focuses more on the disciples' responses than on Jesus' resurrection itself. From these responses, Reeves does not seem to infer anything about the significance of Jesus' resurrection. For example, he does not discuss possible reasons for the women's joy in 28:8, which may be an indication of that significance. Finally, Reeves's literary analysis is focused on the immediate literary context to the neglect of the characterization and plot developed in the earlier parts of Matthew. While the application of literary methods to a particular

---

165. Further analysis of the plot of the Gospel will lead to the conclusion that this future return is more than proof of God's vindication of Jesus.
166. Kingsbury, *Matthew as Story*, 93.
167. Reeves, *Resurrection Narrative*.
168. Reeves, *Resurrection Narrative*, 61.
169. Reeves, *Resurrection Narrative*, 61.
170. Reeves, *Resurrection Narrative*, 61.
171. Reeves, *Resurrection Narrative*, 90.

section of Matthew can bear fruit, his use of these methods neglects one of the primary assumptions of narrative criticism—that a Gospel is literary whole meant to be experienced and understood as such. The results of this study are of limited value for understanding the significance of Jesus' resurrection, not because of the limits of narrative criticism, but because narrative criticism is selectively applied.

John Paul Heil

In *The Death and Resurrection of Jesus: A Narrative-Critical Reading of Matthew 26–28*, John Paul Heil considers the passion and resurrection narratives in Matthew. He shows that many elements in earlier parts of Matthew prepare the implied audience to understand the passion and resurrection of Jesus.[172] He is also more specific when it comes to describing how the implied audience understands the resurrection, including that (1) the teaching that those who lose their lives will save them is confirmed,[173] (2) Jesus is proven to be "the savior who 'will save his people from their sins,'"[174] (3) others "who suffer an unjust death while remaining innocent and obedient to God" will be vindicated,[175] and (4) "the risen Lord continuously empowers us with his divine authority to make true believers of all people."[176]

Heil's application of narrative criticism shows the kinds of contributions that such an approach can make. As with Kingsbury's work, the vindication of Jesus is given more specificity, and conclusions are drawn regarding the effect of Jesus' resurrection on disciples and the implied audience. Heil's work also illustrates that no single study of reasonable length can exhaust the potential contributions of narrative criticism. He provides a detailed discussion of the plot, including patterns within the plot of Matthew 26–28. When it comes to the way in which earlier sections of the Gospel prepare the reader for Jesus' passion and resurrection, Heil's focus is on similar events (e.g., John the Baptist's fate, conflict with the Jews, raising the dead) and on Jesus' predictions of his passion and resurrection (16:21; 17:22–23; 20:18–19). These elements lead the implied

---

172. Heil, *Death and Resurrection*, 7–21.
173. Heil, *Death and Resurrection*, 9.
174. Heil, *Death and Resurrection*, 9.
175. Heil, *Death and Resurrection*, 20.
176. Heil, *Death and Resurrection*, 111.

audience to expect Jesus' death and resurrection. Additional features in the narrative provide a context for understanding their significance more fully. Consideration of other features of Matthew's narrative may lead to additional insights into the way in which the implied audience is prepared to understand the significance of Jesus' resurrection.

Summary

The examples above demonstrate that the contributions of narrative criticism can include (1) additional specificity regarding conclusions contributed by other methodologies, (2) greater emphasis on certain ideas or themes, and (3) greater consideration of the effect of a narrative on the implied audience. The results of narrative criticism may be limited by a failure to consistently apply its principles. In addition, the value of narrative criticism's contributions depends on the ability of narrative critics to base their conclusions not on subjective impressions of a narrative's effect on the implied audience, but on observable features of the narrative which are used as evidence in support of these conclusions.

THE USE OF NARRATIVE CRITICISM IN THIS STUDY

Most of the fifty-five works on Matthew surveyed for the discussion above mention verbal or conceptual connections between Matthew's prologue and resurrection narrative. Connections commonly mentioned include the similarity between 1:23 ("Immanuel . . . God with us") and 28:20 ("I am with you always"), worship (2:11; 28:9, 17), and the presence of the angel of the Lord (1:20, 24; 2:13, 19; 28:2). The mention of these connections demonstrates an awareness on the part of many scholars that the audience is expected to understand the resurrection narrative (Matthew 28) as part of the same story that began in Matthew's prologue (1:1—4:11). In his discussion of intratextuality, Pennington suggests that these kinds of connections invite the audience to hear individual episodes in light of each other and to see how related episodes emphasize a theme.[177] In spite of an awareness of these connections, the works surveyed contain very little—if any—discussion of the significance of these connections for interpretation or of their effect on the audience's understanding. Most appear to ignore, or at least to fail to appreciate, the significance of these

---

177. Pennington, *Reading the Gospels*, 189–92.

connections which the implied audience is expected to notice and which influence its understanding of the narrative.

As noted earlier, the aim of this study is to better understand the significance of Jesus' resurrection in Matthew by giving thorough and sustained consideration to the ways in which Matthew's prologue prepares the implied audience to understand his resurrection. For the purpose of this study, Matthew's prologue will be defined as 1:1—4:11, all of which indisputably precedes the public ministry of Jesus. Although Matthew's prologue is not the only source of information that influences the implied audience's understanding of Jesus' resurrection, it establishes the initial plot and characterization of Jesus and, therefore, make it the necessary starting point for such a study. In ancient literature, a prologue often would be used to prepare the audience to understand what follows.[178] This fact alone makes Matthew's prologue a necessary consideration for understanding its conclusion. As we will see, though, numerous verbal and conceptual links between Matt 1:1—4:11 and Matthew 28 invite—or even require—the two sections to be read as parts of a unified composition in which chapter 28 provides the conclusion to what begins in the prologue.

In this study, we will seek to identify the verbal and conceptual connections between Matthew's prologue and resurrection narrative. The identification of these connections will establish the unity of the narrative, avoiding the criticism that narrative critics unjustifiably assume the integrity of a composition. After the unity of the narrative is established, other narrative features will be analyzed. In order to reach conclusions that are more than subjective impressions, this study's conclusions will be related to observations of character, setting, plot, and point of view within the narrative. These conclusions will explain why and how the implied audience understands the resurrection of Jesus to be a fitting conclusion to the narrative that begins in Matt 1:1—4:11.

---

178. See Hooker, "Beginnings and Endings," 184–202.

2

Verbal and Conceptual Similarities Between Matthew's Prologue and Resurrection Narrative

Introduction

In the previous chapter, it was noted that one objection to narrative criticism is its *a priori* assumption of a narrative's literary unity.[1] Therefore, before a narrative-critical analysis is presented in the following chapters, this chapter will identify and discuss the many verbal and conceptual similarities between Matthew's prologue and resurrection narrative. This discussion will demonstrate a strong and observable connection between the prologue and resurrection narrative and, therefore, establish them as components of a unified narrative. The discussion will also include some preliminary observations regarding the potential effect of the prologue on the implied audience's understanding of the significance of the resurrection narrative.

---

1. Ashton, *Studying John*, 143, 165. The term "literary unity" is used here in a narrative-critical sense to refer to the coherence between the parts of the narrative. It is not being used in the sense that it is used in source or redaction criticism to refer to a text that shows no evidence of stages of development or redaction.

Criteria for Identifying Verbal and Conceptual Similarities

Before discussing these verbal and conceptual similarities, we must consider how to determine whether the presence of a particular similarity is significant or incidental. Does it help in establishing unity between these two portions of the narrative? Does the former narrative affect the implied audience's understanding of the latter narrative? For example, ἰδού ("behold") appears nine times in Matthew's prologue and six times in its resurrection narrative. Nevertheless, its forty-seven occurrences elsewhere in Matthew prevent the reader from concluding that its presence in chapter 28 establishes any special connection to the prologue. The frequent occurrence of ἰδού in narrative texts (fifty-seven times in Luke and twenty-three in Acts, though only seven in Mark and four in John) likewise prevents this similarity from indicating to the implied audience that the two narratives must be read as parts of a unified whole. Therefore, some criteria should be used to determine whether a particular similarity contributes to the implied audience's perception of literary unity.

To our knowledge, no list of criteria for evaluating the significance of verbal similarities within a narrative text has been published. Ashton suggests that "the consistency of style and tone" in John's Gospel could justify reading it in its final form.[2] Richard Hays's criteria for detecting echoes of the OT in the writings of Paul are suggestive of, though not identical to, criteria that could be used for our purposes.[3] Hays explains that his criteria permit only "shades of certainty" regarding the identification of scriptural echoes.[4] Likewise, the use of the following criteria to identify significant verbal similarities in Matthew is not an exact science. They can, however, increase our degree of certainty that (1) the implied audience recognizes a verbal or conceptual similarity as forming a connection between Matthew's prologue and resurrection narrative, and that (2) its understanding of the resurrection narrative is influenced by the presence of that similarity.

1. Frequency. A word or concept occurs frequently in both narratives. The appearance of "angel of the Lord" (ἄγγελος κυρίου) four times

---

2. Ashton, *Studying John*, 147.

3. Hays's criteria are availability, volume, recurrence, thematic coherence, historical plausibility, history of interpretation, and satisfaction (*Echoes of Scripture*, 29–32).

4. Hays, *Echoes of Scripture*, 32.

in Matthew's prologue (1:20, 24; 2:13, 19) makes it more likely that its single appearance in the resurrection narrative (28:2; but also in 28:5 as ἄγγελος) is recognized as somehow connecting the two narratives.

2. Prominence. A word or concept appears prominently in the two narratives, rather than in incidental details less likely to be noticed by the implied audience. For example, the word ἔνδυμα ("clothing") occurs in both the prologue (referring to John the Baptist, 3:4) and the resurrection narrative (referring to the angel of the Lord, 28:3). The actual descriptions of the clothing, however, are quite different from each other, and those descriptions become more prominent than the usage of ἔνδυμα, with the result that the implied audience is unlikely to see a connection formed by the two uses of the same word. In contrast, the phrase "Do not fear" (μὴ φοβηθῇς/μὴ φοβεῖσθε) in the prologue (1:20) and resurrection narrative (28:5, 10) becomes more prominent because it is spoken by supernatural characters. As a result, the implied audience is more likely to see it as forming a connection between the narratives.

3. Precision. A word occurs in both narratives in the same or similar form. Better yet, a phrase occurs with the same wording and word order. For example, πνεύματος ἁγίου ("Holy Spirit") appears five times in Matthew—three times in the prologue (1:18, 20; 3:11) and once in the resurrection narrative (28:19)—despite πνεύματος alone appearing 14 times elsewhere in Matthew.[5] The concentration of this phrase in these two narratives using identical words increases our certainty that the implied audience recognizes it as a connecting phrase.

4. Similarity of use. This criterion encompasses both context and semantic range. A word or concept that occurs in both narratives is more likely to be viewed as forming a connection between the narratives if it appears in a similar context. For example, λίθος ("stone") occurs in both narratives. In the prologue, it refers to (1) stones from which God can raise up children for Abraham (3:9), (2) stones that the devil tempts Jesus to turn into bread (4:3), and (3) stones against which God will not allow his Messiah to strike his foot

---

5. The word order appears to be reversed in Matt 28:19 (τοῦ ἁγίου πνεύματος). In this case, however, the use of the article, which puts "Spirit" in parallel with "Father" and "Son" forces the adjective into the first attributive position.

(4:6). These usages differ from its use in the resurrection narrative, where it refers to the stone that covered the opening to Jesus' tomb (28:2). Therefore, the implied audience is unlikely to view λίθος as connecting the narratives. Likewise, there are instances in which a Greek word is used in both narratives with distinctly different meanings within the word's semantic range. The use of ἐγείρω in Matthew provides an example. In the prologue, ἐγείρω is used five times intransitively with the sense "to rise, to get up" (1:24; 2:13, 14, 20, 21) and once transitively with the sense "to raise up" (3:9). In the resurrection narrative, ἐγείρω (28:6, 7) also has the sense "to raise up," but it clearly refers to the resurrection of Jesus. This distinctly different use prevents the implied audience from viewing the occurrence of the same Greek word, even multiple times, as forming a connection between the narratives.[6]

5. Exclusivity. A word, phrase, or concept is found in both Matthew's prologue and resurrection narrative but rarely elsewhere in Matthew (or in the NT). For example, ἄγγελος κυρίου ("angel of the Lord") occurs only in Matthew's prologue and resurrection narrative (1:20, 24; 2:13, 19; 28:2), strongly suggesting that the two narratives are related.

While these criteria cannot produce absolute certainty, they do provide a degree of objectivity in identifying features that the implied audience regards as connecting Matthew's prologue and resurrection narrative.[7] Each criterion independently contributes to the likelihood that the implied audience will notice a similarity. Frequency and prominence may be the most important criteria, since they best explain why a similarity is noticed by the implied audience. The criteria of precision, similarity of use, and exclusivity may contribute to a similarity being noticed, but

---

6. Some may detect a parallel between 3:9 ("raise up children for Abraham") and the resurrection of Jesus, the personification of Israel (cf. 2:15). This parallel, however, is subtle and does not establish the kind of clear connection between the prologue and resurrection narrative that other verbal similarities establish.

7. An additional criterion, that of reception history, could be helpful here. A survey of prominent patristic scholars (Hilary of Poitiers, Augustine, Chrysostom, Jerome), of the *Opus Imperfectum*, and of Simonetti's two volumes on Matthew in *Ancient Christian Commentary on Scripture* suggests that such literary connections were of little interest to the early church. Therefore, there appears to be too little data to use this as a criterion for our purposes. In footnotes, modern commentators who mention these verbal or conceptual similarities are listed. The similarities discussed in this chapter are each mentioned by at least one modern commentator.

they are more likely to strengthen the sense of connection that results from a similarity's prominence or frequency. The similarities that best satisfy at least one of these criteria are discussed in the following section.

Verbal Similarities between Matthew's Prologue and Resurrection Narrative

This section will discuss verbal similarities between Matthew's prologue and resurrection narrative. The criteria supporting the likelihood of the implied audience noticing each similarity will be noted, and scholars who mention these similarities will be identified in footnotes. These similarities will be discussed in the order in which they first appear in Matthew's resurrection narrative (i.e., chapter 28), since our goal is to determine how the implied audience understands the significance of the resurrection in light of the prologue.

The Angel of the Lord

The phrase "angel of the Lord" (ἄγγελος κυρίου) appears four times in Matthew's prologue (in dreams, 1:20, 24; 2:13, 19), once in the resurrection narrative (in person, 28:2; plus "the angel" in 28:5), and nowhere else in Matthew's Gospel.[8] That the implied audience views these appearances as connecting the prologue and resurrection narrative is supported by the following evidence: its exclusive use in these two narratives; its repeated use; its occurrence with precisely the same wording (ἄγγελος κυρίου); the angel's prominent role (i.e., announcing both the birth and the resurrection of Jesus). The belief that the author wanted to create a connection between the prologue and resurrection narrative is strengthened by the redaction of Mark's νεανίσκον ("young man," Mark 16:5) to ἄγγελος κυρίου (Matt 28:2).

---

8. This verbal similarity is mentioned by M. Davies, *Matthew*, 202; Garland, *Reading Matthew*, 263; Turner, *Matthew*, 681; Stock, *Matthew*, 435; Edwards, *Matthew's Story of Jesus*, 93; Davies and Allison, *Saint Matthew*, 1:206, 3:665; Luz, *Matthew 21–28*, 591, 595; Allen, *Matthew*, 268–69; Osborne, *Matthew*, 1066; Morris, *Matthew*, 735; R. E. Brown, *Birth of the Messiah*, 129, 153; Bonnard, *Matthieu*, 20; Schweizer, *Matthäus*, 343; Gnilka, *Das Matthäusevangelium*, 492; Sonnet, "De la généalogie," 207–8.

"Do not fear"

The "angel of the Lord" issues the same command to Joseph in the prologue (1:20) as he does to the women at the tomb in the resurrection narrative (28:5): "Do not fear" (μὴ φοβηθῇς/μὴ φοβεῖσθε).[9] This command is likely to stand out prominently to the implied audience, given its frequent appearance in the context of theophanies or angelophanies in the OT (e.g., Gen 15:1; 26:24; 46:3; Judg 6:23; Dan 10:12). Jesus repeats the same command to the women in 28:10. This command is not exclusive to the prologue and resurrection narrative. It is spoken by Jesus elsewhere in Matthew (10:26, 28, 31; 14:27; 17:7), where its use may influence its interpretation in 28:5. The concurrence of "the angel of the Lord" with this command, however, along with its prominence, leads the implied audience to view it as connecting the narratives about Jesus' birth and resurrection. This similarity between the prologue and resurrection narrative also results from the author's redactional activity. Mark's young man instead tells the women, "Do not be amazed" (μὴ ἐκθαμβεῖσθε; Mark 16:6) and lacks any encounter between Jesus and the women. Therefore, we can again infer that the author has intentionally established a noticeable verbal connection between the two narratives.

Galilee

After declaring to the women that Jesus has been raised from the dead, the angel commands them to tell the disciples to meet Jesus in Galilee (Matt 28:7). Although Matthean references to Galilee are not exclusive to the prologue and resurrection narrative (the majority occur elsewhere: 4:12, 15, 18, 23, 25; 15:29; 17:22; 19:1; 21:11; 26:32; 27:55), it still figures prominently in both (2:22; 3:13; 28:7, 10, 16).[10] In the prologue, Galilee becomes the home of the child Jesus at the direction of God Himself

---

9. This verbal similarity is mentioned by Luz, *Matthew 21–28*, 591. The difference tenses (aorist in 1:20; present in 28:5, 10) may be accounted for by a change in circumstances. The aorist imperative tends to refer to a specific time and situation, while the present imperative tends to be more generally applicable (see Wallace, *Greek Grammar*, 719–22). Therefore, the command to Joseph in 1:20 may be understood as referring to his particular circumstance. The post-resurrection commands to the women in 28:5, 10, on the other hand, suggest that the resurrection of Jesus makes all fear unnecessary, not just the fear of encountering the angel or the risen Lord on that particular day.

10. This verbal similarity is mentioned by Turner, *Matthew*, 98; W. D. Davies and Allison, *Saint Matthew*, 3:687; Ellis, *Matthew*, 98; Allen, *Matthew*, 268–69.

(2:22). In the resurrection narrative, it is the site of the disciples' reunion with Jesus and of the Great Commission (28:16), an encounter pointed out in advance twice (28:7, 10), so that "Galilee" occurs three times in ten verses. This prominent and frequent use of Galilee contributes to the implied audience's impression that there is a relationship between the prologue and resurrection narrative, and that ideas associated with Galilee are important in both.

Great Joy

When the women depart from the tomb, they do so with "fear and great joy" (28:8). Their "great joy" (χαρᾶς μεγάλης) forms a verbal parallel with the narrative about the magi who, upon seeing the star that will guide them to Bethlehem, rejoice exceedingly "with great joy" (χαρὰν μεγάλην, 2:10).[11] Although "joy" occurs as a noun four other times in Matthew (13:20, 44; 25:21, 23), those four are in parables spoken by Jesus and do not describe participants in the narrative.[12] The exclusive occurrence of joy in Matthew, along with its occurrence in the precise phrase "great joy," forms another significant connection between the prologue and resurrection narrative in the mind of the implied audience.

Worship

On their way to report the resurrection to the disciples, the women encounter the risen Jesus (28:9). In response, they "worshipped" (προσεκύνησαν) him. This was also the response of at least some of the disciples who met Jesus in Galilee (28:17). Worship is also prominent in Matthew's prologue, where the magi made their journey in order "to worship" (προσκυνῆσαι) Jesus as the king of the Jews (2:2, 11), Herod feigned a desire to join them in worship (2:8), and the devil attempted to get

---

11. This verbal similarity is mentioned by Garland, *Reading Matthew*, 263-64; Davies and Allison, *Saint Matthew*, 3:668, 673; Luz, *Matthew 21-28*, 591; Osborne, *Matthew*, 1068.

12. The verb "rejoice" (χαίρω) does appear in Matthew five times in addition to the reference to the magi. One is a command regarding future persecution (5:12). Another, in a parable, refers to the joy of a shepherd who finds his lost sheep (18:13), which reflects the joy of God rather than of humans. The remaining three uses are in stereotyped greetings (26:49; 27:29; 28:9). Joy, therefore, whether expressed by a noun or a verb, is only experienced by human characters in Matthew in the prologue (2:10) and in the resurrection narrative (28:8).

Jesus to worship him (4:9) before Jesus affirmed that only "the Lord your God" is to be worshipped (4:10).¹³ Together, the prologue and resurrection narrative contain seven of the thirteen uses of the verb "worship" (προσκυνέω) in Matthew. Of the other six (8:2; 9:18; 14:33; 15:25; 18:26; 20:20), only 14:33 combines worship with the use of a messianic title (ἀληθῶς θεοῦ υἱὸς εἶ, "Truly you are the Son of God"). As a result, it is possible to distinguish between the use of προσκυνέω to refer to worship of Jesus and its reference to bowing down to make a request.¹⁴ The frequent occurrence, however, of προσκυνέω directed toward Jesus in Matthew compared to the other Gospels calls such a distinction into question, as though Matthew depicts something more than a mere bowing down, or at least "an unwitting anticipation" of the worship of Jesus by the early church.¹⁵ While worship of Jesus in Matthew is not unique to the prologue and resurrection narrative, they contain three of the four occurrences of worship combined with messianic terminology or epiphanic elements.¹⁶ The worship of Jesus in both places, therefore, contributes to the implied audience's view of the prologue and resurrection narrative as connected, especially given the combination of worship with the phrase "great joy." The presence of προσκυνέω in Matthew's resurrection narrative also results from redactional activity (i.e., it is not in Mark), making it likely that the author intended this connection.

Gatherings

The next scene depicts the Jewish leaders' plot to quash the news of Jesus' resurrection (28:11–15). The verb συνάγω ("gather, assemble," 28:12) appears here along with the plural noun ἀρχιερεύς ("chief priests," 28:11), leading several scholars to note a similarity to Herod's gathering of Jewish

---

13. This verbal similarity is mentioned by Carlson, "Reading and Interpreting," 440; Garland, *Reading Matthew*, 27, 265; Turner, *Matthew*, 80, 81, 682; Harrington, *Matthew*, 416; W. D. Davies and Allison, *Saint Matthew*, 3:673, 687; Luz, *Matthew 1–7*, 114; Luz, *Matthew 21–28*, 591, 607, 616; Ellis, *Matthew*, 98; Allen, *Matthew*, 268–69; Osborne, *Matthew*, 1069; Morris, *Matthew*, 37; Talbert, *Matthew*, 312; Cabrido, *Shepherd of Israel*, 53; J. K. Brown, *Matthew*, 7, 26; Moloney, *Resurrection*, 47; Bonnard, *Matthieu*, 417; Gnilka, *Das Matthäusevangelium*, 506.

14. Dunn, *First Christians*, 11–12.

15. Hurtado, *Lord Jesus Christ*, 338; Kim, "Worship," 227.

16. See Kim for a discussion of "epiphanic worship" of Jesus in 2:2, 11; 14:33; 28:9, 17 ("Worship," 230–34).

leaders including "all the chief priests" (2:4).[17] There are differences between these two situations. In the prologue, the gathering is initiated by Herod and includes the "scribes" (γραμματεῖς, 2:4), while in the resurrection narrative it is initiated by the chief priests themselves and includes the "elders" (πρεσβυτέρων, 28:12). There are, however, similarities. Both gatherings occur in the context of hostility against Jesus and include a reference to a leader with Roman authority (Herod in 2:3–4; Pilate, "the governor," in 28:14).

References to the Jewish leaders' opposition to Jesus are common in Matthew (e.g., 12:14; 16:1; 21:45–46; 26:3–4, 57–59; 27:1). As Matthew's first and last examples of this opposition to Jesus, the references to this opposition in the prologue and resurrection narrative stand out to the implied audience. The narrative of Herod's attempt to kill the infant Jesus, in which the chief priests and scribes were at least complicit (i.e., the implied audience views negatively their failure to accompany the magi to worship Jesus), is made prominent by its extreme violence. The narrative of the plot to silence the news of the resurrection is made prominent by its desperate resort to lying and bribes, and especially by its contrast to the worshipful responses to the risen Jesus that come immediately before and after it (28:9, 17). Both the prominence of these gatherings and the similarities between them suggest a connection to the implied audience. In addition, John the Baptist's harsh rebuke of the Pharisees and Sadducees (3:7) has no parallel in Mark. This suggests that the author of Matthew intended to present an early negative characterization of the Jewish leaders that forms a connection between its beginning and end.[18]

Mountains

When the narrative about Jesus and the disciples resumes in 28:16, the disciples go to Galilee, to a particular "mountain" (ὄρος) that Jesus designates for the meeting. Mountains appear in Matthew several times (4:8; 5:1, 14; 8:1; 14:23; 15:29; 17:1, 9, 20; 21:1, 21; 24:3, 16; 26:30; 28:16), especially as the location of important events (the third temptation, 4:8–10;

---

17. Bauer, "Kingship," 316; Turner, *Matthew*, 44–45; Heil, *Death and Resurrection*, 16–17; Ellis, *Matthew*, 98; Allen, *Matthew*, 268–69; Osborne, *Matthew*, 1062, 1075; Léon-Dufour, *Matthieu*, 26.

18. The opposition to Jesus could be discussed as a conceptual similarity. It is discussed here under verbal similarities, however, due to the occurrence of συνάγω and ἀρχιερεύς.

the Sermon on the Mount, 5:1—7:29; the feeding of the 5000, 15:29-38; the Transfiguration, 17:1-9; the Olivet Discourse, 24:3—25:46; the Great Commission, 28:16-20). Therefore, "mountain" alone does not form a unique connection between the prologue and resurrection narrative, although they do contain the first and last of these important scenes.

A connection between these first and last mountain scenes may, however, result from the combination of the mountain setting with the idea of global authority. In the climactic third temptation, the devil offers Jesus "all the kingdoms of the world and their glory" (4:8-9). Different words are used here—"kingdoms" (βασιλεία) and "glory" (δόξα) in the prologue, and "authority" (ἐξουσία) in the resurrection narrative (28:18). Nevertheless, many commentators see a connection between the two statements resulting from the implication of authority in the offer of kingdoms,[19] and perhaps also from the appearance in both places of "all" (πᾶς) and a form of "to give" (δίδωμι). For example, France writes, "When eventually Jesus is able to claim on another mountain . . . that 'all authority has been given to me,' it will be as a result not of kowtowing to Satan but of suffering in obedience to God's purpose, and then it will be all authority not only on earth but also in heaven, an authority which the devil was not able to offer (28:18)."[20]

Baptism

As Jesus issues the Great Commission (28:18-20) to "make disciples of all nations," one of the participles used—with imperatival force—is βαπτίζοντες ("baptizing"; 28:19). The other six occurrences of this verb are in chapter 3 (3:6, 11 x2, 13, 14, 16). Although the baptism commanded in 28:19 would come to be understood and practiced as something

---

19. Rogers, "Great Commission," 395; M. Davies, *Matthew*, 45; W. D. Davies and Allison, *Saint Matthew*, 1:371, 3:682; Luz, *Matthew 1-7*, 153; Boxall, *Discovering Matthew*, 174; France, *Matthew*, 126, 135; Beare, *Matthew*, 544; Osborne, *Matthew*, 135 (raises the possibility, but is not decisive); Meier, *Vision of Matthew*, 61; Morris, *Matthew*, 78; Talbert, *Matthew*, 62; Charette, *Restoring Presence*, 52; Schweizer, *Matthäus*, 35; Lagrange, *Matthieu*, 62; Gnilka, *Das Matthäusevangelium*, 89-90.

20. France, *Matthew*, 135. Cf. Luz on the third temptation: "Of greatest importance, however, is the manifold allusion to the Gospel's final pericope. . . . there finally takes place, again on a mountain (28:16), the proclamation of his power not only over all the kingdoms of the world but over heaven and earth (28:18). The renunciation of power by the earthly Jesus points ahead to the authority of the risen Jesus" (*Matthew 1-7*, 153).

different from the baptism administered by John,[21] there is nothing in Matthew's story world that distinguishes them in the mind of the implied audience. The frequent, exclusive, and prominent use of βαπτίζω in the prologue causes the implied audience to find in 28:19 a reminder of John's baptism.[22] This connection is strengthened by the reference to the Holy Spirit in relation to baptism (3:11; 28:19),[23] although the relationship between baptism and the Holy Spirit is probably different in each case.[24] Several commentators go a step further to point to unique (in Matthew) anticipations of the Trinity both at the baptism of Jesus (3:16-17, where Father, Son, and Spirit are distinctly present) and in the command to baptize disciples (28:19, where baptism is to be in the "name of the Father, and of the Son, and of the Holy Spirit").[25] Matthew 3:16-17 and 28:19 do not contain a fully developed Trinitarian theology as stated in the Nicene Creed. Nevertheless, the implied audience is likely to notice the concurrence of Father, Son, and Holy Spirit in the context of baptism, and this concurrence strengthens the connection in its mind between the prologue and resurrection narrative.

21. W. D. Davies and Allison state that the two baptisms are distinctly different as a result of the references to Jesus in the various NT phrases that mention Christian baptism (Matt 28:19; Acts 2:38; 8:16; 10:48; 19:5; Rom 6:3; Gal 3:27; cf. Did. 7.1, 3; 9.5; *Saint Matthew*, 3:685). A key question is whether forgiveness of sins was associated with John's baptism. Luz explains that the general consensus of both ancient and modern scholars is that John's baptism lacked the forgiveness associated with Christian baptism, although he argues that such a distinction is not justified since (1) confession of sins is associated with John's baptism (3:6), and (2) Matthew does not explicitly connect forgiveness with Christian baptism (Luz, *Matthew 1-7*, 136). Keener views both baptisms as signifying repentance and treats them as equivalent ("Matthew's Missiology," 10-11).

22. This verbal similarity is mentioned by Lee and Viljoen, "Ultimate Commission," 74-75; Harrington, *Matthew*, 416; Pregeant, *Matthew*, 187; W. D. Davies and Allison, *Saint Matthew*, 1:299, 3:684-85; Luz, *Matthew 21-28*, 632; France, *Matthew*, 99; Mitch and Sri, *Matthew*, 372; Osborne, *Matthew*, 1081; Morris, *Matthew*, 748; J. K. Brown, *Matthew*, 30; Moloney, *Resurrection*, 55.

23. Lee and Viljoen, "Ultimate Commission," 74-75; M. Davies, *Matthew*, 43, 207; Charette, *Restoring Presence*, 95; J. K. Brown, *Matthew*, 30; Bonnard, *Matthieu*, 20.

24. See, for example, W. D. Davies and Allison, *Saint Matthew*, 3:684-85, who comment on 28:18 that "any real connexion with 3.11 appears unlikely," contra M. Davies, *Matthew*, 207; Mitch and Sri, *Matthew*, 372; and Charette, *Restoring Presence*, 95, 126.

25. Lee and Viljoen, "Ultimate Commission," 74-75; Luz, *Matthew 21-28*, 632; Mitch and Sri, *Matthew*, 371; Morris, *Matthew*, 68, 748; Charette, *Restoring Presence*, 126; Moloney, *Resurrection*, 55; W. D. Davies and Allison, *Saint Matthew*, 1:340, 3:687; Turner, *Matthew*, 119; Talbert, *Matthew*, 313. This was also noticed earlier in the history of the church by, for example, Augustine, *Sermons*, 259; and Jerome, *Commentary on Matthew*, 70-71.

Son

The word "son" (υἱός) appears eighty-nine times in Matthew, of which ten are in the prologue (1:1 x2, 20, 21, 23, 25; 2:15; 3:17; 4:3, 6) and one in the resurrection narrative (28:19). Of the ten occurrences in the prologue, just four refer to Jesus as God's Son (2:15; 3:17; 4:3, 6). Since the occurrence of "son" in 28:19 is in relation to God as the Father, it is not clear that the other uses of "son" in the prologue ("son of David," "son of Abraham") are evidence of a connection to the resurrection narrative. Nevertheless, despite the decreased frequency (i.e., four instead of ten occurrences) and the lack of exclusivity within the Gospel, the prominence of this term leads the implied audience to see it as contributing to a connection between the two narratives.[26] The term is used in 2:15 to refer to Jesus as God's Son in fulfillment of Hos 11:1, where Jesus is presented as the new or ideal Israel.[27] In 3:17, God, speaking from heaven, calls Jesus his "beloved son." Furthermore, the devil uses Jesus' sonship as the basis of the first two temptations ("If you are the Son of God . . ."; 4:3, 6), where Jesus demonstrates filial obedience.[28] The theme of Jesus as the "son of God" is so prominent in Matthew that Kingsbury argues that it is the dominant point of view regarding Jesus.[29] Although Jesus is referred to as the "son of God" elsewhere in Matthew (8:29; 14:33; 16:16; 17:5; 27:54), the implied audience recalls that he was first referred to as such in the prologue, forming a connection between the two narratives in its mind.

Holy Spirit

The use of "the Holy Spirit" (τοῦ ἁγίου πνεύματος) in the baptismal formula (28:19) creates an additional connection between the prologue and

---

26. This verbal similarity is mentioned by Carlson, "Reading and Interpreting," 442; Rogers, "Great Commission," 387; Heil, *Death and Resurrection*, 11–12; Turner, *Matthew*, 57; Stock, *Method and Message*, 50–51; W. D. Davies and Allison, *Saint Matthew*, 1:339; Allen, *Matthew*, 269–70.

27. Luz, *Matthew 1–7*, 121; W. D. Davies and Allison, *Saint Matthew*, 1:263–64; France, *Matthew*, 81. Schreiner argues that the entire Gospel of Matthew portrays Jesus as the new and better Israel who "fulfills the mission of Adam, Abraham, Moses, David, Jeremiah, Elijah, and many more" (*Matthew*, 239).

28. Luz, *Matthew 1–7*, 151–53; W. D. Davies and Allison, *Saint Matthew*, 1:367; France, *Matthew*, 124.

29. Kingsbury, *Matthew as Story*, 52.

resurrection narrative in the implied audience's mind.[30] This connection meets the criterion of precision, since the same phrase occurs three times in Matthew's prologue (1:18, 20; 3:11; albeit without the definite article) and once in the resurrection narrative (28:19). The only other occurrence of the phrase in Matthew differs in that it uses the second attributive position (τοῦ πνεύματος τοῦ ἁγίου, 12:32). Thus, the implied audience views references to the Holy Spirit as an additional connection between those sections.

"God with us" and "I am with you"

The final verbal similarity between Matthew's prologue and resurrection narrative to be discussed here is the one most commonly cited by commentators. It is the *inclusio* formed by "Immanuel . . . God with us" in 1:23 and "I am with you always" in 28:20.[31] These are not precise verbal parallels (μεθ' ἡμῶν ὁ θεός, 1:23; ἐγὼ μεθ' ὑμῶν, 28:20). The differences, however, are made necessary by the context, given the speaker and audience, as well by the literalness of the translation from the Hebrew of Isa 7:14, where the precise order of עִמָּנוּ אֵל is maintained. The other main difference between the two phrases is a shift from God to Jesus as the one who is with his people. Various aspects of Matthew's narrative prepare the reader to see this as an appropriate shift. The birth and naming of Jesus fulfill the Immanuel promise of Isa 7:14, to which Matthew adds the

---

30. See Turner, *Matthew*, 64; J. K. Brown, *Matthew*, 17; and the footnotes in the discussion of "Baptism" above for others who mention the references to the Holy Spirit in both the prologue and the resurrection narrative.

31. This verbal similarity is mentioned by Lee and Viljoen, "Ultimate Commission," 75; Carlson, "Reading and Interpreting," 439; McDonald, "I Am with You," 66; Schneider and Huizenga, "Das Matthäusevangelium," 23; Bauer, "Kingship," 311; Willis, "Matthew's Birth Stories," 45; Krentz, "Missionary Matthew," 31; Kupp, *Matthew's Emmanuel*, 175, 219; Kingsbury, *Matthew as Story*, 41–42; Kingsbury, *Matthew* (Proclamation Commentaries), 28; Garland, *Reading Matthew*, 6, 265; Turner, *Matthew*, 34, 690–92; Harrington, *Matthew*, 416; Stock, *Method and Message*, 30, 439–41; Edwards, *Matthew's Story of Jesus*, 13, 93; Heil, *Death and Resurrection*, 9; W. D. Davies and Allison, *Saint Matthew*, 1:213, 3:686–87; Luz, *Matthew 1–7*, 96; Luz, *Matthew 21–28*, 597, 616, 634; Ellis, *Matthew*, 28, 98; Allen, *Matthew*, 25, 269–70, 280; Boxall, *Discovering Matthew*, 90, 174; France, *Matthew*, 49; Mitch and Sri, *Matthew*, 47; Osborne, *Matthew*, 79, 1082; Meier, *Vision of Matthew*, 214; Senior, *Matthew*, 90, 174–75; Morris, *Matthew*, 31, 749–50; Alkier, "From Text to Intertext," 8; Cabrido, *Shepherd of Israel*, 30; J. K. Brown, *Matthew*, 16, 31; R. E. Brown, *Birth of the Messiah*, 153; Moloney, *Resurrection*, 45–46, 56; Sonnet, "De la généalogie," 207–8; Charette, *Restoring Presence*, 109; Schweizer, *Matthäus*, 351; Gnilka, *Das Matthäusevangelium*, 21; R. Reeves, *Matthew*, 566.

translation "God with us" (Matt 1:23). Jesus receives worship (2:11; 28:9, 17) while affirming that worship should be directed to God alone (4:10). Jesus is closely identified with God through "son of God" language (2:15; 3:17; 28:19; cf. 11:27). Although the "son of God" concept is not exclusive to Jesus in Matthew (cf. 5:9, and the implication of 6:9), "my beloved son" (ὁ υἱός μου ὁ ἀγαπητός) in 3:17 (cf. 17:5) implies a unique relationship to the Father. Jesus also appears to claim omnipresence in 18:20, where he promises to be present among any two or three gathered in his name.

Although "with you/us" language occurs only once in the prologue and once in the resurrection narrative, in both cases it is very prominent. One appears in conjunction with words from the prophet Isaiah (Matt 1:23; Isa 7:14) and evokes other "with you" language from the OT (e.g., Gen 26:3, 24; 28:15; 31:3; Exod 3:12; Deut 2:7; 20:4; 31:6, 8, 23; Josh 1:5, 9; 3:7; Judg 6:12, 16; 2 Sam 7:3, 9), and the other appears in the final words spoken by the risen Jesus (28:20). The implied audience can hardly miss this *inclusio*. Even though questions remain as to exactly how the continued presence of the risen Son of God is to be equated with the Immanuel presence of God, it is clear that the prologue and the resurrection narrative are related and must be read together to be properly understood.

Conclusion

To summarize, in Matthew's resurrection narrative (28:1–20), over the course of just twenty verses, or a mere 329 words, the implied audience encounters seventeen occurrences of thirteen different words or phrases that are very similar to words or phrases found in the Gospel's prologue.[32] There are many other words that appear in both the prologue and resurrection narrative, some of which are cited by commentators.[33] The use of

---

32. The repetitions of "angel" in 28:5 (cf. "angel of the Lord" in 28:2), of Galilee three times (28:7, 10, 16), and of worship (28:9, 17) result in the four additional occurrences of distinct words or phrases.

33. Other words occurring in both the prologue and resurrection narrative that are identified by commentators as possibly connecting the two are "brothers" (ἀδελφοί; 1:2, 11; 28:10), Sonnet, "De la généalogie," 208; "Mary" (Μαρία; 1:16, 18, 20; 2:11; 28:1), Sonnet, "De la généalogie," 207–8; "Jews" (Ἰουδαῖοι; 2:2; 28:15), Senior, *Matthew*, 169, and Bonnard, *Matthieu*, 415; "governor" (ἡγεμών; 2:6; 28:14), Cabrido, *Shepherd of Israel*, 47; "report" (ἀπαγγέλλω; 2:8; 28:8, 10, 11), Luz, *Matthew 21–28*, 591, and Gnilka, *Das Matthäusevangelium*, 499; "go before" (προάγω; 2:9; 28:7), Cabrido, *Shepherd of Israel*, 47; "seeing" (ἰδόντες; 2:10; 28:17), Carter, "To See the Tomb," 202–3; and "heaven"

the criteria described above, however, allows us to speak with a degree of certainty and objectivity about the implied audience's recognition of these similarities. The claim that the implied audience is expected to view the prologue and resurrection narrative in Matthew as two parts of a single, unified narrative is not based on the occurrence of words that are too common to be recognized as forming such a connection. Together, the verbal similarities discussed above convince the implied audience that Matthew's prologue and resurrection narratives are related to one another.[34] In addition, it understands that the prologue, which forms the beginning of the story, contains information that will contribute in important ways to its understanding of the resurrection narrative that concludes the story. At least four of these similarities are the results of redactional activity on the part of Matthew's author, suggesting that the author intentionally established connections between the prologue and resurrection narrative that the implied audience is expected to notice.

Conceptual Similarities between Matthew's Prologue and Resurrection Narrative

The criteria described above are admittedly more useful for evaluating verbal similarities than conceptual similarities.[35] The presence or absence of a particular word is an objective fact, whereas the presence of a concept may be debated. It is difficult to speak of precision as a criterion when comparing concepts that may be presented in very different ways. At minimum, conceptual similarities are expressed using different words; otherwise, they would be verbal similarities. Therefore, an argument for literary unity based only on conceptual similarities would be

---

(οὐρανός; 3:3; 28:18), Schweizer, *Matthäus*, 23. There is also an interesting concurrence in 4:6 of "angels," "foot," and "stone," which may be related to 28:2–9, where the "angel" of the Lord (28:2), the "stone" that had covered the tomb (28:2), and the "feet" of Jesus (28:9) are all mentioned. It would be difficult to prove, however, that the implied audience is expected to notice this concurrence of terms.

34. It may be better to say that these similarities confirm the implied audience's assumption that the beginning and the end of the story should be read as parts of a single story. It is worded as it is, however, due to the objection of some that such an assumption is not appropriate.

35. For the purpose of this study, "conceptual similarity" is defined broadly as any similarity between Matthew's prologue and resurrection narrative that does not result from use of the same word or words. Such similarities may result from the use of synonyms, implications of certain words or actions, or similar circumstances or events.

less convincing. Fortunately, we can point out conceptual similarities between Matthew's prologue and resurrection *in addition to* the verbal similarities present in them. The recognition of conceptual similarities strengthens the impression of the implied audience that these two parts of Matthew are related. While it is possible to point to several possible conceptual similarities,[36] the four discussed below are those most likely to be recognized by the implied audience.

Preservation of Jesus' Life

Matthew's implied audience observes that God preserves the life of Jesus in both the prologue (2:12–14) and the resurrection narrative. In the prologue, the birth of Jesus is followed almost immediately by King Herod's attempt to destroy him (2:7–8, 13, 16).[37] God intervenes to spare Jesus from death by communicating to the magi (2:12) and to Joseph (2:13) through dreams. In the resurrection narrative, Jesus had not been spared from death (cf. 27:46). Nevertheless, "Jesus, who had been crucified" (28:5) "has been raised" (28:6). The divine passive, ἠγέρθη (28:6) indicates that God is the one who raised Jesus. Although there are differences between the two sets of circumstances—Jesus is spared from death in one but raised from death in the other—the implied audience recognizes that, in both cases, God intervenes to preserve the life of Jesus. In both cases, the angel of the Lord is involved in the preservation of Jesus' life, first by issuing warnings (2:12, 13), and later by revealing (28:2) and announcing (28:5–6) that Jesus had been raised. In addition to the similarities between these events, their prominence—as God's initial and ultimate rescues of Jesus—contribute to the implied audience's recognition that they form a connection between the prologue and the resurrection narrative.

---

36. Others mentioned by commentators, but not discussed here, are the correlation of "beginning" (1:1) and "end" (28:20), Bauer, "Genealogy," 159; the concept of righteousness seen in 3:15 (Jesus' baptism was "to fulfill all righteousness") and 28:19 ("teaching them to obey everything . . ."), Luz, *Matthew 1–7*, 142; and possible Moses motifs in 4:1–11 and 28:16–20, Rogers, "Great Commission," 388–89, 392–98.

37. This conceptual similarity is mentioned by Derickson, "Chiastic Structure," 427, and Willis, "Matthew's Birth Stories," 45.

Hostile Gatherings

In Matt 28:11-15, after Jesus' resurrection, the Jewish leaders gather in response to the guards' report about "all that had taken place" (28:11). Several commentators observe that in the details of this event there are conceptual similarities to events in Matthew's prologue. Allen points out that there is an apologetic motif to prevent a possible scandal both here (i.e., explaining away the rumor that Jesus' disciples had stolen his body, 28:15) and in the statement in 1:25 that Joseph kept Mary a virgin (lit. "did not know her," οὐκ ἐγίνωσκεν αὐτήν) until after she had given birth to Jesus.[38] Other commentators note similarities between this gathering and Herod's response to the visit of the magi (2:1-18).[39] Both of these events involve Jewish leaders (2:4; 28:11-12), rulers with Roman authority (2:3; 28:14), and soldiers (28:11; implied in 2:16). Herod and all Jerusalem are troubled when they hear of the birth of the "king of the Jews" (2:3) and, although it is not stated explicitly, the response of the Jewish leaders shows that they are troubled by the report of Jesus' resurrection (28:12-14). Both events involve a secret meeting (explicit in 2:7; implicit in 28:12-14). Finally, both events involve lies. Herod lies to the magi about his intention to worship Jesus (2:8), and the soldiers are instructed to lie about the reason that Jesus' tomb is empty (28:13). The cumulative effect of these similarities leads the implied audience to view the prologue and the resurrection narrative as parts of a single story in which political and religious authorities consistently try to stop God from accomplishing his purpose in sending Jesus, but they ultimately fail.

Authority and Kingship

Finally, there are two concepts in Jesus' words in the Great Commission (28:18-20) that recall concepts introduced in the prologue. The first is Jesus' claim that "all authority in heaven and on earth" has been given to him (28:18). This statement was discussed above in relation to the connection formed by the mention of mountains in 4:8 and 28:16. The concept of authority, however, is also found in other parts of Matthew's prologue. Although there was no uniform messianic expectation prior

---

38. Allen, *Matthew*, 268-69.

39. Aspects of this conceptual similarity are mentioned by Pregeant, *Matthew*, 191, 193-94; W. D. Davies and Allison, *Saint Matthew*, 3:673; Osborne, *Matthew*, 1075; Heil, *Death and Resurrection*, 16-17.

to the coming of Jesus,[40] his introduction in 1:1 as "Christ" or "Messiah" (Χριστός) in conjunction with the phrase "son of David" implies a messianic figure who possesses ruling authority.[41] Thus, the first verse of Matthew's Gospel begins to define Χριστός within the range of existing expectations. That Χριστός in Matthew's story world implies kingship, and therefore authority, is confirmed when Herod, in response to the magi's question about the location of the birth of the "king of the Jews" (2:2), asks where the Χριστός is to be born (2:4). The chief priests and scribes answer by quoting Mic 5:2, 4, which they understand to refer to the Messiah (though the word מָשִׁיחַ is not present in that text), indicating that they expect the Messiah to have ruling authority over Israel (2:6). Matthew 1:1 continues by referring to Jesus as the "son of David," which the implied audience (which knows the OT) recognizes as a reference to the descendant of David whose kingdom will be established forever (2 Sam 7:12–13). The "son of God" language found in Matthew's prologue (2:15; 3:17; 4:3, 6) is understood not only to indicate a filial relationship between Jesus and God the Father, but also kingship (Ps 2:7–12; cf. 2 Sam 7:14) and the authority associated with it. In these ways, the concept of authority is prominent in Matthew's prologue. Jesus' claim of authority in 28:18 is therefore understood by the implied audience to be related to the prologue's presentation of Jesus, which also uses language implying authority.

Inclusion of Gentiles

A second concept found in Jesus' Great Commission that is also present in the prologue is that the scope of Jesus' mission through his disciples is "all nations" (πάντα τὰ ἔθνη, 28:19). Hare and Harrington argue that πάντα τὰ ἔθνη should be understood as "all the gentiles," exclusive of Israel, although this interpretation is informed by their understanding of Matthew's *Sitz im Leben*, which lies outside of its story world.[42] Meier's analysis of the use of ἔθνος/ἔθνη in Matthew, where he concludes that it

---

40. Charlesworth, "From Messianology to Christology," 5, 35; Longman, "The Messiah," 28–29.

41. This conceptual similarity is mentioned by Lee and Viljoen, "Ultimate Commission," 66–71; Carlson, "Reading and Interpreting," 436; Turner, *Matthew*, 34, 80, 689; Stock, *Method and Message*, 50–51; W. D. Davies and Allison, *Saint Matthew*, 3:687; Charette, *Restoring Presence*, 37; Cabrido, *Shepherd of Israel*, 30; France, *Matthew*, 1113.

42. Hare and Harrington, "Make Disciples," 359, 366–67.

should be translated "nations" in 28:19 (he even prefers "peoples"), better accounts for the contexts in which it is used.[43] He also recognizes the consistent use of πάντα τὰ ἔθνη to include Israel when it occurs as a result of Matthew's redactional activity (24:9, 14; 25:32; 28:19).[44]

While the phrase "all the nations" does not appear in Matthew's prologue, the concept is found there in multiple places. First, many detect it in 1:1, where Jesus is called the "son of Abraham," which likely recalls Gen 22:18 (cf. 12:3; 18:18) and God's promise to bless "all the nations" (πάντα τὰ ἔθνη in LXX) of the earth "in" Abraham's "seed" (or "offspring," זֶרַע).[45] The women who appear in Matthew's genealogy (Tamar, 1:3; Rahab and Ruth, 1:5; "the wife of Uriah," 1:6) are often understood to highlight the inclusion of gentiles among the people of God.[46] If the implied audience understands these women to be gentiles, it results in a prominent gentile motif in the genealogy. Rahab and Ruth, and most likely Tamar, were gentiles, although Bathsheba may not have been, making the gentile motif more subtle, although one that is still present.[47] In Matthew, the first people to respond properly to Jesus with worship are magi (2:1–11), whose title, origin ("the east"), interest in astrology, and

43. Meier, "Nations or Gentiles," 97–101. Cf. Lee and Viljoen, "Target Group," 94.

44. Meier, "Nations or Gentiles," 102.

45. This conceptual similarity is mentioned by Lee and Viljoen, "Ultimate Commission," 66; Carlson, "Reading and Interpreting," 435; Bauer, "Kingship," 323; Kingsbury, *Matthew as Story*, 47; Stock, *Method and Message*, 24; W. D. Davies and Allison, *Saint Matthew*, 3:687; Boxall, *Discovering Matthew*, 79, 174. Other commentators point out that the phrase "son of Abraham" also emphasizes Jesus' status as a true Israelite (W. D. Davies and Allison, *Saint Matthew*, 1:158; Luz, *Matthew 1–7*, 82; Kingsbury, *Matthew as Story*, 47). Huizenga, "Matthean Jesus," 70, argues that "son of Abraham" in 1:1 rather introduces an Isaac motif that continues throughout Matthew's Gospel.

46. This conceptual similarity is mentioned by Krentz, "Missionary," 29; Turner, *Matthew*, 691; France, *Matthew*, 37; Osborne, *Matthew*, 70, 1069; Schweizer, *Matthäus*, 9.

47. Rahab was a resident of Jericho prior to the arrival of the Israelites (Josh 2:1). Ruth is identified as a Moabitess (Ruth 1:4). Tamar's ethnicity is not indicated. Given that she was close in age to the second generation after Jacob (Gen 38:6) and that Judah, her father-in-law, had not made her marriage within the clan a priority (cf. Gen 38:1–2), she was probably a gentile. Philo, *Virt*. 221, referred to Tamar as being from Palestinian Syria (cf. Bauckham, "Two Problems," 320). Bathsheba was married to a Hittite (2 Sam 11:3), but her ethnicity is not mentioned, and her father had a Hebrew name (Eliam, 2 Sam 11:3). Other possible explanations for the presence of the women in the genealogy are that that their presence supports a Pharisaic messianic expectation, that they are all sinners, and that their marital unions were all irregular, with the latter two options highlighting God's ability to send the Messiah through less than ideal people and circumstances (see discussions in W. D. Davies and Allison, *Saint Matthew*, 1:170–72; and Heil, "Women," 544–45).

gifts all suggest that they are gentiles.[48] Their worship, contrasted with Herod's opposition to Jesus and the Jewish leaders' apathy toward him, contributes to the development of the concept of the gentiles' inclusion in God's mission through Jesus. In addition, the devil's offer of "all the kingdoms of the world and their glory" (4:8) necessarily includes all nations. Finally, Jesus' presence in Galilee (2:22; 3:13)—later called "Galilee of the gentiles" (4:15; cf. Isa 9:1)—suggests that God's plan through Jesus includes the gentiles. Together, these elements of the prologue prepare the implied audience to understand "all nations" in 28:19 as conceptually related to the beginning of the narrative and, therefore, to see the resurrection narrative in general, and the Great Commission in particular, as bringing to fulfillment a prominent theme from the prologue.

Conclusion

In addition to the seventeen occurrences of verbal similarities Matthew's prologue and resurrection narratives, the implied audience encounters four significant conceptual similarities that strengthen the perceived connection between the beginning and the end of that Gospel. Three of these conceptual similarities are found closely associated with one another in Jesus' final words (28:18–20). In addition, these similarities do not appear in just one part of Matthew's prologue; they are present in nearly every section of it—the title or opening (1:1), the genealogy (1:2–17), the visit of the magi (2:1–12), the slaughter of the innocents and flight to Egypt (2:13–23), the baptism of Jesus (3:13–17), and the temptation of Jesus (4:1–11). Those sections of the prologue lacking clear conceptual similarities to the resurrection narrative (1:18–25; 3:1–12) do, however, contain verbal similarities to the resurrection narrative. The result, then, is that Matthew's resurrection narrative is understood by the implied audience to be connected to every part of the prologue.

The verbal and conceptual similarities between Matthew's prologue and resurrection narrative are substantial. Evidence of this is that some

48. This conceptual similarity is mentioned by Bauer, "Kingship," 319; Garland, *Reading Matthew*, 265; Heil, *Death and Resurrection*, 13–14; Pregeant, *Matthew*, 186; W. D. Davies and Allison, *Saint Matthew*, 3:673; Ellis, *Matthew*, 98; Allen, *Matthew*, 268–69; Boxall, *Discovering Matthew*, 76; France, *Matthew*, 37, 67; Mitch and Sri, *Matthew*, 36; Osborn, *Matthew*, 1069, 1080; Senior, *Matthew*, 169; Cabrido, *Shepherd of Israel*, 51; J. K. Brown, *Matthew*, 26; R. E. Brown, *Birth of the Messiah*, 182; Keerankeri, "Birth of the Messiah," 847–48. R. E. Brown, discusses their likely origin, which is Parthia or Persia, Babylon, or Arabia or the Syrian desert (*Birth of the Messiah*, 167–70).

scholars refer to the Great Commission (28:16–20) as a summary of the entirety of Matthew's Gospel,[49] while another can refer to the infancy narrative as "the Gospel of Matthew in miniature."[50] The nature of the relationships established by these similarities may not be immediately obvious to the implied audience. Their existence, however, invites and compels the implied audience to reflect on them and to be guided by them in its effort to understand the significance of Jesus' resurrection.

Similarities between Matthew's Prologue and Resurrection Narrative: Possible Significance for Interpretation

It seems clear that the implied audience of Matthew's Gospel is expected to recognize that its prologue and resurrection narrative are linked together through numerous verbal and conceptual similarities. As a result, it views these two portions of the Gospel not only as parts of a single narrative, but also as being uniquely connected; their understanding of the resurrection narrative is therefore informed and influenced by the content of the prologue.

What is not clear is *how* the content of the prologue informs and influences the implied audience's understanding of the resurrection narrative. This lack of clarity is illustrated by the diverse ways in which the significance of the Immanuel *inclusio* (1:23; 28:20) has been interpreted. It has been described as "artistry" without comment on its significance for interpretation.[51] Some indicate that 1:23, along with the Gospel's commentary on the Immanuel theme, result in the implied audience not being surprised by the promise in 28:20.[52] Some suggest that the *inclusio* shows that what was true at 1:23 remains true at 28:20.[53] Others detect some change or development so that 28:20 does more than simply reiterate or confirm what 1:23 initially said about Jesus.[54]

---

49. Lee and Viljoen, "Ultimate Commission," 75; Krentz, "Missionary Matthew," 24; Scaer, "Relation," 261; Harrington, *Matthew*, 416.

50. Keerankeri, "Birth of the Messiah," 848.

51. Edwards, *Matthew's Story of Jesus*, 93.

52. Lee and Viljoen, "Ultimate Commission," 75.

53. Luz, *Matthew 21–28*, 597; Allen, *Matthew*, 269–70; France, *Matthew*, 49; Senior, *Matthew*, 90.

54. Krentz, "Missionary Matthew," 31; Heil, *Death and Resurrection*, 9; Bauer, "Kingship," 311; Turner, *Matthew*, 690.

The Immanuel *inclusio* is the most commonly discussed similarity between Matthew's prologue and resurrection narrative. Although most commentators recognize the presence of this *inclusio*, there remains a lack of consensus regarding its significance for interpretation. This lack of consensus may result from a lack of reflection on the role of these statements within the overall narrative. Do the two statements refer to something that has been consistently true throughout the entire narrative? Do they reflect something that was initially true, but later jeopardized or reversed, then finally restored to its original state? Or do they reflect some type of progress or development so that, while it always was true, the latter expression of the truth includes some modification or improvement?

While most scholars will notice the *fact* that certain similarities exist between parts of a narrative, narrative criticism provides tools for understanding and evaluating the possible *significance* of these similarities. These tools include attention to plot, which aids our understanding of *how* the parts are related, and consideration of evaluative point of view, by which earlier parts of the narrative establish guidelines for evaluating later parts. One must be careful not to limit interpretive interest to explaining the relationships between verbal and conceptual similarities. After all, the presence of these similarities in Matthew's prologue and resurrection narrative has confirmed narrative criticism's presumption of the unity of the two parts of that Gospel. As a result, everything in them is understood to be related to the rest since they comprise the beginning and the end of the same story.

We conclude this chapter with a series of questions provoked by the similarities noted above. This discussion was not intended to draw conclusions, but rather to reflect on how narrative criticism may help to answer such questions, through the analysis of character, setting, plot, and point of view in the rest of this dissertation.

First, how might the appearance of certain motifs (such as the angel of the Lord, "Do not fear," worship, great joy) exclusively or primarily in the contexts of Jesus' birth and resurrection indicate that these two events are unique, or of some special quality, within the Gospel as a whole? This special quality could be the result of more direct divine activity or presence, of the significance of these events for salvation history, or of their apocalyptic nature.

Second, what is the significance of the concentration of Matthew's references to Galilee near its beginning and end? If, as Luz suggests, the significance of Galilee is that it is a place of refuge that offers protection from the Jewish leaders,[55] its appearance at the beginning and end could have the effect of showing that opposition to Jesus continued even after his resurrection. Alternatively, it could suggest that through his disciples, Jesus continues to shine light in the darkness in Galilee of the gentiles (cf. 4:12–16).

Third, "great joy" (χαρὰ μεγάλη) occurs only in 2:10 and 28:8. Should we conclude, then, that Matthew shows that a special time of joy began with the birth of Jesus and continued, uninterrupted, through his resurrection and beyond? Or is it better to understand that great joy was an especially appropriate response to the birth and resurrection of Israel's Messiah, but that there was some threat to or interruption of this joy between these two great events?

Another similarity with possible significance for interpretation is the opposition of the Jewish leaders. Is the presence of such opposition at the beginning and end an indication of a theme that runs straight through the Gospel and that exists in much the same way throughout? Or should the implied audience detect a development and transformation of the Jewish leaders' opposition to Jesus?

How should one interpret the relationship between the first and last mountain scenes in Matthew? Is Matthew merely marking these events as among the more significant events in the Gospel?[56] Do the mountain scenes in Matthew demonstrate Jesus' superiority to Moses?[57] Are the first (4:8–9) and last (28:18) of greater significance? Do they indicate, for example, that Jesus had obtained, through obedience rather than through worship of the devil, something greater than, but inclusive of, what had been offered in 4:9?[58]

The concept of authority appears in the prologue especially as an implication of Jesus' characterization as the royal Son of David (which Matthew associates with "Messiah", Χριστός, at 2:2, 4, by identifying the Messiah with the "king of the Jews"), and then in the resurrection narrative in his claim of "all authority" in 28:18. How should one understand the distinction between the authority associated with David's throne and "all authority in heaven and on earth"? One possibility is to view the latter

---

55. Luz, *Matthew 21–28*, 621.

56. See Charette, as an example of those who point out that key events in Matthew often happen on mountains (*Restoring Presence*, 115).

57. Rogers, argues that the Great Commission is the culmination of the theme of Jesus' superiority to Moses ("Great Commission," 398).

58. See, for example, France, *Matthew*, 135.

as an alternative to the former, so that Jesus is understood to do something different from, though perhaps greater than, what was expected of the Son of David. Another possibility is to view the latter as including the former, so that Jesus is understood to do all that was expected of the Son of David, and perhaps more that was not expected. Another question related to this authority is whether Jesus has always possessed "all authority" or came to possess it only at the end of the Gospel. If the latter is the case, how did he come to possess it? Was it a result of his obedience in general or more specifically of his death and resurrection?

Finally, the concept of the gentiles, or nations, implicit in the prologue and explicit in the Great Commission (28:20) may be significant for interpretation. Should one view the directive to make disciples of "all nations" as expected and possible under the conditions found in the prologue? Or should the gentile mission be seen as an intention expressed in the prologue but unable to occur under the conditions found in the prologue (when the devil could claim to possess "all the kingdoms of the world and their glory," 4:8)? If the latter of these options is the case, what brought about a change in these conditions? How and why might the death and resurrection of Jesus have changed these conditions?

The verbal and conceptual similarities between Matthew's prologue and resurrection narrative demonstrate the unity between those passages. They also suggest ways that those passages may be related and invite the implied audience to consider the significance of these relationships when interpreting the resurrection narrative. Some possible interpretations of the relationships are described above. In order to determine how the implied audience is expected to understand the significance of Jesus' resurrection in light of Matthew's prologue, we must go beyond simply identifying these similarities and the tools of narrative criticism to use. In the following chapters, the characterization, settings, plot, and point of view of Matthew's prologue and resurrection narrative will be analyzed with the goal of understanding the way in which the prologue influences the implied audience's understanding of the significance of Jesus' resurrection.

3

Characterization Part One

Introduction and Jesus the Messiah

Introduction

The first literary element to be analyzed in this study is characterization. This is both because the presentation of a character affects the implied audience's understanding of the narrative's plot and because Matthew's narrative begins with characterization of Jesus (1:1). Most discussions of characterization devote considerable space to the way that characters are developed (showing and telling) and to the different types of characters (round, flat, or stock; static or dynamic).[1] Since the goal of narrative criticism is to determine the narrative's effect on the implied audience, it is surprising that these discussions contain little explanation of the ways in which characterization produces this effect. Therefore, before discussing the characters in Matthew's prologue (1:1—4:11) and resurrection narrative, it is necessary to outline several possible ways that the presentation of a character can lead to the implied audience's response.

---

1. Powell, *What Is Narrative Criticism?*, 51–67; Resseguie, *Narrative Criticism*, 121–65; Kingsbury, *Matthew as Story*, 9–28. Merenlahti argues that a character's degree of development is determined by the need to present them as consistent with the narrative's ideological point of view ("Characters in the Making," 49–50).

How Characterization Leads to the Implied Audience's Response

1. Characterization often presents characters' responses as model responses. The implied audience knows a positive response, such as the magi's worship of Jesus (2:9-12), is also expected of it.[2] It also knows that negative responses, such as Herod's attempt to destroy Jesus (2:16), should be rejected. In the Gospels, it is almost always a character's response to Jesus, the protagonist, that is of interest.[3] Model responses may be expressed in actions or words. Positive responses reflect an ideological (or evaluative) point of view that the implied audience is expected to adopt.[4] The implied audience more easily identifies with characters which are more fully developed and with those presented positively.[5]

2. Some characters indirectly affect the implied audience by contributing to the design of the plot or to the development of some theme.[6] Some characters, referred to as "stock characters" or "walk-ons," are developed so little that they are more like props in the narrative.[7] These characters lack a vividness that enables the implied audience to identify with them. Other characters, such as the angel of the Lord or the Holy Spirit, although not stock characters, are in a class (i.e., non-humans) that prevents the implied audience's identification with them.

3. Some characters contribute to the characterization of other characters. A foil character indirectly affects the implied audience by emphasizing one or more traits of another (or others).[8] The centurion who demonstrates "great faith" in Matt 8:5-9 presents a response to be imitated. It is the contrast, however, between his—a gentile's—believing response to Jesus and the unbelieving responses of many

---

2. Lehtipuu, "Characterization and Persuasion," 104-5.

3. Williams, "Characterization of Jesus," 125-26; Bennema, "Comprehensive Approach," 57-58.

4. Lehtipuu, "Characterization and Persuasion," 104.

5. Lehtipuu, "Characterization and Persuasion," 104; Howell, *Inclusive Story,* 229.

6. Culpepper, "Weave of the Tapestry," 35. See also Resseguie, *Narrative Criticism,* 125.

7. Powell, *What Is Narrative Criticism?,* 55; Resseguie, *Narrative Criticism,* 125; Kingsbury, *Matthew as Story,* 10.

8. Powell, *What Is Narrative Criticism?,* 66.

Jews that is more significant to the plot and to the effect on the implied audience.[9] A character may also contribute to the characterization of another through his or her testimony about or association with the other (e.g., John's testimony about Jesus in 3:11–12).

4. The presentation of a character can guide the implied audience's evaluation of real persons.[10] Matthew's narrative invites its implied audience to relate certain characters to people in its own experience. The claim that Jesus' followers had stolen his body (28:15) was still being circulated at the time of the Gospel's composition. In addition, Jesus assures the Eleven and those, like those in implied audience, who would become his disciples that he would be present with them until the end of the age (28:20). These statements from the closing verses of Matthew relate the narrative and certain characters in it to the implied audience's own time and circumstances,[11] influencing its response to Jesus and to Jewish leaders they encounter.[12]

5. Characterization can increase or clarify the significance of an event when the event's significance is related to the person(s) performing or affected by it. When Jesus says, "Go Satan" (ὕπαγε, σατανᾶ) to the devil (4:10), the implied audience is impressed, but not surprised, by Jesus' forcefulness. When he says nearly the same thing, however, to Peter—"Get behind me, Satan" (ὕπαγε ὀπίσω μου, σατανᾶ; 16:23)—the words have added significance. If the apostle could act as an adversary to Jesus, then what prevents other disciples from doing the same?

6. Another effect of characterization is related to the expectations associated with the character's presentation. For example, in Matthew, a little girl (9:25; cf. 9:18, 24) and Jesus (28:7) are both raised (ἐγέρθη) from death. The lack of information about the little girl

---

9. Jesus points out this contrast in Matt 8:10–12.

10. Williams makes this point regarding Jesus, since "the reality of Jesus' Lordship extends into the time and world of his audience" ("Characterization of Jesus," 125–26). Cf. Luz, "for the readers it is not a stranger who speaks in the Gospel but their own Lord" (*Matthew 1–7*, 17). Cf. Kupp, *Matthew's Emmanuel*, 236.

11. Cf. Luz (*Matthew 1–7*, 42), who refers to this phenomenon as "transparency."

12. Howell suggests that Jesus or other characters address the implied audience directly (e.g., Matt 5:13; 7:24, 26; 8:27; 13:51; 16:24; 26:54; *Inclusive Story*, 219–29). It is difficult to prove that the implied audience is expected to understand words spoken in the narrative as being addressed to it, since nothing in the text explicitly places them in the story world. The implied audience's ability to identify with those directly addressed within the story world eliminates the need to prove that it is addressed directly.

limits the implied audience's understanding of the significance of her raising. Her return to life apparently enabled nothing more than the resumption of an ordinary life. The narrative significance of Jesus' raising, on the other hand, is much greater. He is characterized as the promised Messiah (1:1) through whom God's kingdom has come near (4:17; cf. 3:2) and who promises to execute God's judgment and reward (7:21-23; 19:28; 25:31-33).[13] Therefore, his return to life enables him to perform the functions associated with his characterization. Characterization leads the implied audience to have specific expectations for a character, and these expectations are confirmed, threatened, or undermined as the plot unfolds.

To summarize, characterization affects the implied audience's response in six ways.

1. Characterization can present positive or negative model responses—along with their corresponding ideological points of view—to be adopted or rejected by the implied audience.

2. Characterization may indirectly produce an effect on the implied audience by advancing the plot or developing a theme.

3. The characterization of one character may contribute to the characterization of other characters through testimony about or association with the other character, or by serving as a foil.

4. Characterization may guide the implied audience in evaluating real people who can be identified with characters in the narrative.

5. Characterization can increase or clarify the significance of actions performed due to the significance of the person performing or receiving the action.

---

13. Although Matthew normally—but not exclusively (cf. 6:10, 33; 12:28; 13:41, 43; 16:28; 19:24; 21:31, 43; 26:29)—uses the term "kingdom of heaven," we will generally avoid that term because (1) we can confidently view it as equivalent in meaning to "kingdom of God" (cf. Mark 1:15; 4:11, 30; 10:14-15, 23; see Luz, *Matthew 1-7*, 135), (2) it lends itself to being understood (wrongly, in our view) as referring to a purely heavenly or spiritual (i.e., non earthly) kingdom (e.g., Foster, "Why on Earth," 487-99), and (3) language such as "God's kingdom," "Davidic kingdom," and "the kingdom" better reflects the continuity that exists between the points of view of the OT and Matthew's story world.

6. Characterization establishes expectations associated with a character, and subsequent events confirm, threaten, or undermine those expectations.[14]

As the characters in Matthew's prologue and resurrection narrative are discussed in this chapter and the next, an effort will be made to discern the implied audience's response to the presentation of each character. We will exclude persons who form part of the background to the narrative, but who do not actually appear as "actors" in the narrative (e.g., David, Archelaus).

Jesus the Messiah

Jesus is the first and most important character introduced in Matthew's Gospel. Therefore, our narrative-critical analysis of characters begins with him. As many have noted, it is necessary to go beyond the various titles attributed to Jesus, since he is presented as having some traits that are not included in the meanings of those titles.[15]

Matthew's Initial Characterization of Jesus (1:1)

Matthew begins by telling the implied audience that this narrative is "The book of the genealogy (or 'generations,' γενέσεως) of Jesus (the) Messiah" (1:1).[16] Whether this phrase refers only to the genealogy (1:2–17), to Matthew's infancy narrative or prologue, or to the entirety of the Gospel, it clearly identifies Jesus as its central figure. The phrase βίβλος γενέσεως (cf. LXX of Gen 2:5; 5:1) suggests to the implied audience that this narrative is related to the Genesis narrative.[17] The genealogy (1:2–16) will

---

14. Effects 5 and 6 may sometimes overlap, but they are stated separately here to encourage narrative critics to look for both phenomena.

15. Luz, *Matthew 1–7*, 70; Luz, *Matthew 21–28*, 639–40; W. D. Davies and Allison, *Saint Matthew*, 3:720–21; Boring, "Narrative Christology," 359; Donaldson, "Vindicated Son," 102.

16. I have chosen to translate Χριστός as "Messiah" to reflect the conviction that the implied audience, with a Jewish background and knowledge of the OT, understands this title as having messianic connotations. While a case can be made for thinking of the audience as an "implied hearer" as opposed to an "implied audience" (e.g., Yamasaki, *John the Baptist*, 39–41), I will use the standard terminology of "implied audience."

17. W. D. Davies and Allison, *Saint Matthew*, 1:159; Hieke, "Frauen und Männer," 4.

clarify that Jesus' life continues—and will eventually bring to a climax—that earlier narrative.

"Jesus the Messiah" (Ἰησοῦ Χριστοῦ; 1:1) is the first of many titles attributed to Jesus in Matthew. Some suggest that Χριστοῦ functions not as a title, but as a surname.[18] The implied audience, encountering the title apart from the proper name "Jesus" in the same context (1:16, 17; with the definite article in 1:17), understands it as a title also in 1:1.[19]

What is the significance of the title Χριστός? Its inherent meaning is "anointed one." It was used in the OT especially with reference to the anointing of kings (1 Sam 2:10; Ps 18:50; Isa 45:1), but also of priests (Lev 4:5) and prophets (1 Kgs 19:16).[20] In the OT, it did not refer to an eschatological figure, but it did sometimes refer to such a figure in early Jewish literature.[21] References to an eschatological Messiah fail to reveal either a universal expectation or a uniform understanding of such a figure.[22] Therefore, we cannot assume that the implied audience derives much specific information from the attribution of the title "Messiah" to Jesus other than that "he has been anointed by God to bring salvation history . . . to its climax."[23] One effect of Matthew's Gospel on the implied audience is to clarify what kind of Messiah Jesus is. While the remainder of the narrative will answer that question, the effect of calling him "the Messiah" first (i.e., the primacy effect) ensures that the implied audience

---

18. Luz argues that Matthew always uses the article when Χριστός is a title (*Matthew 1-7*, 70). Since, however, only here and at 1:18 in Matthew does the proper name Ἰησοῦς occur with Χριστός (Χριστός being anarthrous in both places), it is unclear how Matthew would denote the title along with the proper name. The close association of Χριστοῦ here with υἱοῦ Δαυίδ ("son of David") suggests that it is to be understood as a title and not (merely) as a surname.

19. Some scholars, while noting that Χριστός was on its way to being understood as a name, concede that it retained its messianic connotation in the first century (W. D. Davies and Allison, *Saint Matthew*, 1:155; Quesnel, "De quelques avatars," 60). Others conclude that Χριστός here is either both name and title (Kingsbury, *Matthew as Story*, 46-47) or "clearly much more" than a sort of surname (France, *Matthew*, 34). Fred W. Burnett argues that Χριστός is a title and not a proper name because it connotes, whereas proper names only denote ("Characterization and Christology," 591).

20. Charlesworth, "From Messianology to Christology," 11-12. Cf. Carter, *Matthew: Storyteller, Interpreter, Evangelist*, 169.

21. Charlesworth, "From Messianology to Christology," 3-4, 7. Examples of early Jewish literature referring to an eschatological Messiah include T. 12 Patr. (T. Sim. 3; T. Levi 5); Pss. Sol. 17-18; 4 Ezra 12; 2 Bar. 40, 72.

22. Charlesworth, "From Messianology to Christology," 3-4, 14, 28. Cf. Carter, *Matthew: Storyteller, Interpreter, Evangelist*, 170; Vinson, "King of the Jews," 247-48.

23. Bauer, "Major Characters," 358.

will understand all that he does and all that happens to him in light of this role (cf. Matt 11:2; 16:16, 20; 27:17, 22).[24]

Matthew 1:1 identifies Jesus as "son of David." That Jesus is "son of David" (cf. 9:27; 12:23; 15:22; 20:30–31; 21:9) confirms the common—but not universal—expectation that the Messiah is the promised Davidic king (2 Sam 7:12–16),[25] as most "anointed ones" in the OT were kings.[26] Although it is not yet clear whether Jesus is the first of a new Davidic dynasty or will rule forever himself,[27] Matthew's implied audience knows that Jesus' role involves kingship.[28] In the genealogy that follows (Matt 1:2–16), David is referred to as "David the king" (1:6), highlighting the significance of David in this context and of Jesus being "the son of David."[29]

Jesus is also "the son of Abraham" (1:1). The implied audience understands that Jesus is "the son of Abraham" in some unique way, since any "son of David"—and any male Jew—is also a "son of Abraham." The most natural identification of a unique "son of Abraham" is derived from the promises to Abraham regarding his "seed" or "offspring" and the blessing of the nations (Gen 12:3; 22:18). The Hebrew verbs in these promises (niphal and hithpael forms of ברך) are ambiguous, since they may be understood as passive ("they will be blessed") or reflexive ("they will bless themselves"), leading to debate over how the promises should

---

24. France, *Matthew*, 33. Boring points out that "the variety of titles in Matthew converge on the royal image of Jesus-as-king" ("Narrative Christology," 363). Note that Matthew's opening verse, along with the genealogy and birth narrative—especially the visit of the magi—focus the implied audience's attention on his role as the Messiah in contrast to Mark's opening verse, where "Son of God" could become the focus of attention.

25. France, *Matthew*, 35; W. D. Davies and Allison, *Saint Matthew*, 1:159–60; Luz, *Matthew 1–7*, 70; Carter, *Matthew: Storyteller, Interpreter, Evangelist*, 170; Eloff, "Exile," 81; Vinson, "King of the Jews," 247–48.

26. Cf. W. D. Davies and Allison, *Saint Matthew*, 1:156.

27. Cf. Roberts, "Old Testament's Contribution," 51.

28. The importance of Jesus' identification as "son of David" for understanding Matthew's narrative is established in Zacharias, *Matthew's Presentation*. Zacharias concludes that Matthew redefines "son of David" as "the humble king and the healing shepherd," as opposed to "the violent Messiah" seen, for example, in Pss. Sol. 17 (*Matthew's Presentation*, 191). This conclusion, however, makes too little of passages such as Matt 2:6 (within its original context of Micah 5); 3:10–12; and 13:40–42, which anticipate some violence in Jesus' future activity. We agree with Zacharias that Matthew presents Jesus as the son of David who will establish God's kingdom, but we are persuaded that the prologue (at least) requires a particular understanding of the means by which he will do so.

29. Brossier, "Les évangiles," 20.

be understood.³⁰ In the LXX, these verbs are translated using the future passive ἐνευλογηθήσονται, removing this ambiguity. This is the translation (Gal 3:8; Acts 3:25)—and the interpretation (Gal 3:9-14)—of these promises that is taken up in the NT. Therefore, it is assumed to be the understanding within Matthew's community and in his Gospel's story world.

Some suggest that the reference to Jesus as "son of Abraham" is an indication of a Jesus-as-Isaac motif by which the gentile mission is emphasized, since Isaac is the one through whom all nations would be blessed (Gen 22:18).³¹ This motif, if present at all, is too subtle to assume the implied audience notices it. Moreover, an emphasis on the gentile mission does not require a Jesus-as-Isaac motif, since the inclusion of gentiles is indicated in more obvious ways (cf. Matt 1:5; 2:1-11). Others suggest that this title points to Jesus being worthy of father Abraham,³² being a true Israelite,³³ or completing the history of Israel that began with Abraham.³⁴ None of these options, however, raises the significance of the title to a level comparable to that of "son of David" which it accompanies. Therefore, it is best to adopt the majority view among scholars, which is that "son of Abraham" refers to God's promise to Abraham in Gen 22:18 (cf. Gen 12:3). Jesus, then, is the "seed" or "offspring" of Abraham through whom "all the nations of the earth" (cf. Matt 28:19) will be blessed, extending his significance beyond the single nation of Israel.

Matthew 1:1 presents Jesus as the eschatological "anointed one" sent by God to bring salvation history to its intended goal. He is the descendant of David through whom God will reestablish David's kingdom (cf. 12:28; 16:28; 20:21; 26:29). He is the descendant of Abraham through whom God will bless Israel and all the nations of the earth. This initial characterization guides the implied audience throughout the narrative; additional information, though it may clarify or supplement this characterization, will not nullify or supersede it.

---

30. For a recent treatment of this debate, including references to the views of many scholars on this debate, see Lee, "Once Again," 279-96.

31. See Erickson, "Joseph," 38; cf. Huizenga, "Obedience unto Death," 516. They mention that both Jesus and Isaac are promised children who are born under irregular circumstances, and that the wording of Matt 1:21 is very close to the LXX of Gen 17:9.

32. W. D. Davies and Allison, *Saint Matthew*, 1:158.

33. W. D. Davies and Allison, *Saint Matthew*, 1:160.

34. Kingsbury, *Matthew as Story*, 47.

The Messiah's Genealogy and Birth (1:2–25)

The importance of Matthew's opening statement is reinforced by the genealogy that follows it (1:2–16).[35] Jesus' descent from both Abraham and David is established.[36] The genealogy concludes by referring to Jesus as "the Messiah" (1:16), emphasizing the importance of this title for his characterization. Jesus is again referred to as "the Messiah" in a summary of the genealogy that includes four crucial moments in Israel's history—Abraham (that history's beginning), David (a high point as the kingdom was established with God's chosen king), the deportation to Babylon (a low point as the kingdom was dissolved), and the coming of the Messiah (implying the restoration of that kingdom). The division of Israel's history into three equal periods of fourteen generations suggests that Jesus the Messiah had come at the appointed time.[37] Three references to the "deportation to Babylon" (1:11, 12, 17) with no mention of a return lead the implied audience to view the exile as not yet ended—a problem the Messiah must solve.[38] This is consistent with Jesus' characterization as the promised king and develops the expectation that he will reestablish the kingdom lost at the time of the exile.

Although the birth of Jesus is not narrated, the circumstances surrounding his birth contribute to his characterization. That Mary became pregnant "by the Holy Spirit" (1:18) informs the implied audience that Jesus is born as result of God's divine activity. Although there are miraculous conceptions in the OT (e.g., Gen 21:1–7; Judg 13:2–24; 1 Sam 2:5, 19–21), there are no virginal conceptions. The implied audience concludes that Jesus, like other miraculously conceived children, will play an important role in God's purposes. Since Jesus' conception is more miraculous, the audience suspects that Jesus may be greater than others born through such conceptions, but there is no precedent to allow a more specific expectation. Although Matthew does not link conception by the Holy Spirit

---

35. R. E. Brown, *Birth of the Messiah*, 137–38.

36. Kingsbury, "Birth Narrative," 164.

37. W. D. Davies and Allison, *Saint Matthew*, 1:187; cf. Edwards, *Matthew as Story*, 13. The implied audience accepts the narrator's accounting of the generations despite the numerical discrepancy.

38. Eloff, "Exile," 82–84; Baxter, "Mosaic Imagery," 71–72; W. D. Davies and Allison, *Saint Matthew*, 1:187; Repschinski, "He Will Save," 253. Wright makes the controversial claim that Second Temple Jews viewed themselves as still in exile (*People of God*, 385–86). Here, we claim only that this is the point of view within Matthew's story world.

to Jesus being "the Son of God" (as in Luke 1:35), the implied audience is not surprised that Jesus is later called God's Son (Matt 2:15; 3:17).[39]

Additional contributions to the implied audience's understanding of Jesus result from the angel's encounter with Joseph (1:19–23). God's intervention through the "angel of the Lord" (1:20) to ensure that Joseph would not divorce Mary makes two contributions. First, the angel speaking to the father about the unborn child reminds the implied audience of OT narratives about miraculous conceptions (Gen 18:9–15; Judg 13:8–20),[40] reinforcing the instinct to view Jesus' conception as similar to those OT examples. Second, the implied audience understands that this intervention ensures Jesus' descent from David (cf. Matt 1:16) and, therefore, his right to David's throne, thus emphasizing his role as the royal "son of David."

The angel instructs Joseph to name the child "Jesus" ('Ιησοῦς; 1:21; Heb. יְהוֹשׁוּעַ, "Yhwh is salvation"). The reason for this name—"he will save his people from their sins" (1:21)—is the first explicit indication of what Jesus will do.[41] "Jesus" is the natural grammatical antecedent of "he."[42] Given the prior characterization of Jesus, the implied audience accepts that this man, rather than God, is called the one who saves. That some group is called "his people" reflects Jesus' status and authority as messianic king. In the context provided by the genealogy (1:2–16), the implied audience understands "his people" as referring to the Jewish people.[43]

What is the salvation that Jesus would accomplish? Some scholars say that Jesus does not intend to reign over an earthly kingdom, viewing this salvation as consisting only of forgiveness of sins through his sacrifice.[44]

---

39. France, *Matthew*, 49–50. This appears to be another deliberate redactional decision of Matthew's author, leading to the implied audience's initial focus on Jesus as "Messiah" rather than as "Son of God." Ironically, Bauer says that 1:16 presents Jesus as the Son of God ("Genealogy," 155), although all that it says is that he was born to Mary, whose husband Joseph was. The ways in which "Son of God" might have been understood in a Jewish context are indicated below in the discussion of Matt 3:17, where God calls Jesus his "son."

40. Conrad, "Annunciation," 662.

41. W. D. Davies and Allison, *Saint Matthew*, 1:155.

42. France, *Matthew*, 53.

43. Repschinski, "He Will Save," 255–56; Carter, "Save His People," 389–90.

44. M. Davies, *Matthew*, 32; Bauer seems to limit Jesus' kingship to functions of a shepherd, especially self-sacrifice to save those in danger, but he ignores other royal functions ("Kingship," 310–12). Kingsbury, *Matthew as Story*, 92; Luz, *Matthew 21–28*, 639; Jones, "Subverting," 271.

This view fails to consider that the implied audience's understanding of sin's consequences is informed by the OT.[45] Foreign oppression had often been experienced and understood as God's discipline when his people sinned (Judg 2:11–15; 10:6–8; 1 Sam 12:9; 2 Kgs 17:19–20; 24:18–20; Jer 25:1–11). This is why Ps 79:9 can speak of salvation and forgiveness as deliverance from foreign oppression (cf. Jer 42:11; 46:27–28). Matthew's point of view is that the sins of God's people had led to their exile (Matt 1:11, 12, 17).[46] A relationship between sin and loss of kingdom is also seen in Matt 21:43, where the chief priests and the Pharisees (cf. 21:45) will lose the kingdom because they had failed to "produce its fruit." Since sin leads to exile, salvation from sin includes the removal of foreign oppression.

Language that speaks of sin as personally alienating the sinner from God—which appears to shape some Matthean scholars' understanding of salvation—is typical in Paul's theology (e.g., Rom 5:1–11), but not in Matthew's story world. It is more consistent with Matthew's narrative to understand "he will save his people from their sins" to mean that Jesus, the messianic, Davidic king, would permanently reestablish the kingdom that God's people had lost because of their sins.[47] This requires Jesus to bring about both forgiveness *and* the end of foreign oppression.[48]

Matthew 1:22–23 states that "all this" happened to fulfill Isa 7:14. Since Isa 7:14 LXX refers to a παρθένος giving birth and to the naming of the child, "all this" should be taken to refer to all of Matt 1:18–21. The claim that Jesus' birth fulfills OT prophecy indicates to the implied audience that Jesus is an extraordinary individual with a unique role in salvation history.[49] The content of that prophecy makes an additional contribution to the characterization of Jesus.

---

45 Repschinski, "He Will Save," 256.

46. Donaldson, "Vindicated Son," 113–14.

47. Carter says, "Matthew 1:21, 23 makes the Christ's mission explicit. It does not consist of the use of military power against Herod or the Romans. It does, however, have profound consequences for transforming all of life including the political and societal structures" (*Matthew: Storyteller, Interpreter, Evangelist*, 171). Cf. Carter, "Save His People," 399–401; Repschinski, "He Will Save," 256; Hagner, *Matthew 1–13*, 19; Wright, *People of God*, 385.

48. Carter, "Save His People," 401. Contra Bauer, who says that Herod was wrong to view Jesus as a threat to his rule ("Kingship," 314).

49. That this prophecy was fulfilled already in the OT (cf. Isa 8:3–8) contributes to the idea that Jesus recapitulates Israel's history as the true and faithful Israel.

According to Matt 1:23, Jesus' name will be called "Immanuel, which is translated 'God with us.'" The implied audience will learn later that Jesus is the way God will be present with his people (28:20; cf. 18:20). At this point, however, it is clear only that Jesus' birth is at least a sign of God's presence, in the way that the birth of Isaiah's son was a sign to Ahaz that God would be with Judah to deliver it from the kings of Aram and Israel (Isa 7:16). In Isaiah 7, God's presence was experienced as he overcame the threat of foreign oppression.[50] Therefore, the presence of God associated with Jesus here is most naturally understood by the implied audience to mean that God will again overcome foreign oppression so that his kingdom will be reestablished. The implication of Matt 1:23—since verse 21 fulfills Isa 7:14—is that the names "Jesus" and "Immanuel" are somehow synonymous.[51] This suggests to the implied audience that the salvation which Jesus will accomplish includes not only forgiveness and restoration after exile, but also the restoration of God's presence, which has both relational and political implications.

The Visit of the Magi, Herod's Response, and the Flight to Egypt (2:1–23)

Several elements in the story of the magi (2:1–12) contribute to the characterization of Jesus. First, the magi refer to Jesus as the "King of the Jews" (2:2; cf. 27:11, 37), which is equated with the term "Messiah" (2:4).[52] For the first time, the title "king" is attributed to Jesus. This attribution strengthens the implied audience's understanding of Jesus as the messianic, Davidic king, as does the quotation of Mic 5:2 in Matt 2:6, where the Messiah's vocation ("ruler," "shepherd my people Israel") is stated.[53] Second, the appearance of a special, guiding star in conjunction with

---

50. Other OT promises of God's presence transcend mere relational presence by relating that presence to a person's success in accomplishing what God had called them to do (Gen 26:3; 28:15; Exod 3:12; Deut 31:23; Josh 1:5; Judg 6:16; 1 Kgs 11:38; Isa 43:2; Jer 1:8; cf. Gen 39:2–3, 21–23; 1 Sam 3:19; 18:14; 2 Chr 17:3–5).

51. In both scriptures, a son is born and is given a name, suggesting that some relationship exists between those names.

52. "Messiah" is a more natural term for Jews to use, while "King of the Jews" is more natural for gentiles.

53. Cabrido argues that Jesus is presented as a shepherd throughout Matthew's Gospel, though he admits that this is not the most prominent characterization of Jesus (*Shepherd of Israel*, 29). He detects this theme in places where the implied audience is unlikely to notice it.

Jesus' birth points to the divine origin and purpose of this extraordinary child. Third, Herod's response to Jesus' birth ("troubled," 2:3; seeking to destroy Jesus, 2:13) makes it clear to the implied audience that he understands Jesus as a threat to his reign. In theory, Herod could be wrong (i.e., Jesus is not a threat).[54] The narrative, however, gives no indication that he has misunderstood Jesus, and there are ample indications that Jesus' reign has a political, earthly dimension (see above). The goal of the magi is to "worship" Jesus (2:2, 11), indicating that he is (at least) a king. The implied audience, whose community worships Jesus, understands this worship as more than "paying homage" and Jesus as more than just a king (cf. 8:2; 9:18; 14:33).[55] Finally, the "exceedingly great joy" (2:10) of the magi, who are gentiles from the east, reinforces what "son of Abraham" (1:1) suggested—that the Jews' Messiah would bring God's blessing to "all the nations of the earth" (Gen 22:18). The implications of his arrival are so great that "exceedingly great joy" is warranted, even if not all rejoiced (Matt 2:3–8, 13).

Herod's "slaughter of the innocents," which was intended to "destroy" Jesus (2:13), also contributes to the characterization of Jesus. First, it makes clear that Herod saw him as a threat to his political power, and perhaps to a dynasty through his sons (cf. 2:22; 14:1–3). Second, Jesus, whom the implied audience knows to be God's Son, is shown to be vulnerable like all children are. God sends his angel to warn Joseph to flee to Egypt with Jesus and Mary (2:13), showing that Herod's plan could have resulted in Jesus' death. This warning also shows that Jesus' physical survival, at least for a time, is more necessary for God's plan than is the survival of other children.[56] Jesus' vulnerability and the importance of his

---

54. E.g., Bauer, who concludes that Herod misunderstands Jesus' kingship because, "the Matthean Jesus rejects all political aspirations and refuses to understand his kingship in political terms" ("Kingship," 314). See, however, Matt 25:31–46, where "eternal life" (25:46) is equated with inheriting a kingdom (25:34) with physical characteristics (25:31, 34). In Matthew, "kingdom of heaven" (βασιλεία τῶν οὐρανῶν) is a circumlocution for "kingdom of God" (βασιλεία τοῦ θεοῦ; see parallels, such as Matt 4:17 and Mark 1:15) and is understood as "God's kingdom" rather than as the kingdom "which is" or "located in" heaven. That kingdom had "come near" (3:2; 4:17).

55. Bauer, "Kingship," 321.

56. While modern readers are sometimes disturbed by the moral problem resulting from God's protection of his own Son and not of other children, the implied author is unconcerned with defending God's action. From a narrative-critical perspective, the implied audience trusts the reliable narrator and infers that this is not a problem. Throughout history, however, real readers have proposed solutions to this perceived problem, including that these children had the honor of being martyrs for Jesus (see the discussion in Luz, *Matthew 1–7*, 121–22).

survival are again emphasized in Matt 2:22, when Herod's son Archelaus is perceived as a threat to Jesus. Third, this incident leads to another statement about Jesus fulfilling the OT (2:15). The statement—"Out of Egypt I called my son" (Hos 11:1)—both presents Jesus as the true or ideal Israel and prepares for later declarations of Jesus' sonship.[57]

In Matt 2:19–23, Jesus returns from Egypt. The instruction that Joseph take the child to Israel (2:19–20) indicates to the implied audience that God's purpose for Jesus requires him to be in Israel among God's people. This is consistent with, but does not require, the expectation that Jesus would reestablish the kingdom of Israel and rule over it. The obscure reference to the "prophets" who said, "He shall be called a Nazarene" (2:23), continues the theme of Jesus fulfilling prophecy and/or scripture.[58] While scholars have not identified the source of this quotation, the implied audience knows the source or accepts the statement as reliable. Either way, the point is made that Jesus' life accords with what God had said about his Messiah in advance.

The presentation of Jesus in Matthew's prologue appears to contain allusions to Moses, especially in his deliverance as an infant, his presence in Egypt, and the strong echo of Exod 4:19 in Matt 2:20.[59] Other allusions to Moses appear in the temptation scene (4:1–11), especially Jesus' forty-day fast (4:2; cf. Exod 34:28; Deut 9:9, 18) and his repeated use of Deuteronomy to respond to the devil. These allusions strengthen the implied audience's view of Jesus as authoritative and leads them to view Jesus—rather than the Jewish leaders who claimed Moses' authority (Matt 23:2)—as God's spokesman. While some elements of Matthew's narrative present Jesus as being like Moses, some scholars point out that the implied author passed up many opportunities to forge an even

---

57. Matthew 2:15 raises the possibility of Jesus' divine sonship without asserting it. It is a true statement, even if Jesus is only understood to be God's Son as Israel had been. Garland understands it to mean that "Jesus will enact a new exodus" (*Reading Matthew*, 30), but here it refers to Jesus already having exited Egypt.

58. Knowles argues that, since God rarely speaks in Matthew, it is in these quotes from the OT that the voice of God is heard ("Plotting Jesus," 128).

59. Allison, *New Moses*, 140–65; Crossan, "From Moses to Jesus," 21–27; Baxter, "Mosaic Imagery," 70–71; Kensky, "Moses and Jesus," 45–46. Crossan and Kensky include elements found in the Midrashim, which provide Mosaic parallels that are not found in Exodus. Note the similar wording of Exod 4:19 (τεθνήκασιν γὰρ πάντες οἱ ζητοῦντές σου τὴν ψυχήν, "for all those who were seeking your life have died") and Matt 2:20 (τεθνήκασιν γὰρ οἱ ζητοῦντες τὴν ψυχὴν τοῦ παιδίου, "for those who were seeking the life of the child have died").

stronger connection between Jesus and Moses.[60] This warns us against overemphasizing the influence of these similarities on the implied audience's understanding of Jesus.

The Baptism of the Messiah (3:1–17)

John the Baptist says several things that contribute to the implied audience's understanding of Jesus.[61] John's message—"Repent, for the kingdom of heaven is at hand" (3:2)—points to Jesus and his mission. Jesus was first called "the Messiah," (1:1) and then "King of the Jews" (2:2). Now, the "kingdom of heaven"—over which God's anointed king will reign—is declared to be "at hand" or "near." The implied audience understands that the nearness of God's kingdom is the result of the presence of its king.

By quoting Isa 40:3, Matt 3:3 says that John's ministry prepares "the way of the Lord." It is unclear whether "the Lord" here refers to Jesus or to God the Father. If it refers to Jesus, then he appears to be equated with Yhwh in Isa 40:3. For the implied audience, which already worships Jesus, this provides a scriptural basis for that worship. Within the narrative, the reference to Isa 40:3 at least raises the possibility that Jesus is more than a mere man.

In Matt 3:11–12, John speaks to the Pharisees and Sadducees about Jesus. John, a great prophet whose ministry was prophesied in the OT (3:3) says that Jesus is "mightier than" he.[62] John is not even worthy to remove Jesus' sandals (3:11). Jesus will also do what John cannot. Jesus will baptize them "with the Holy Spirit and fire" (3:11). Jesus' ability to baptize with the Holy Spirit suggests that he is more than just a special human being.[63] He has the authority to distribute the blessing of the Holy Spirit. In the context of verse 12 (where Jesus will burn chaff), the implied audience understands Jesus' baptism "with fire" as his judgment. According to John, Jesus is the agent of God's eschatological judgment (cf. 25:31–46),[64] a characterization that further develops the implied audience's understanding of Jesus' messiahship. In addition to reestablishing

---

60. Bornkamm, *Studien*, 135; Luz, *Matthew 21–28*, 620.

61. Since his ministry fulfills scripture (Matt 3:3; cf. Isa 40:3) and he comes in the mold of Elijah the prophet (Matt 3:4), John is a reliable character whose testimony regarding Jesus is accepted as true.

62. Bauer, "Major Characters," 358.

63. Cf. Joel 2:28–29, where the distribution of the Spirit is a prerogative of Yhwh.

64. M. Davies, *Matthew*, 42; Yamasaki, *John the Baptist*, 95.

and ruling over God's kingdom, he will carry out God's judgment, determining who will enter that kingdom. John's warning (3:10) informs the implied audience that the Pharisees and Sadducees are in danger of experiencing the judgment that Jesus will carry out, preparing it for the coming conflict between the Jewish leaders and Jesus.

The implied audience has yet to "see" Jesus do anything,[65] but knows that Jesus is the eschatological, anointed, Davidic king of Israel (1:1; 2:2, 6) who will save his people from their sins (1:21), reestablish the kingdom (1:1; cf. 1:17), bring God's blessing to all nations (1:1), and execute God's eschatological judgment (3:10–12). The implied audience has also learned that Jesus is more than a mere man (3:11), although it is not yet clear how much more. This exalted presentation of Jesus contrasts sharply with the humility of his first "appearance" as an adult. In submission to God, Jesus comes "to be baptized" (3:13). When John objects (3:14), Jesus insists on fulfilling all righteousness by expressing his submission (3:15). In this passage, Jesus is presented as humble and righteous. The implied audience may not fully understand how Jesus' baptism was necessary to "fulfill all righteousness" (3:15), but it does understand that Jesus is fully committed to righteousness, in contrast to others in the narrative (cf. 3:7–8; 5:20; 6:2, 5, 16).

When Jesus is baptized, two things happen that contribute to his characterization. First, he sees the heavens opened and "the Spirit of God descending like a dove and coming upon him" (3:16). The coming of the Holy Spirit on Jesus is understood as his anointing (cf. Isa 61:1; Matt 12:18, 28), providing the supernatural power to carry out his mission.[66] The Spirit's coming also points to Jesus as the "shoot from Jesse's stem" who will reign righteously and bring back the remnant of Israel (Isa 11:1–12), conforming to the expectations of the Messiah (cf. 1QSb, 4Q161, 4Q174). The concurrence of Spirit, water, and bird imagery may lead the implied audience to detect a subtle reference to Gen 1:2, which would point to Jesus as the bringer of a new creation.[67]

Second, "a voice out of the heavens"—the implied audience knows this is God's voice—says, "This is my beloved son, in whom I am well-pleased" (3:17). While Matt 2:15 suggests that Jesus may be the "Son of God" in a special way, Matt 3:17 makes clear that he is. Several (mutually

65. Cf. Weaver, "Rewriting," 380.
66. Kingsbury, *Matthew as Story*, 52.
67. Cf. W. D. Davies and Allison, *Saint Matthew*, 1:334. This, however, is not a prominent motif in Matthew.

non-exclusive) meanings of "Son of God" here have been suggested.[68] It could refer to Jesus as the ideal Israel, as the use of Hos 11:1 in Matt 2:15 suggests (cf. Exod 4:22).[69] It could refer to Jesus as *a* king of Israel (1 Chr 28:6; cf. Ps 2:7),[70] or as *the* messianic king (depending on the interpretation of texts like 2 Sam 7:12–16 and Ps 2:7; cf. 4QFlor 10–14).[71] It could also refer to Jesus' unique, filial relationship with God the Father.[72] Since Jesus has already been presented as the ideal Israel (Matt 2:15), as Messiah (1:1; cf. 1:16–17), and as Davidic king (1:1; 2:2), the implied audience will naturally understand "Son of God" to include at least these three possibilities.[73] The fourth possibility (i.e., the unique Father-Son relationship), though not required by the narrative, is likely to be included in the implied audience's understanding, since it consists of members of Matthew's worshipping community. By calling Jesus his son, God clearly aligns himself with him. Now, all who oppose Jesus (9:34; 12:14, 24; 16:1; 19:3; 21:15–16; 22:15; 26:3–4, 14–16, 59; 27:20) oppose his Father, but all who obey him obey his Father.

Because God himself has declared Jesus to be his "son" (3:17; 17:5; cf. 8:29; 16:16; 26:63–65; 27:54), Kingsbury has concluded that "Matthew's christology is preeminently a Son-of-God christology."[74] This view risks ignoring the interpretive significance of other aspects of Matthew's characterization of Jesus. There is no indication that it is necessary or proper to identify one aspect of Matthew's Christology as more important than others.[75] If one must identify a preeminent Christology, that expressed by the implied author or by Jesus are legitimate alternatives to that expressed by God.[76] Narrative critics must pay special attention to characterization as it relates to the development of the plot. While Jesus' characterization as "Son of God" provides theological background regarding his divine origin, other aspects of his characterization—especially "Messiah" and

---

68. Based on OT and deuterocanonical usage, "Son of God" may also refer to an angel (Job 1:6; 2:1; possibly Gen 6:2, 4; Dan 3:25) or (merely) to any righteous Israelite (Sir 4:10; Wis 2:18), but neither of these possibilities fits with the existing characterization of Jesus. See the discussion in Fitzmyer, *Wandering Aramean*, 104–5.

69. Luz, *Matthew 1–7*, 120–21; M. Davies, *Matthew*, 40.

70. Luz, *Matthew 1–7*, 120–21; Hauerwas, *Matthew*, 48.

71. W. D. Davies and Allison, *Saint Matthew*, 1:263.

72. Kingsbury, "Figure of Jesus," 11.

73. Kingsbury, "Figure of Jesus," 10–11; Quesnel, "De quelques avatars," 68–69.

74. Kingsbury, "Figure of Jesus," 3, 11; Kingsbury, *Matthew as Story*, 52.

75. W. D. Davies and Allison, *Saint Matthew*, 1:157, n. 33.

76. Hill, "Figure of Jesus," 42.

"son of David"—are associated with expectations that the plot may or may not confirm.[77] Therefore, it is important that Jesus' status as "Son of God" not be emphasized to an extent that other aspects of Jesus' characterization end up being neglected.[78]

The recent work of J. R. Daniel Kirk examines the emphasis of Matthew's Christology.[79] He argues that the exalted status of Jesus in Matthew, as well as in Mark and Luke, is best explained through the paradigm of an "idealized humanity."[80] To the Jewish mind, such a figure can be associated with God and receive worship or attribution of OT references to God.[81] Kirk's work is helpful in its recognition that Matthew's Christological emphasis is not on some inherently divine status possessed by Jesus, but rather on the roles that he performs in his humanity—his sacrificial death, eschatological reign, embodiment of Israel, authoritative teaching, and receiving of authority.[82] Kirk goes too far, however, in his denial that Matthew presents Jesus as divine. For example, his argument that the virginal conception does not necessarily contribute to a divine understanding of Jesus is overly dependent on Greco-Roman—and not Jewish—sources and fails to appreciate the uniqueness of Jesus' conception in comparison to those of idealized humans in the OT (e.g., Adam, David, Moses).[83] Moreover, his argument about Jesus' authority to forgive in Matt 9:1–8 fails to appreciate that the resulting allegation of blasphemy (9:3) is evidence that his claim was interpreted as one belonging to divinity (cf. 26:63–65).[84] Nevertheless, Kirk is correct that the emphasis in Matthew is on what Jesus does and will do as a human figure. This is what is crucial to the plot of the Gospel.[85]

---

77. "Matthew's Christology does not focus on the metaphysics of Jesus' person, but on Jesus' role in God's restoration of the divine sovereignty of the Creator, the ultimate establishment of God's justice throughout creation" (Boring, "Narrative Christology," 365).

78. While one connotation of "Son of God" is a messianic one, Kingsbury's emphasis is on "the unique filial relationship that Jesus has with God" ("Figure of Jesus," 3). Jesus' resurrection and establishment of God's kingdom are then understood as "proof" of God's vindication rather than essential functions of his office.

79. Kirk, *Attested by God*.

80. Kirk, *Attested by God*, 570.

81. Kirk, *Attested by God*, 570.

82. Kirk, *Attested by God*, 573–74.

83. Kirk, *Attested by God*, 370–72.

84. Kirk, *Attested by God*, 281–82. Cf. Shively, review of *Attested by God*, 637–39.

85. Kirk, *Attested by God*, 378–79.

The Temptation of the Messiah (4:1–11)

In the final scene of Matthew's prologue, Jesus is tempted by the devil (4:1–11).[86] The concurrence of a wilderness setting, temptation or testing, and bread (4:3) recalls the testing of Israel (cf. Exod 16:4). Since Jesus passes the "test," the implied audience understands Jesus as the ideal Israel and faithful Son of God (cf. 2:15). This temptation occurs immediately after God declared from heaven that Jesus is his well-pleasing Son (3:17), and it is the Holy Spirit who leads him into the desert to be tempted (4:1). Therefore, the implied audience understands that this temptation does not result from any sin or failure by Jesus and is not inconsistent with God's pleasure.

The implied audience knows that Jesus was hungry (4:2), so the temptation to turn stones into bread (4:3) offered something truly desirable, making it a genuine temptation. This first temptation sets a precedent that does not appear to the implied audience to be broken by the other two, even if it is not explained why the second and third temptations are desirable to Jesus. The narrator says that Jesus was led into the wilderness "to be tempted" (4:1), leading the implied audience to view all three as genuine temptations.[87] Therefore, the implied audience understands Jesus to be, like every other human, vulnerable to temptation and familiar with the experience of unfulfilled desire.

As mentioned above, Jesus' forty-day fast and his repeated references to Deuteronomy in this scene contribute to his identification with Moses. He has the same type of devotion to the Lord and self-discipline as did the great OT leader and prophet. The implied audience wonders how else Jesus will be like Moses. Would he deliver the people of Israel? Would he transmit the law, or a new law, to the people on God's behalf? In addition, is Jesus only like Moses (cf. Deut 18:15) or is he superior to him?[88]

The devil's first two temptations of Jesus are based on Jesus' status as "Son of God" (Matt 4:3, 6). The devil's words help clarify what it means for Jesus to be the "Son of God." The implied audience understands that

---

86. While πειράζω can mean either "tempt" or "test," the implied audience knows that this is a temptation since the devil hopes that Jesus will fail the "test" (cf. Exod 16:4, where the Lord hopes that Israel would pass the "test").

87. If the devil alone referred to this as temptation, the implied audience could conclude that the devil was wrong about Jesus' vulnerability to temptation.

88. Allison, *New Moses*, 267–68; Baxter, "Mosaic Imagery," 70–73; Kensky, "Moses and Jesus," 45–46; Crossan, "From Moses to Jesus," 27.

the "Son of God" has special powers (4:3) and privileges (4:6; cf. 4:8–9) that surpass those of an "ideal Israel" or a Davidic king (cf. 4:23–24; 8:16, 26–27; 9:1–8; 11:2; 14:15–21; 15:32–38). These powers and privileges are characteristic of a divine being, such as one with a unique, filial relationship with God. The devil tempts Jesus to use those powers and privileges for his own benefit; but he refuses to do so.[89] In the process, Jesus affirms that God's word—and not bread—is best for imparting life (4:4; cf. Deut 8:3). The implied audience understands Jesus to have resisted the temptation while rightly valuing God's word over food. Jesus' quotation of the OT also shows his consistency with and submission to the OT (cf. Matt 5:17; 7:12; 22:35–40). This will be important in Jesus' conflicts with Jewish leaders, who neglect parts of the OT (15:3–9; 23:23) while Jesus obeys it. Finally, Deut 8:3 does not put food and God's word in opposition to each other; it teaches reliance on God's provision, which Jesus demonstrates by refusing to provide for himself. In this way, he is shown to possess the faith demanded of Israel despite his extreme hunger, the absence of prohibitions against eating, and his power as the Son of God to provide food for himself.

Having observed Jesus' commitment to scripture, the devil tempts Jesus a second time, using scripture as "bait" (Matt 4:5–6; cf. Ps 91:11–12). It is not clear whether the temptation to throw himself from the highest point of the temple to be caught by angels is a temptation to prove to himself, to the devil, or to those near the temple that he is God's Son. In any case, the implied audience knows that this is a temptation and that Jesus responds wisely and biblically. Jesus knows that Ps 91:11–12 refers to salvation from the danger of external threats, rather than to self-inflicted harm. He understands that the devil asks him to test God. This was not an invitation to obey God faithfully and to trust him for protection, but to "force" God to protect him. Jesus quotes Deut 6:16, using scripture properly rather than perverting its intention. He is again shown to be faithful and obedient to the OT, and as trusting God, rather than testing him as Israel had.[90]

The third temptation offered to Jesus is to receive "all the kingdoms of the world and their glory" (Matt 4:8). To obtain these, Jesus must "fall

---

89. Donaldson says that Jesus' sonship entails humble obedience rather than royal sovereignty ("Vindicated Son," 117). Sonship and suffering, however, are not mutually exclusive, and Jesus does appear to view sovereignty as part of sonship (cf. Matt 25:31–46).

90. Kingsbury, *Matthew as Story*, 56; Garland, *Reading Matthew*, 30.

down and worship (or 'pay homage to')" the devil (4:9). This temptation, unlike the first two, is not based on Jesus' status as "Son of God."[91] That status provides no basis for bowing to the devil, who is too smart to remind Jesus of his status when making his appeal.[92] Some point to other Matthean passages (17:24–27; 20:25–28; 22:15–22; 27:27–31, 41–42) and conclude that Jesus has no interest in worldly power or authority.[93] If that is the case, then this is no real temptation. The placement of this as the final, climactic temptation, however, leads the implied audience to view this as the greatest of the three temptations and, perhaps, of all possible temptations. The implied audience knows that Jesus came to "shepherd" Israel (2:6) and that he is humble enough to submit to John's baptism (3:13–15). Therefore, the temptation is not to possess "all the kingdoms of the world and their glory" merely for his own benefit or to "lord it over" them like other rulers (cf. 20:25). Jesus had come to reclaim the world's peoples that they might be free from the devil's authority and share in God's blessings (cf. "son of Abraham," 1:1). The devil has offered Jesus a much easier way to obtain those kingdoms than the one by which he would ultimately obtain them (cf. 20:28). Since, however, that easier way would require Jesus to bow to the devil, rather than to the Lord who alone deserves worship and glory, Jesus refuses. Again, quoting from Deuteronomy, Jesus rejects the devil's offer.[94] Jesus chooses obedience to God over anything the devil can offer. The implied audience will later understand this choice to be a demonstration of his love for his people, since it was a choice that ultimately leads to the cross (cf. 16:21).

As the temptation scene concludes, the implied audience observes Jesus' authority and special status as Son of God. When Jesus says, "Depart, Satan" (4:10), the devil obeys (4:11). This demonstrates Jesus' authority over the devil (cf. 8:28–32; 9:32–33; 10:1; 17:18).[95] Since Jesus does not order the devil to leave sooner, the implied audience knows

---

91. The absence of "if you are the Son of God" in conjunction with the third temptation may lead the implied audience to expect one more temptation in the future. As Jesus hung on the cross dying, the words of those passing by ("If you are the Son of God, come down from the cross," 27:40) provide that expected final temptation (cf. Luz, *Matthew 21–28*, 538).

92. W. D. Davies and Allison, *Saint Matthew*, 1:372.

93. Kingsbury, *Matthew as Story*, 48; Kingsbury, "Figure of Jesus," 9; Bauer, "Kingship," 314–15. Cf. Luz, *Matthew 21–28*, 639.

94. Jesus appears to paraphrase or interpret Deut 6:13, since the Greek in Matt 4:10 does not appear to quote the LXX or to precisely translate the MT.

95. Kingsbury, *Matthew as Story*, 56.

that he voluntarily chose to endure temptation for the benefit of others, perhaps as an example for them to follow, and perhaps to reveal himself in a unique way. Finally, the scene concludes with angels serving (or "ministering to") Jesus (4:11), demonstrating the truth of Ps 91:11–12. The angels did come to Jesus' aid, not because Jesus forced God to send them, but because he trusted God to provide at the right time and in the right way.

The Resurrection of the Messiah (28:1–20)

Between Matthew's prologue and resurrection narrative there is much that contributes to the characterization of Jesus. Jesus is called "Messiah" at important moments (16:16; 27:17) and his miracles are described as "the works of the Messiah" (11:2). He is called "son of David" at his Triumphal Entry (21:9) and refers to himself in this way while debating the Pharisees (22:41–45). The theme of God's kingdom (i.e., "kingdom of heaven") permeates the narrative (4:17; 7:21; 10:7; 12:28; 13:1–52; 16:28; 21:31; 24:14; 26:29), confirming the implied audience's expectation that Jesus' mission is to establish that kingdom. At times, the implied audience is reminded that Jesus will fulfill the OT (5:17; 26:54). Though Jesus is not called "son of Abraham," the theme of gentile inclusion does appear (8:11; 10:18; 12:17–21; 15:21–28; cf. 10:5–6). Jesus is called the "Son of God" by demons (8:29), the disciples in the boat (14:33), Peter (16:16; as a royal title), God the Father (17:5), and a Roman centurion (27:54). Jesus "saves" people (cf. 1:21) in a concrete sense (8:25–26; 9:21–22; 14:30–31; 27:42), rather than a purely spiritual sense. In his teaching, he presents the standard of righteousness by which he will personally judge others (5:20; 6:1; 7:21–23). Though the devil does not "appear" in the narrative, Jesus' authority over him is seen in his authority over demons and unclean spirits (8:16; 9:32–33; 17:18; cf. 10:1). Therefore, as the implied audience comes to Matthew's resurrection narrative, the characterization of Jesus established in the prologue, and the expectations associated with that characterization, provide the context for understanding the resurrection's significance.

Of course, Matthew's resurrection narrative contributes further to the characterization of Jesus. The narrative surrounding his resurrection begins with apocalyptic elements—a "great earthquake" (28:2) and the "angel of the Lord" in bright white clothing (28:3; cf. Dan 7:9; 10:6). These elements suggest that the resurrection of Jesus is an apocalyptic event and leads the implied audience to expect a previously unseen spiritual reality to be revealed.[96]

The words of the angel of the Lord in Matt 28:5–7 contribute to the characterization of Jesus. The angel describes Jesus as "having been crucified" (ἐσταυρωμένον; 28:5). The implied audience knows that Jesus had been put to death and, though he had predicted both his death and resurrection, apart from a miracle, he would still be dead in the tomb. The angel then says that Jesus is not there but has been raised as he had predicted (28:6). This reversal of Jesus' death, which is the work of God as indicated by the divine passive ἠγέρθη,[97] is apocalyptic in that it reveals in the present age the resurrection that will characterize the age to come (cf. Dan 12:1–4). It also advances the plot, since a dead Messiah lacks the ability to perform the functions (e.g., ruling, judging) that the implied audience expects based on the prologue (Matt 1:1; 2:2, 6; 3:11–12) and that Jesus says he will perform in the future (7:21–23; 10:32–33, 40–42; 13:41–43; 25:31–46).

The dominant expectation created by the prologue is that Jesus will establish the messianic kingdom and reign as its king. Therefore, the implied audience understands all opposition to him (cf. 9:34; 12:14, 24; 16:1; 19:3; 21:15–16; 22:15; 26:3–4, 14–16, 59; 27:20) as threatening that expectation. While the redemptive nature of Jesus' death is a minor theme in Matthew (cf. 20:28; 26:28), the prominence of messianic kingdom expectations causes the implied audience to view Jesus' death as the ultimate threat to—and end of—those expectations. His resurrection, then, is understood as his victory over that threat and the confirmation that nothing can prevent Jesus from doing what he said he would do. That his resurrection took place "just as he said" (28:6; cf. 16:21; 17:23; 20:19) reminds the implied audience of Jesus' foreknowledge and strengthens his characterization as one to whom God has revealed the future.

---

96. Cf. the definition of "apocalypse" in J. J. Collins, which includes revelation "mediated by an otherworldly being to a human recipient" about a transcendent reality. In Collins's definition, the transcendent reality "envisages eschatological salvation" and "involves another, supernatural world" (*Apocalypse*, 9). The apocalyptic elements in Matt 28:2–3 bring that salvation and supernatural world into the time and location of the narrative.

97. Many versions translate ἠγέρθη using the intransitive "he is risen," implying that Jesus raised himself. The passive transitive "he has been raised" better reflects the Greek and emphasizes that God raised Jesus. As W. D. Davies and Allison (*Saint Matthew*, 3:667) point out, several other NT texts "make the resurrection God's act" (Acts 3:15; 4:10; Rom 4:24; 8:11; 10:9; 1 Pet 1:21; etc.).

The angel then instructs the women to inform Jesus' disciples that he has been raised and that they would see him in Galilee (28:7). These words indicate that Jesus is visible in his risen state and prepare the implied audience to expect some significant, post-resurrection event before the narrative concludes. The women depart "with fear and great joy" to deliver this message to the disciples (28:8). The implied audience understands their fear as a response to an event of divine origin.[98] Their "great joy" reflects the restoration of their hope. Since their hope that Jesus would establish and reign over the messianic kingdom appeared to have died with Jesus, his resurrection means that they could once again hope for those things.

Before the women can deliver the angel's instructions to his disciples, they personally encounter Jesus (28:9-10). The women worship Jesus (28:9), indicating to the implied audience that Jesus, especially in his risen state, is worthy of worship. Their taking hold of Jesus' feet (28:9) is an act of veneration, but it also indicates to the implied audience that Jesus is not a ghost, since he can be touched (28:9).[99]

This description of Jesus is not like the one in the transfiguration narrative (17:2), nor is it apocalyptic like that of the angel of the Lord in this pericope (28:2-3). He is not described as resurrected to a glorified state as in other Gospels (cf. Luke 24:15-16, 31, 36-37, 51; John 20:14-15, 19, 26). Matthew's narrative emphasizes the continuity between Jesus' physical state before and after his crucifixion. The implied audience's understanding of the qualitative difference between Jesus' resurrection and, for example, the raising of the girl in 9:25 results not from the description of the risen Jesus or the language used to refer to his being raised (ἠγέρθη; 28:6), but from the eternal nature of the promises about him (cf. 1:1; 2 Sam 7:12-13) and from Jesus' promise in Matt 28:20. The implied audience, therefore, is not led to understand Jesus' resurrection as his glorification to a state different from his previous one, which could result in different expectations of Jesus. It understands Jesus' resurrection as the reversal of his death and the resumption of the life that he had prior to his crucifixion, confirming the expectations that existed before his death.[100]

---

98. Cf. Luz, *Matthew 21–28*, 607.

99. W. D. Davies and Allison, *Saint Matthew*, 3:669.

100. In this study, references to Jesus' resurrection as the resumption or restoration of his life are not meant to imply that his resurrection was merely a resuscitation (cf. 9:25; 10:8; 27:52). The NT provides evidence of both continuity (28:9; John 20:27-29) and discontinuity (Luke 24:15-16; John 20:15-16, 19) between Jesus' physical states

This restoration of his life brings about the restoration of his disciples' hope that he will do all that he had promised.

In the final scene of Matthew's Gospel, Jesus appears to and speaks with the eleven disciples (28:16). This scene contains no description of Jesus' physical appearance to indicate that his state is other than what it had been prior to his crucifixion. Even though some of the disciples doubt,[101] they all worship him (28:17), as the two women had (28:9), reemphasizing for the implied audience that Jesus is worthy of worship.

As Jesus speaks to his disciples, he claims to possess "all authority in heaven and on earth" (28:18). Some scholars observe that the wording of Matt 28:18 recalls that of Dan 7:14.[102] The implied audience therefore understands that Jesus is the heavenly Son of Man who will reign over all peoples forever. The authority given to Jesus is more extensive than what the devil had offered (Matt 4:9–10), since that included only the world's kingdoms.[103] Jesus' universal authority is the basis of his command to "make disciples of all nations" (28:19). Since Jesus previously tells his disciples not to preach to the nations/gentiles (10:5–7; cf. 15:24) and refuses the devil's offer of "all the kingdoms of the world and their glory" (4:8–9), the implied audience understands that Jesus has only recently been given universal authority.[104] The giving of this authority is naturally understood by the implied audience to be related to Jesus' death and resurrection although this is not explained. It is Jesus' reception of this authority, not the details of the "transaction," that the implied audience must understand.

Jesus' possession of universal authority is a development in the plot.[105] This increased authority allows him to command his disciples to make

---

before and after his death and resurrection. Matthew's narrative appears to emphasize the continuity and deemphasize the discontinuity by omitting references to occasions when Jesus was not recognized or when he appeared or disappeared unexpectedly. This emphasis on continuity leads the implied audience to maintain the expectations they had of Jesus prior to his death and resurrection. An emphasis on discontinuity could result in an abandonment of those expectations and a search for new ones. Matthew's narrative does, however, provide hints of discontinuity in Jesus' claim of universal authority (Matt 28:18) and his promise of eternal presence with his disciples (28:20). Cf. Nicklas, "Resurrection," 18.

101. On the disciples doubting, see the discussion on the eleven disciples in chapter 4.

102. France, *Matthew*, 1112; W. D. Davies and Allison, *Saint Matthew*, 3:679; Hauerwas, *Matthew*, 248–49. The wording, however, is not identical in the two texts.

103. France, *Matthew*, 1113.

104. Cf. Kirk, *Attested by God*, 380.

105. Contra Burnett, who says that Jesus always had this authority ("Characterization

disciples of all nations (28:19), rather than of the Jews only (cf. 10:5-6). His command that they teach the nations all that he had commanded them indicates that Jesus' authority is not only political authority. It is also teaching authority, which he is shown to possess elsewhere in Matthew (cf. 7:29), but which was delegated to the disciples until after his resurrection (cf. 10:7-8).

Jesus' final words to his disciples are about his abiding presence with them. "And behold, I am with you always to the end of the age" (28:20). These words, which recall Matt 1:23 ("Immanuel... God with us"), make a final contribution to the characterization of Jesus. Jesus promises to be "with" his disciples as God has been with his people. He would never again be taken away as he was taken away by the crucifixion. By these words, the implied audience understands that Jesus has abilities that only divine beings possess. Jesus implicitly claims omnipresence and immortality. Jesus' presence "with" his disciples will enable their success in making disciples, as God's presence in the OT had enabled the success of his people.[106] Jesus' final words are understood by the implied audience as extending into its time and applying to it.[107] As disciples of Jesus the Messiah, they are commissioned to make more disciples of Jesus, the one who possesses all authority.[108] Jesus' own presence with the implied audience will ensure success in fulfilling that commission.[109]

---

and Christology," 595).

106. W. D. Davies and Allison, *Saint Matthew*, 3:687.

107. Kupp, *Matthew's Emmanuel*, 236.

108. This command (Matt 28:19) is viewed by some as applicable only to the apostles or to their generation, rather than to all Christians for all times. It is best to conclude, though, that the implied audience understands it to apply to it because: (1) It expects the conclusion of the narrative to be relevant to them. (2) The eleven disciples alone could not make disciples of "all nations" in their lifetimes. (3) The implied audience lives near or after the end of the apostolic age and knows that disciples still need to be made among the nations. (4) The command to make disciples (28:19) can be understood as part of "all that I commanded you" (28:20), which future disciples are to be taught. After a helpful discussion of the reception history of this command, Luz (*Matthew 21-28*, 626-28) concludes that this command is "transparent"—that it applies to the church throughout history.

109. Hauerwas, *Matthew*, 249.

Summary of Effects of Jesus' Characterization on the Implied Audience

We can say, above all, that the implied audience is expected to accept the evaluative point of view that Jesus is worthy of full submission, worship, and obedience because:

1. He is the promised, eschatological Messiah (Χριστός) of Israel.
2. He continues the OT narrative and fulfills the promises made to Abraham and David.
3. He will reestablish God's kingdom and return God's people from exile, saving them from their sins and restoring God's presence. He will reign not as a tyrant, but as a shepherd.
4. He is a threat to earthly rulers, who are under the devil's authority and guilty of oppression.
5. He is the ideal Israel who has been faithful where Israel has not.
6. He will carry out God's eschatological judgment.
7. He has a unique, filial relationship to God as the "Son of God."
8. He is like, but greater than, Moses.
9. He is more powerful than, and has authority over, the devil.
10. God raised him from the dead so he could fulfill the purposes for which he was sent.
11. He possesses universal authority.
12. With divine attributes, he is with his disciples to enable them to carry out his commission.

The submission, worship, and obedience due Jesus is due both from characters in the narrative's story world and from those in the implied audience's world. The characterization of Jesus informs the implied audience's evaluation of responses to him by characters in the narrative. In addition, because of (1) Jesus' resurrection, (2) his promise to be with his disciples to the end of the age, and (3) its membership in a community of disciples, Jesus' characterization calls for the implied audience's own believing response to him.[110]

---

110. W. D. Davies and Allison, *Saint Matthew*, 3:688–89.

Jesus' characterization also affects the implied audience's understanding of the significance of events in Matthew's narrative. Herod's attempt to kill Jesus is a threat to the hope that Jesus will reestablish God's kingdom. Likewise, the growing opposition to Jesus on the part of the Jewish leaders represents a threat to kingdom hopes and not simply to Jesus' teaching and healing ministry. The implied audience also understands Jesus' resurrection as the restoration of those hopes and the guarantee that they will be fulfilled.

The characterization of Jesus also teaches the implied audience that when Jewish leaders in its own day oppose or reject Jesus or his disciples, it must always follow Jesus rather than those leaders. Jesus' superiority to Moses and John the Baptist provides a rationale for choosing Jesus and rejecting the Jewish leaders who claim allegiance to Moses. The implied audience also expects Jesus, the risen Messiah, to establish God's kingdom on earth in the future. In the meantime, while it works to make disciples of all nations, the implied audience is comforted by his promise of his presence. Finally, although Jesus is primarily one to whom the implied audience must respond, he is also one whose example should be followed. His vulnerability to death and temptation provides a basis for the implied audience's identification with Jesus' humanity. Although the implied audience cannot identify with Jesus as messianic king, it can identify with him as one who humbly submits to God and obeys his will.[111]

---

111. See Pennington, *Reading the Gospels*, 219.

4

Characterization Part Two

Other Characters in Matthew's Prologue and Resurrection Narrative

Introduction

Chapter 3 presented an analysis of the characterization of Jesus in Matthew's prologue and resurrection narrative. This chapter presents an analysis of the other characters in these two sections of that Gospel. Again, the goal of this analysis is to determine the effect of the presentation of those characters on the implied audience's understanding of Matthew's resurrection narrative. The characters are discussed in the order in which they first appear in the narrative. Commentaries on Matthew rarely provide analysis of these characters *as* characters. Surprisingly, this is even true of commentaries that employ narrative-critical methodology. The observations that commentators do make about these characters are considered in this analysis.

Joseph

Joseph, husband of Mary and Jesus' legal father, appears in Matthew only in the infancy narrative. He is first mentioned in the genealogy of Jesus, where he is said to be descended from both Abraham and David (1:16). Joseph was betrothed to Mary (1:18) and had not been sexually intimate with her (1:18, 25) when she became pregnant. His abstinence and willingness to end their betrothal (apparently believing that Mary had been immoral) are consistent with his being called "righteous" (1:19).[1] Joseph was instructed to name Jesus (1:21), by which he effectively adopted Jesus, making Jesus a legal heir to David's throne.[2] Joseph responded obediently and refrained from sexual intimacy with Mary until after Jesus' birth (1:24–25), accepting his role as a servant of God and of his Son (2:13–15, 19–23).[3]

The characterization of Joseph affects the implied audience in three ways. First, Joseph's righteousness, which combines devotion to the Law with compassion,[4] will serve to highlight the flaws in the righteousness of the scribes and Pharisees pointed out later (5:20; 9:11–13; 12:1–8; 23:23). Second, Joseph serves as one example of a faithful response to Jesus, modelling self-denial and sacrifice for the sake of Jesus (cf. 16:24). Finally, as a Jewish man (1:20) he is one of several examples proving that not all Jews oppose Jesus and that Jewish contemporaries of the implied audience may also respond to him in faith.

Mary

Mary, the mother of Jesus, is not as prominent in Matthew's infancy narrative as in Luke's. Matthew does not mention her conversation with an angel, her visit to her cousin Elisabeth (cf. Luke 1:26–56), or the circumstances of Jesus' birth (cf. Luke 2:1–7). Of the ten verbs associated with her in Matthew's infancy narrative, only two are active with Mary as the subject (Matt 1:21, 25),[5] four are active with Mary as the object (1:19, 20, 24, 25), and four are passive (1:16, 18 x2, 20). Joseph is frequently the subject—and Mary and/or Jesus the object(s)—of verbs involving the entire family (1:24, 25; 2:14, 21). The two active verbs with Mary as subject refer to her giving birth (τέξεται in 1:21, ἔτεκεν in 1:25), keeping the implied audience's focus on Jesus, the one Mary bore. In Matthew's infancy narrative, Mary simply gives birth to Jesus the promised Messiah. The implied audience understands Mary to be Jewish because of her betrothal

---

1. Morris, *Matthew*, 28; Turner, *Matthew*, 65.
2. Brossier, "Les evangiles," 20; Kingsbury, "Birth Narrative," 164; Morris, *Matthew*, 29.
3. Kingsbury, *Matthew as Story*, 27; W. D. Davies and Allison, *Saint Matthew*, 1:208.
4. Morris, *Matthew*, 28; Cf. Turner, *Matthew*, 65.
5. In Matt 1:21, τέξεται is in the middle voice with active meaning.

to a "son of David" (1:20) and her typically Jewish name (Μαρία, cf. מרים, Miriam; Μαριάμ in some MSS).

For the most part, Mary functions as an agent, even if she is the agent through whom the Messiah entered the world. The implied audience is unable to identify with Mary's unique circumstances, and her response is not developed enough to provide a model for the implied audience's own response. One effect of Mary's characterization on the implied audience is the result of her Jewishness. Mary, a Jewish woman, is one of several examples in Matthew that prove that not all Jews rejected Jesus and that God has not rejected all Jews. The implied audience, therefore, knows that Jewish individuals in their (i.e., the audience's) own time could be part of God's plan and that Jesus' commission to "make disciples of all nations" (28:20) includes Jews.

Holy Spirit/Spirit of God

The Holy Spirit is mentioned in three pericopes in Matthew's prologue, as well as in the resurrection narrative. The Spirit performs significant actions but is not described in detail, which suggests that the implied audience already understands the Spirit's nature and significance. The term "Holy Spirit" occurs rarely in the OT (Ps 51:11; Isa 63:10, 11) and in early Jewish literature (Wis 9:17; 4 Ezra 14:22),[6] but it is equivalent in meaning to the more frequently used terms "Spirit of the Lord" and "Spirit."[7] The OT usage does not require a Trinitarian understanding of the Holy Spirit, but it does present the Spirit as, at least, God's agent, presence, or creative power which enables people to accomplish his purposes.[8] Everything done by the Spirit is understood as done at the initiative of God himself, since it is *his* Spirit.

In Matthew, the Holy Spirit is the means of Jesus' conception in Mary's womb (1:18, 20). The implied audience does not know exactly how this conception occurred but does understand that the pregnancy is

---

6. The phrase also appears in Sus 1:45 in reference to the spirit of a person, rather than of God.

7. "Holy Spirit" in Ps 51:11 refers to what is called "the Spirit of the Lord" in 1 Sam 16:13-14. Isaiah 63:10-11 mentions the Holy Spirit's activity in the days of Moses, although the language in Num 11:16-30 is simply "the Spirit" and Num 11:29 indicates that this is the Spirit of the Lord. Cf. Goldingay, *Isaiah 55-66*, 395.

8. Baumgärtel, "πνεῦμα, πνευματικός," 362-63; Goldingay, *Isaiah 55-66*, 395; Tate, *Psalms 51-100*, 23-24; Tsumura, *First Samuel*, 287; W. D. Davies and Allison, *Saint Matthew*, 1:200.

God's will and work. The Holy Spirit's role in Jesus' conception explains how Mary could give birth to the Messiah while still a virgin, in fulfillment of (Matthew's interpretation of) Isa 7:14.

The Holy Spirit participates in Jesus' baptism scene, being referred to there as "the Spirit of God" (πνεῦμα τοῦ θεοῦ, 3:16). This common OT term evokes the creation narrative (Gen 1:2) and the anointing of Jesse's "branch" who would be a righteous ruler (Isa 11:2 LXX). After Jesus is baptized, he sees the Spirit "descending like a dove and coming upon him." Although Matt 3:16 has the Spirit "coming" (ἐρχόμενον) upon Jesus, rather than "coming mightily" (ἐφήλατο) as upon David (1 Sam 16:13), Matthew's choice of the preposition "upon" (ἐπί) recalls many OT narratives in which God sends his Spirit "upon" people to empower them (Num 11:25; Judg 3:10; 1 Sam 10: 6, 10; 11:6; 16:13).[9] Therefore, Matt 3:16 leads the implied audience to view Jesus as anointed and empowered by God to do his will according to the OT pattern.[10] Since Jesus' role in executing eschatological judgment had just been mentioned in 3:12, the implied audience understands that Jesus is empowered by God *at least* to carry out that judgment.

The only reference to the Holy Spirit in Matthew's resurrection narrative is in 28:19. The disciples of Jesus are to baptize future disciples "in the name of the Father and of the Son and of the Holy Spirit." Whether "in the name of" is a reference to the disciple's new identity—belonging to, or having a new relationship with, the Father, Son, and Holy Spirit—or to baptism as it was practiced within Matthew's community (cf. Did. 7.1),[11] what matters for the purpose of this study is the way in which Father, Son, and Holy Spirit are associated here. The implied audience is not surprised to find the Holy Spirit associated with God the Father.[12] There is no precedent in the OT or Matthew, however, for placing the two on par. The association of the Son, Jesus, with the Father and the Holy Spirit, while not requiring a Trinitarian view,[13] seems to exceed the implications of Jesus' reception of the Spirit (3:16) and provides a basis

---

9. Matthew's change to ἐπί from εἰς (cf. Mark 1:10) forms a stronger parallel between this event and similar OT events.

10. Kingsbury, *Matthew as Story*, 52; Garland, *Reading Matthew*, 37; M. Davies, *Matthew*, 43.

11. See the discussions in W. D. Davies and Allison, *Saint Matthew*, 3:685, and Luz, *Matthew 21–28*, 632.

12. See discussion above on the usage of "Holy Spirit," "Spirit," and "Spirit of the Lord" in the OT.

13. W. D. Davies and Allison, *Saint Matthew*, 3:686; Luz, *Matthew 21–28*, 632.

for later Trinitarian expressions.[14] One of the last ideas that the implied audience encounters in Matthew is that Jesus should be viewed alongside God and his Holy Spirit. He is associated with the two as closely as they are associated with one another.

The primary effect on the implied audience of the Holy Spirit's characterization in Matthew's prologue and resurrection narrative is its contribution to the characterization of Jesus. The Spirit's association with Jesus' conception (1:18, 20), baptism (3:16), and temptation (4:1) demonstrates that these events are divinely ordained. Jesus' reception of the Holy Spirit shows that he is divinely empowered to do God's will. Finally, the close association of Jesus with the Father and the Holy Spirit points to his exalted status.

Angel of the Lord

The angel of the Lord appears three times—all three in dreams—in Matthew's prologue (1:20; 2:13, 19), and once physically in the resurrection narrative (28:2–7). The simple references to the angel of the Lord in the infancy narrative presume that the implied audience has prior understanding of this character. The OT occurrences of the term "angel of the Lord" often appear to equate the angel with Yahweh himself (e.g., Gen 16:7–13; Exod 3:1–16).[15] In the OT, the angel of the Lord frequently delivers messages to human beings (e.g., Gen 16:7–12; 22:1–18; Exod 3:2; Num 22:32–35; Judg 2:1–4; 1 Kgs 19:7; 2 Kgs 1:3–4). The angel of the Lord also acts in contexts of war for Israel and against its enemies (Isa 37:36; Ps 34:7; 35:5–6) or even against Israel itself (1 Chr 21:11–30). While OT examples raise the possibility that the angel of the Lord in Matthew is Yahweh himself, characters' responses to the angel (with the possible exception of Matt 28:4) do not lead Matthew's implied audience to that conclusion. The "angel" (or "messenger," ἄγγελος) of the Lord simply functions as a divine messenger.[16]

This angelic messenger delivers to Joseph commands and an explanation of Mary's pregnancy (1:20–21), ensuring that he would not divorce Mary.[17] The angel then delivers a warning and a command that

---

14. See, for example, Basil the Great, *Hom. Spir.* 10.24; 17.43.
15. White, "Angel of the Lord," 302.
16. Turner, *Matthew*, 66; W. D. Davies and Allison, *Saint Matthew*, 1:206.
17. Betrothal was legally binding in a way that engagement in Western cultures is

spare Jesus' life from Herod's wrath (2:13) and, later, instructions to return to Israel after Herod's death (2:19–20). In these cases, the angel of the Lord communicates to humans on God's behalf, directing their actions and ensuring the success of God's plan. Therefore, the angel of the Lord contributes to the implied audience's understanding that Jesus' birth, survival, and eventual presence in Israel are vital to God's plan.[18] The information communicated by the angel is accurate, confirming the reliability of the angel of the Lord and preparing for his announcement of Jesus' resurrection to be viewed as a reliable announcement.[19]

The angel of the Lord figures prominently in the first part of Matthew's resurrection narrative (28:2–7). His physical appearance is like lightning, and his clothes are white as snow (28:3), recalling the imagery of Dan 7:9 (cf. 10:6).[20] The women's response (Matt 28:8), however, does not suggest that the angel is Yahweh himself (i.e., "the Ancient of Days" in Dan 7:9). The angel's appearance terrifies the guards, who shake and become like dead men (28:4), and induces the women's initial, fearful response (28:5).[21] The angel's arrival and removal of the stone from in front of Jesus' tomb are associated with a "great earthquake" (28:2). This violent impact reminds the implied audience that the "angel of the Lord" is capable of far more than delivering messages. It is, however, the role of a messenger that the angel fulfills by announcing Jesus' resurrection. He is a reliable messenger, sent by the Lord to explain to the disciples why the tomb is empty and where they must go to see, and receive instruction from, the risen Jesus (28:5–7).

The implied audience is influenced by the appearance of the "angel of the Lord" in conformity with the OT pattern, strengthening the impression that Jesus' story continues the OT narrative. The angel's repeated intervention in Jesus' circumstances emphasizes Jesus' vital role

---

not. Therefore, legal action, akin to a divorce, was required to end a betrothal. See Isaksson, *Marriage and Ministry*, 137–41.

18. Viljoen, "Angel of the Lord," 7–8.

19. Knowles argues that the voices of angels in Matthew are relativized, especially by quotes from OT prophets in the infancy narrative. He says that this is done to prevent the angels from being viewed as competing with the authority of Jesus ("Plotting Jesus," 122–23). Since, however, angels are shown to be in the service of Jesus (2:13, 19–20; 4:11), it is unlikely that the implied audience would detect any competition. It is better to view the OT quotes as emphasizing that the "angel of the Lord" brings about the will of God as it has been prophesied.

20. W. D. Davies and Allison, *Saint Matthew*, 3:666; Turner, *Matthew*, 681.

21. Fear is typical in narratives with heavenly appearances. Cf. J. J. Collins, *Apocalypse*, 6; Talbert, *Matthew*, 311.

in God's plan. Most importantly, when Jesus is raised, his resurrection is announced by this divine messenger who has been shown to be a reliable witness. The implied audience, therefore, understands the resurrection to be divinely revealed truth and not an inference or invention of the disciples. The association with Jesus' resurrection of the same angel associated with his birth and escape from Herod leads the implied audience to view Jesus' resurrection as integral to—not just an epilogue to—this Gospel. The angel's role in preparing for Jesus' commission to his disciples (28:19–20) also highlights the importance of that commission.

God/Father/Lord

It is only in Matthew 3:17 that God the Father is directly involved in either Matthew's prologue or resurrection narrative.[22] His presence and activity, however, are easily inferred by the implied audience in several other places.[23] God is behind actions attributed to the Holy Spirit, such as the virginal conception of Jesus (1:18, 20), Jesus' spiritual anointing (3:16), and the leading of Jesus into the wilderness to be tempted (4:1). He is also the source of the messages delivered by the angel of the Lord (1:20–21; 2:13, 19–20; 28:5–7),[24] as well as of other messages revealed in dreams (2:12, 22). Other supernatural occurrences, such as the appearance of the star in the east (2:2) and the earthquake associated with the empty tomb (28:2) are naturally attributed to God. The implied audience understands that God is the cause of these events, contributing to the characterization of God as willing and able to intervene in human affairs and actively directing the course of Jesus' life.[25]

Matthew's prologue contains other elements that contribute to the characterization of God. The prominent motif of fulfilled scripture (1:22–23; 2:15, 17–18, 23; 3:1–3; cf. 8:17; 12:17; 13:14, 35; 21:4; 26:56; 27:9) shows that God is faithful to his word. Matthew 1:23 indicates that Jesus' birth is at least a sign that God will be with his people, demonstrating

---

22. Knowles, "Plotting Jesus," 121; Cf. Sanchez Navarro, "Revealer of the Son," 72–73.

23. Viviano outlines ways in which God is present throughout Matthew, albeit discreetly, giving prominence to Jesus ("God," 341–54).

24. The angel's final words, "Behold, I have told you," in 28:7 suggest that his mission was to deliver this message.

25. Sanchez Navarro, "Revealer of the Son," 80–81; Garland, *Reading Matthew*, 13; Luz, *Matthew 1–7*, 124.

his commitment to them.²⁶ John the Baptist's statement that God has the power (δύναται) to raise up from stones children for Abraham (3:9) emphasizes his supernatural power, his faithfulness to his promises (cf. Gen 15:5), and his sovereign freedom to exclude from his kingdom faithless and fruitless descendants of Abraham.

In the pericope of Jesus' temptation by the devil, both Jesus and the devil quote the OT when speaking about God (Matt 4:4, 6, 7, 10). The use of OT quotations shows that God is to be understood in the first century in a way that is consistent with his presentation in the OT.²⁷ That both Jesus and the devil appeal to the authority of God's word contributes to his characterization as the ultimate authority.

In Matthew's prologue and resurrection narrative, there are limited descriptions of God's direct activity. We will include the divine passives found in 28:6–7,²⁸ which inform the implied audience that God, the Father of Jesus, is responsible for Jesus' resurrection. God had spared Jesus from death in the prologue, ensuring that his purpose in sending the Messiah would not fail. Later, he did not spare him from death, instead permitting his death before restoring him to life again. The only action attributed to God in these passages using an active verb is found in Matt 3:17. The implied audience knows that "the voice out of the heavens" is that of God himself,²⁹ investing those words with great significance. As discussed above, the words spoken ("This is my beloved son, in whom I am well pleased.") contribute to the characterization of Jesus by identifying him so closely with God that one's response to Jesus is a response to God. Although God is not yet called "Father" in Matthew's prologue, the references to Jesus as his Son (2:15; 3:17; 4:3, 6) do characterize him as Jesus' Father. "Father" becomes a—if not *the*— primary way that Jesus refers to God in the rest of Matthew (e.g., 6:9; 7:21; 20:23; 26:53), giving

---

26. Luz, *Matthew 1–7*, 96; France, *Matthew*, 49.

27. The OT quotations in Matt 4:4, 6, 7 are identical to the LXX wording of their sources (Deut 8:3; Ps 91:11–12; Deut 6:16). The quotation of Deut 6:13 in Matt 4:8, however, does not match the wording of either the LXX or the Hebrew text.

28. ἠγέρθη should be translated "he was raised," rather than "he has risen," which sounds like an active voice intransitive instead of a passive. Cf. W. D. Davies and Allison, *Saint Matthew*, 3:667; Osbourne, *Matthew*, 1067; Charlesworth, "Resurrection," 157.

29. Kingsbury, *Matthew as Story*, 51–52; Sanchez Navarro, "Revealer of the Son," 85.

the implied audience a more specific way of referring to God and, at the same time, emphasizing God the Father's relationship with Jesus.[30]

When Jesus commands the eleven to baptize new disciples (28:19), the implied audience is not surprised that they should be baptized in the name of the "Father." His is the "name" with which his people are expected to identify. What is surprising is that this "name" is shared by the Father with the Son and the Holy Spirit.[31] This, along with the worship of Jesus in various places in Matthew, raises questions in the implied audience's mind about the nature of God. Though not requiring a developed Trinitarian view, this does associate other characters with God in a way not seen in the OT.

The characterization of God the Father in Matthew's prologue and resurrection narrative directs the implied audience to view God as sovereign, faithful to the promises he made in the OT, dedicated to the well-being of Jesus, and possessing a unique Father-Son relationship with Jesus. Matthew's presentation of God the Father also contributes to the characterization of Jesus. His unique relationship to the Father shows that he is something more than a physical descendant of David and of Abraham, even if that "something more" is not yet carefully defined.[32] This close identification of Jesus and God adds significance and authority to the words that Jesus speaks,[33] makes his sacrificial death for sinners (1:21; 20:28) both surprising and merciful, and causes opposition to Jesus to be understood as opposition to God himself.[34] When God raises Jesus from the dead, he demonstrates that nothing—not even death—can or will prevent him from accomplishing what he has purposed to do in and through Jesus, including some things not accomplished prior to his death and resurrection (cf. 1:1, 11, 21; 2:2, 6; 3:2, 11–12; 25:31–46).

---

30. Viviano holds the view that "Father" is God's specific name in Matthew in the way that Yahweh is his specific name in the OT ("God in Matthew," 341).

31. See the brief discussion in W. D. Davies and Allison, *Saint Matthew*, 3:685–86.

32. Kingsbury, *Matthew as Story*, 11; Kingsbury, "Figure of Jesus," 11; Cf. France, *Matthew*, 49; Quesnel, "De quelques avatars," 61.

33. Edwards, *Matthew's Story of Jesus*, 17; Quesnel, "De quelques avatars," 61; Kingsbury, *Matthew as Story*, 52.

34. This last item results in a uniformly negative evaluation of Jewish leaders in the narrative. See Burnett, "Anti-Jewish Ideology," 156.

Herod

Herod (the Great) is first mentioned in Matt 2:3. Because two generations of Herod's descendants had also governed in and around Israel after his death, the mere mention of his name reminds the implied audience of the murders and immorality that characterized the Herodian dynasty that had not yet ended when Matthew was written.[35] While historians caution that Herod was a complex individual and not as unambiguously evil as he appears to be in the Gospels,[36] his appearance in Matthew is focused on just once incident. This incident is included not out of any special interest in Herod himself, but because it demonstrates for the implied audience both the opposition that Jesus faced and the plight of his people. Even if the implied audience's outside knowledge of Herod might lead them to view him less negatively as a historical person than he is presented in Matthew, it would not undermine his role in the narrative (i.e., story) world. The implied audience also knows that Herod, since he was not a Davidic king, was an illegitimate king whom God would eventually replace.

The implied audience learns that Herod was "troubled" (2:3) by the magi's arrival and their search for the "King of the Jews" (2:2). Herod, the "King of the Jews" by the Roman Senate's decree,[37] felt threatened by a rival with a legitimate claim to that title (cf. 2:1–18).[38] The troubled king's ability to gather "all the chief priests and scribes of the people" (2:4–6) on short notice shows that his authority was recognized and respected by the Jewish leaders, even if he ruled by imposing fear in others (cf. 2:16–18).[39]

As Matthew's narrative continues, the implied audience gets the impression that Herod is deceitful and untrustworthy because he calls the magi "secretly" (2:7) and plots to protect his position.[40] This impression is confirmed when God warns the magi not to return to Herod (2:12) and when the angel of the Lord informs Joseph of Herod's murderous intent (2:13). Before anything is said about Herod's slaughter of young children

---

35. On the Herodian dynasty, see Josephus, *Ant.* 14–15. The phrase in 2:1—"in the days of Herod the king"—implies that the audience has knowledge of Herod from outside the narrative (cf. Powell, *Chasing the Eastern Star,* 92).

36. See, for example, Vermes, *True Herod,* xi, 100–6; Richardson and Fisher, *Herod,* 15, 409.

37. Josephus, *J.W.* 1.14.4–8.

38. France, *Matthew,* 1113; Weaver, "Power and Powerlessness," 183.

39. Weaver, "Power and Powerlessness," 183; Bauer, "Kingship," 308.

40. Bauer, "Kingship," 308; Kingsbury, *Matthew as Story,* 48.

(2:16–18), the implied audience is told in 2:15 that Jesus outlived Herod, showing that he—like every earthly ruler—is ultimately powerless against God. That powerlessness is further emphasized in 2:16, where Herod is "tricked" by the magi.[41]

Matthew 2:16–18 shows the magnitude of Herod's rage and of his willingness to use violence for his own benefit.[42] He had initially planned to kill only Jesus with the help of intelligence obtained from the magi (2:8, 12). Unable to obtain that intelligence, and unaware that Jesus had already been taken from the area, Herod did not take the time to identify Jesus by some other means, but "sent and slew all the male children," not only in Bethlehem itself, but also in the surrounding area (2:16). Herod desperately attempts to eliminate his rival at any cost. His willingness to kill many children—and to accept the political consequences of the slaughter—reveal the firmness of Herod's opposition to the kingship of Jesus and of his commitment to preserving his own reign. The slaughter presents Herod as similar to Pharaoh (Exod 1:8–22), from whose slaughter God had rescued Moses.

Matthew's characterization of Herod affects the implied audience in multiple ways. First, it contributes to the characterization of Jesus. Herod's way of ruling, using deception and violence, makes him a foil to Jesus, who will give his life for the benefit of others (Matt 20:28), rather than taking the lives of others for his own benefit.[43] Herod's response also shows that Jesus' kingship is a threat to the reigns of earthly kings. After Jesus is raised, when he establishes God's kingdom, he will possess authority previously held by other kings.

This characterization of Herod also contributes to the setting of Matthew's Gospel. It shows that, at the time of the Messiah's birth, God's people lived under foreign oppression that could include great suffering. By showing what life was like under a king like Herod, the implied author shows the implied audience the radical difference that would result from the arrival of God's kingdom in the person of the Messiah.[44]

---

41. Bauer, "Kingship," 308–9; Weaver, "Rewriting," 381. Cf. Hauerwas, *Matthew*, 38.

42. Edwards, *Matthew's Story of Jesus*, 14; Weaver, "Power and Powerlessness," 183–84.

43. M. Davies, *Matthew*, 40; Bauer, "Kingship," 307–8.

44. Carter, *Matthew: Storyteller, Interpreter, Evangelist*, 171. Cf. Charlesworth's explanation of the development of messianology ("From Messianology to Christology," 3–4).

Magi

When the term "magi" (μάγοι) appears in Matt 2:1, it is not explained, indicating that the implied audience is already familiar with the term either through the OT or their own experience.[45] These magi are understood by the implied audience to be gentiles, not only because they are "from the east" (2:1),[46] but also because they bring the gifts of the nations (cf. Isa 60:1–6).[47] Magi are not kings, but servants of kings.[48] They are considered foolish and are sometimes objects of "sympathy or ridicule" (cf. Dan 2:1–12; Acts 13:6–11).[49] They advise kings (Dan 1:20) and interpret dreams (2:1–10) and other phenomena (5:5–15), apparently using magical practices. It is not surprising, then, that these magi respond to a sign observed in the sky (Matt 2:2). What *is* surprising is that God reveals his work to gentiles who are engaged in such forbidden practices (cf. Lev 20:6, 27; Exod 22:18; Isa 44:24–25), who seek guidance from the stars rather than from the true God (cf. Isa 8:19–20).

The magi are presented as trusting of King Herod,[50] providing him with the timing of the star's appearance (Matt 2:7) and, indirectly, the general location of the child (2:2–6). They also seem willing to give him the child's exact location once they discover it (2:8–9). Their trust is consistent with their enthusiastic response to the birth of Israel's Messiah and with an expectation that those in Israel would share their enthusiasm. The magi, therefore, serve as foils who highlight the violent opposition of Herod to the Messiah, as well as the apathy of the Jewish leaders and

---

45. In the OT, μάγοι appear in Daniel (2:2, 10, LXX and Theodotion; also in 1:20; 2:27; 4:7; 5:7, 11, 15 in Theodotion). The term translates אשׁף ("conjurer," "enchanter"), most often in conjunction with "magicians" and "Chaldeans." In Dan 2:27, it appears to be distinct from "wise men." In Dan 5:7, "wise men" appears to be an umbrella term that includes μάγοι. In Acts 13:6, 9, the singular μάγος refers to a magician on the Mediterranean island of Cyprus, suggesting that the activity of of μάγοι was not limited to the east.

46. Their reference to Jesus as "king of the Jews," rather than as "our king," suggests that they are gentiles and not from some community of Jews in the east.

47. R. E. Brown identifies their most likely origins as Parthia or Persia, Babylon, or Arabia or the Syrian desert (*Birth of the Messiah*, 167–70). The absence of a more specific origin than "the east" may suggest to the implied audience that such a response to Jesus is possible in many locations among many nations.

48. Powell, "Magi as Kings," 472; Turner, *Matthew*, 79.

49. Powell, *Chasing the Eastern Star*, 142, 152; Cf. Philo, *Mos.* 1.48–53.

50. Ironically, the magi do not appear to be particularly discerning in their interactions with Herod.

Israel.[51] Although they are not kings, by bringing gifts to the Messiah and worshiping, they perform acts toward the Messiah that foreign kings should (cf. Ps 72:10–11; Isa 60:3).[52]

After visiting Jerusalem and learning that Bethlehem was where the child should be, the magi are again guided by the star (Matt 2:9). Their response to the star was joyful (2:10), since it provides them assurance that they will find the "King of the Jews." The repetitive description of their joy emphasizes its magnitude. The magi "rejoiced exceedingly with great joy" (ἐχάρησαν χαρὰν μεγάλην σφόδρα, 2:10). The implied audience knows that joy is the proper response of all who understand that the Messiah has arrived.

The characterization of the magi produces an effect on the implied audience in three ways. First, it contributes to the theme of the inclusion of gentiles in God's purposes and kingdom. Second, it contributes to the characterization of Herod, and especially of the Jewish leaders, by means of the contrasting responses to Jesus' birth. Finally, their worshipful and joyful response to Jesus provides an example for the implied audience to follow[53]—an example also seen in the responses of those who encounter the risen Jesus (28:8–9, 17).

The first responses to Jesus in Matthew's Gospel are the sharply contrasted responses of Herod and the magi.[54] Both are responses to the claim that Jesus is the Messiah, the King of the Jews. Neither the magi nor Herod are representative of ordinary Jews. The implied audience, though, begins to wonder how the Jews will respond to Jesus as the plot unfolds.

Jerusalem/Judea/The District around the Jordan

Matthew's prologue contains two phrases that refer to ordinary Jews (i.e., those not in positions of authority or influence). While these terms technically refer to geographical areas, the implied audience understands them to refer to the inhabitants of those areas.

When Herod heard that the magi were seeking the King of the Jews, he was "troubled" (ἐταράχθη) along with "all Jerusalem" (2:3). Some

---

51. Kingsbury, *Matthew as Story*, 26; Morris, *Matthew*, 38–39.

52. Powell, *Chasing the Eastern Star*, 137, 159; W. D. Davies and Allison, *Saint Matthew*, 1:251.

53. Heil, *Gospel of Matthew*, 7; Kingsbury, *Matthew as Story*, 48.

54. Bauer, "Kingship," 307–8; Bornkamm, *Studien*, 141–42.

scholars view Jerusalem's response as negatively as Herod's and, therefore, as prefiguring those who will be responsible for Jesus' death.⁵⁵ The verb ταράσσω, however, is not inherently negative. It simply denotes disturbance or confusion.⁵⁶ It is used positively in reference to Jesus (John 11:33; 12:27; 13:21) and neutrally or positively in reference to others (Matt 14:26; Luke 1:12). The inhabitants of Jerusalem are understandably stirred up by the report of the Messiah's birth. Was this news true? If it was true, would it mean salvation or judgment for them? The implied audience is left wondering how ordinary Jews will eventually respond to the Messiah.

The implied audience begins to learn about the response of ordinary Jews in Matt 3:1–6, where "Jerusalem" (3:5) reminds the implied audience of "all Jerusalem" in 2:3. This is not a response to Jesus, but to John the Baptist's preaching of the "kingdom of heaven." When John appears resembling Elijah (3:4) and preaching the arrival of the kingdom, large numbers of ordinary Jews respond positively. Going to John, they are baptized while confessing their sins (3:5–6). The implied audience infers from 3:7 that their submission to baptism is an effort to flee the wrath of God associated with the arrival of his kingdom. Nothing in the narrative suggests that their response was inadequate or insincere.⁵⁷ The implied audience, therefore, expects many ordinary Jews to respond positively to Jesus himself, the messianic king in whose person the kingdom of God arrived (cf. 12:28).

The characterization of ordinary Jews in Matthew's prologue affects the implied audience in multiple ways. First, the disturbance among them in 2:3 leads the implied audience to watch carefully for their eventual response. Second, since the implied audience's first impressions of ordinary Jews are somewhat positive (2:3; 3:1–6), they see their Jewish contemporaries as capable of responding positively to Jesus. Finally, the initial characterization of ordinary Jews as neutral or positive contributes to the negative characterization of the Jewish leaders. It will be under the influence of these leaders that many ordinary Jews in Matthew end

---

55. See, for example, Brossier, "Les evangiles," 22. Cf. R. E. Brown, *Birth of the Messiah*, 182–83; Luz, *Matthew 1–7*, 137.

56. "ταράσσω," BDAG, 990.

57. In Luke 3:7, "brood of vipers" refers to the crowds, rather than to only the Pharisees and Sadducees, suggesting that Matthew's author may have had access to, but did not include, a negative evaluation of the crowds' response.

up opposing Jesus (cf. 27:20, 25), despite their initial neutral or positive response to the news of his kingdom.

Jewish Leaders (Chief Priests, Scribes, Pharisees, Sadducees, Elders)

In Matthew's Gospel, various groups of Jewish leaders play prominent roles. These groups will be treated as a single "character" because of their consistent opposition to Jesus.[58] Much of their characterization is developed in the middle parts of Matthew. Our analysis of the prologue and resurrection narrative includes their initial and ultimate characterization.

The first Jewish leaders to appear in Matthew are "the chief priests and the scribes of the people" in 2:4.[59] The implied audience first encounters Jewish leaders as associated with and submissive to the evil King Herod. Although their submission likely results from fear (cf. 2:12-20), those expected to lead for the good of the people are portrayed as cooperating with the oppressive Roman ruler (2:4-6).[60] After telling Herod where the Messiah would be born (2:5), the chief priests and scribes disappear from that pericope, and they do not reappear together again until they indignantly rebuke Jesus at the temple after his triumphal entry (21:15-16). Some scholars condemn them as participants in Herod's plan to kill Jesus,[61] but this goes beyond what the implied audience is told in the narrative. Herod met with the magi "secretly" (2:7), suggesting that the chief priests and scribes were unaware of his plan. The implied audience knows that these leaders, as members of "all Jerusalem" (2:3), were aware of the claim that the "King of the Jews" had been born (2:2) and that they apparently made no effort to investigate the claim or to join the

---

58. Kingsbury, "Developing Conflict," 58; Cf. Bauer, "Major Characters," 367, n. 10. The Pharisees, though not having official authority like other groups, were very influential among the people. They are included here because, like the groups with official authority in Matthew, they oppose Jesus and influence the people in cooperation with these other groups. Cf. Kampen, *Matthew*, 24-25; Scaer, "Sadducees," 145.

59. Although having less power than the chief priests and elders, the scribes, as members of the "retainer class," possessed influence over the people. See Saldarini, *Pharisees*, 161. In Matthew's story world, the scribes' influence is seen in their teaching role (7:29), their association with other influential groups (2:4; 5:20; 26:57; 27:41), and their sitting in the "chair of Moses" (23:2).

60. Kingsbury, "Developing Conflict," 65; Bauer, "Kingship," 316.

61. R. E. Brown, *Birth of the Messiah*, 182-83. This also seems to be implied by Luz, who says that they become Herod's "accomplices" (*Matthew 1-7*, 113).

magi in worship.⁶² They either did not believe the scriptures (i.e., Mic 5:2; cf. Matt 2:6) or had no interest in their fulfillment. They do not yet actively oppose Jesus, but their apathetic response to the report of the Messiah's birth establishes an initially negative view of them.

The implied audience next encounters the Jewish leaders when the "Pharisees and Sadducees" arrive at the Jordan River where John is baptizing (3:7).⁶³ The phrase ἐπὶ τὸ βάπτισμα αὐτοῦ is ambiguous in meaning. It could mean that they had come "for his baptism" (i.e., to be baptized; cf. NASB), "to his baptism" (i.e., to observe it; cf. KJV, ESV, NAB), or even "against his baptism" (i.e., to oppose it). John's response suggests that they had come to be baptized. Baptism's association with repentance in light of the arrival of God's kingdom (3:2) is understood as an effort to "flee from the coming wrath" (3:7), and this is what John understands the Pharisees and Sadducees to be doing. Since John is a reliable witness, his words "brood of vipers" (3:7) accurately reflect God's own view of the Pharisees and Sadducees. They are not trustworthy shepherds, but evil, dangerous snakes.⁶⁴ John's command to produce "fruit worthy of repentance" (3:8) indicates that they were failing to live out submission to God's will.⁶⁵ John condemns them for assuming that their Jewishness, regardless of their actions, obligates God to include them in his kingdom (3:9).⁶⁶ John's words in 3:10–12 indicate that the Pharisees and Sadducees face severe judgment if they do not change their behavior.⁶⁷

It is significant that John the Baptist distinguishes between the Jewish leaders and ordinary Jews. In Luke 3:7–9, John's harsh words are directed toward the Jewish crowds, but in Matt 3:7–9 they are directed only toward the Pharisees and Sadducees. This distinction, made early in the Gospel, allows the implied audience to view ordinary Jews as distinct from their leaders for the remainder of the narrative. Between the prologue and resurrection narrative, all five groups of leaders—chief priests (21:15, 23–27, 45–46; 26:3–5, 14–15, 47, 59; 27:1–2, 12, 20, 41), elders

62. Kingsbury, "Developing Conflict," 65; Cabrido, *Shepherd of Israel*, 30; Bornkamm, *Studien*, 141–42.

63. An alliance between the Pharisees and Sadducees is unusual and, therefore, to be viewed as motivated only by their mutual opposition to Jesus (cf. Josephus, *Ant.* 13.10.6; 18.1.14).

64. Kingsbury, "Developing Conflict," 60; Yamasaki, *John the Baptist*, 87.

65. Hauerwas, *Matthew*, 46; Morris, *Matthew*, 58–59.

66. Morris, *Matthew*, 59; W. D. Davies and Allison, *Saint Matthew*, 1:307–8.

67. Kingsbury, *Matthew as Story*, 19; Kingsbury, "Developing Conflict," 60; Cf. Bauer, 'Major Characters," 35–36.

(21:23; 26:3–4, 47, 57; 27:1–2, 12, 20, 41), scribes (9:3; 12:38; 15:1–2; 21:15; 26:57; 27:41), Pharisees (9:11, 34; 12:2, 14, 24, 38; 15:1–2, 12; 16:1; 19:3; 21:45–46; 22:15, 34–35),[68] and Sadducees (16:1; 22:23)—are presented as opposing Jesus, with this opposition leading to Jesus' passion. As the leaders become more aggressive in their opposition (cf. 12:14), the crowds can appear more neutral, more capable of a believing response to Jesus, and less culpable than their leaders.[69]

After the Jewish leaders apparently succeed—their opposition to Jesus leading to his death—they make a final appearance in Matthew's resurrection narrative. In Matt 28:11–15, the "chief priests" (28:11) hear about the empty tomb and consult with "the elders" (28:12) to formulate a response. The chief priests, in the report of some who had guarded the tomb, are told "all that had happened" (28:11). "All that had happened" must include the earthquake and the appearance of the angel of the Lord, which had terrified the guards (28:2–4).[70] It must also include that the tomb was empty, since the leaders' response was focused on explaining the empty tomb (28:13).[71] It almost certainly includes, or implies, the resurrection of Jesus. Given the large bribe paid to the soldiers to claim that Jesus' body had been stolen, the implied audience understands that both parties know that this explanation is a lie.[72] It was a risky lie for the soldiers to tell, since sleeping on duty was punishable by severe discipline or death.[73] Those paying and receiving the bribe must have known that there was a different explanation for the empty tomb. They knew that Jesus had predicted his resurrection (27:63), which is why the guards had been deployed in the first place (27:64–66). Jesus' resurrection remained

---

68. Note that, despite their prominence through most of the Gospel, the Pharisees are not depicted as being involved in Jesus' trial or crucifixion, although they must have been present and aware of it (cf. 27:62). W. D. Davies and Allison consider this the result of the "historical memory" that the Pharisees "were not responsible for Jesus' execution" (*Saint Matthew*, 3:653).

69. See especially Matt 27:20–23, where "the chief priests and the elders" influence the crowds to call for Jesus' crucifixion.

70. Morris, *Matthew*, 741; Luz, *Matthew 21–28*, 610.

71. "[E]ven the priests could not deny this fact" (Luz, *Matthew 21–28*, 1104); Morris, *Matthew*, 741.

72. Furthermore, because the Romans severely punished grave-robbers, it is implausible that those who had recently deserted Jesus in fear would have the courage to steal his body (R. E. Brown, *Death of the Messiah*, 1294).

73. See Justinian, *Digest* 49.16 for a list of offenses and their punishments under Roman military law, including capital punishment for desertion. This was a "self-incriminating" lie (W. D. Davies and Allison, *Saint Matthew*, 3:671).

the best explanation for the empty tomb, even if it that explanation was difficult to believe. The implied audience, therefore, understands that the chief priests and elders have been informed that Jesus may have risen from the dead and of the supernatural events associated with the empty tomb.

The response of the chief priests and elders to the possibility of Jesus' resurrection completes Matthew's characterization of them. Having failed to destroy Jesus the Messiah permanently, they desperately try to prevent others from believing in his resurrection. They pay the guards "a considerable sum of money" to lie (28:12). The implied audience infers that this is a misappropriation of funds meant for a more noble purpose (cf. 26:14–15; 27:6). They invent the lie that the guards would tell (28:13). The implied audience notices the irony that those who requested a guard to prevent a "greater deception" by the disciples (27:64) now invent a greater deception themselves.[74] Their foolishness and desperation are seen in the implausibility of the lie that they invent.[75] Since the guards agree to the leaders' plan, the implied audience accepts as plausible the leaders' claim that they would satisfy the governor if he heard the false report. Their claim to be able to influence the governor,[76] as they did during Jesus' trial (27:18–26), leads the implied audience to view those Jewish leaders—and not the Romans—as those most responsible for Jesus' death and, even after his resurrection, those most opposed to his mission.

The implied audience notices the remarkable hardness of heart of the chief priests and elders. These leaders know that Jesus claimed to be the Messiah and eschatological Son of Man (26:63–68; cf. Dan 7:13–14) and that he had predicted his resurrection (Matt 27:63). But even when confronted with an unbiased report of his (possible) resurrection (28:11), rather than repenting and acknowledging him as Lord and Messiah—or at least investigating the matter—they persist in their opposition and desperately try to keep others from believing in him. They appear to have no interest in the truth or in God's plan, wanting only to preserve their own position of power and influence (cf. 27:18), even at the expense of the ordinary people who will hear their lie.[77]

---

74. Heil, *Death and Resurrection*, 104; Cf. Turner, *Matthew*, 685; W. D. Davies and Allison, *Saint Matthew*, 3:671.

75. Hauerwas, *Matthew*, 247; Luz, *Matthew 21–28*, 610–11.

76. Hauerwas calls this claim a lie (*Matthew*, 248). The entire plan, however, could unravel if it was a lie.

77. Luz, *Matthew 21–28*, 1104; W. D. Davies and Allison, *Saint Matthew*, 3:670.

The characterization of the Jewish leaders affects the implied audience in several ways. First, it helps the implied audience to understand the setting in which Jesus lived and ministered. In addition to being subject to foreign oppression (2:13–23), God's people were suffering the consequences of their own corrupt and evil leadership. They needed to be rescued from their leaders. Second, since Jesus' willingness to "give his life as a ransom for many" (20:28) sharply contrasts with the efforts of other leaders to seek their own good at the expense of others, the Jewish leaders serve as a foil to Jesus.[78] Third, the characterization of the Jewish leaders sheds light on events in the plot. Their use of authority and influence to oppose the Messiah—instead of welcoming him—is a significant obstacle which adds suspense to the plot. Fourth, the Jewish leaders provide an example of a negative response that must be avoided.[79] Finally, the characterization of the Jewish leaders guides the implied audience's response to Jewish leaders in their own day (cf. 28:15). Those leaders, who did not represent all Jews, were understood as continuing to oppose God's work through Jesus. They were not to be trusted and were enemies of the gospel, even though enemies were to be loved (cf. 5:44).

Infants

In Matt 2:16, Herod is shown to be lying about his intention to worship the newborn King of the Jews. His true intention is reflected in his next act: the murder of all the male children aged two and under in Bethlehem's vicinity. The implied audience understands that Herod did not know about Jesus' flight to Egypt (2:13–15) and, therefore, interprets this massacre as an attempt to kill Jesus despite the magi's lack of cooperation (2:12).

The implied audience knows nothing about these children other than their age range, gender, location, and fate. They are presumed to be innocent and undeserving of this violent death. Their primary effect on the implied audience is in displaying the wickedness of Herod.[80] They

---

78. Bauer, "Major Characters," 366; Cf. Bond, *Caiaphas*, 124.

79. Bauer, "Major Characters," 366; Carter, *Matthew: Storyteller, Interpreter, Evangelist*, 213.

80. Although not directly relevant to the resurrection narrative, Matthew's use of language elsewhere to refer to the weak and vulnerable (παιδίον, μικρός, ἐλάσσων) indicates that (1) such language refers to members of the church (cf. 11:25; 18:3, 6; 25:40, 45), with whom these infants may be identified, and (2) despite their slaughter, these

also contribute to the implied audience's understanding of the political setting into which Jesus was born, and in which God's people lived during Herod's reign.[81] This was an example, even if an extreme one, of the brutality to which the people were subject—and to which they would continue to be subject until God sent the Messiah to set them free.

JOHN THE BAPTIST

John figures prominently in Matt 3:1–17. He is introduced with a title—"the Baptist" (3:1)—and is described as preaching a message of repentance based on the arrival of "the kingdom of heaven" (3:2). The simple use of the title "the Baptist" assumes that the implied audience has prior knowledge of John. The next two verses (3:3–4) lead the implied audience to evaluate John very positively. John's ministry was prophesied by Isaiah (3:3; cf. Isa 40:3)—giving it God's strong endorsement—and was preparation for the coming of the Lord (Matt 3:3; cf. Isa 40:3). The description of John in 3:4 casts him in the mold of the prophet Elijah (cf. 2 Kgs 1:8).[82] On the basis of 3:3–4, then, the implied audience understands that John is a reliable character and will accept everything John says as truth, including his statements about other characters.[83]

John's preaching is well-received despite his unusual appearance and diet (3:4). Large numbers of ordinary Jews go to John in the wilderness to be baptized while confessing their sins (3:5–6). The implied audience observes John's boldness and directness when he rebukes the Pharisees

---

children are neither insignificant nor forgotten (cf. 10:42; 18:1–6, 10–14; 19:13–14). Cf. Weren, "Children in Matthew," 61–62.

81. Several considerations suggest that the implied audience understands this as typical of Herod's behavior. First, as the only narrated event in which Herod is involved, it is natural to understand it as typical, rather than exceptional. Second, Herod's ability to quickly gather all the chief priests and scribes (2:4) is consistent with his already being feared, which can be explained by his similar actions in the past. Third, the warning to the magi (2:12), since it was not necessary for Jesus' rescue (cf. 2:13–14), suggests that the magi themselves were in danger from Herod. Finally, that Joseph was instructed to remain in Egypt until Herod died (2:19–20) portrays Herod as an ongoing threat to Jesus, as well as to anyone else who appears to threaten his reign.

82. Yamasaki, *John the Baptist*, 84; Morris, *Matthew*, 55.

83. Edwards, *Matthew's Story of Jesus*, 16; Yamasaki, *John the Baptist*, 83, 147. Yamasaki suggests that the implied audience may briefly doubt John's reliability because he uses a title for Jesus that the narrator does not ("one coming after me," 3:11) and because he questions Jesus regarding his coming for baptism (3:14). He concludes that John's reliability is ultimately preserved, and that John had only misunderstood the timing of eschatological judgment (*John the Baptist*, 95–96).

and Sadducees with harsh language (3:7–10). Since the Pharisees and Sadducees remain "on stage" long after John's death (14:3–12), their characterization through John's words, rather than the characterization of John, is of greater significance in the narrative. The implied audience understands John's condemnation of the Jewish leaders to be consistent with God's opinion of them,[84] introducing the theme of conflict between the Jewish leaders and God. This conflict raises the question as to how God will establish his kingdom despite the opposition of these leaders—a question that will be answered by the end of Matthew's Gospel.

John also contributes to the characterization of Jesus (3:11–12, 14). When John encounters Jesus, his humble statement ("I need to be baptized by you," 3:14) sharply contrasts with his boldness toward the Jewish leaders. John knows that Jesus is superior to him (cf. 3:11) and is willing, therefore, to submit to Jesus even without understanding why Jesus should be baptized by him (3:15). It is the superiority of Jesus, rather than the humility of John, that is important as the narrative unfolds.[85]

The primary effect on the implied audience of John the Baptist's characterization is to contribute, as a reliable witness, to the characterization of other characters. The crowds who come to John's baptism are understood to respond appropriately to his message. The Pharisees and Sadducees are understood to be subject to God's wrath unless they produce the fruit of repentance. Jesus is understood to be the eschatological judge—a role that, once he has died, he can only fulfill as a result of his resurrection. Finally, John, a Jew who responds positively to Jesus, contributes to the implied audience's understanding that their Jewish contemporaries may also respond positively to him.

The Devil

When the devil is introduced in Matt 4:1, the implied audience is expected to know already who he is. In the LXX, the Greek διάβολος normally translates the Hebrew שָׂטָן (satan, adversary). Although שָׂטָן in the OT is not necessarily a proper name, the LXX's rendering of it as ὁ διάβολος (e.g., 1 Chr 21:1; Job 1:6–7) indicates that some understood it to refer to a particular evil being. Therefore, the implied audience understands "the

---

84. Yamasaki, *John the Baptist*, 147; Edwards, *Matthew's Story of Jesus*, 16.

85. The absence of John's "I need to be baptized by you" (Matt 3:14) in Mark (1:9–11) and Luke (3:21–22) suggests that the implied author of Matthew intends to emphasize Jesus' superiority to John.

devil" to be Satan, the angelic being who became God's chief adversary (cf. Mark 1:13; Matt 12:26). Although the OT does not explain how the devil came to be God's adversary, early Jewish literature points to his envy—including his desire to be exalted like God (Wis 2:24; 2 En. 29). This same desire appears to motivate his offer to exchange the world's kingdoms for Jesus' worship (Matt 4:8–9). The devil was subordinate to God in the OT (Job 1:12 LXX), and he continues to be in Matthew, since his opportunity to tempt Jesus comes from the Holy Spirit (Matt 4:1).

Matthew's presentation of the devil is consistent with the implied audience's prior knowledge. He is "the tempter" (ὁ πειράζων, 4:3), identifying his method of opposing God's people. Though he is not necessarily omniscient, he does know that Jesus is the "son of God" (4:3, 6; cf. 3:17).[86] He is aware of Jesus' hunger (4:3) and seeks to exploit it and any sense of entitlement Jesus may have as "son of God." The devil uses scripture to tempt Jesus (4:6). He seeks to replace God as the object of Jesus' worship (4:9). The devil appears to have superhuman powers when he stands Jesus on the pinnacle of the temple (4:5) and then takes Jesus to a high mountain to show him all the world's kingdoms (4:8).[87] When Jesus calls him "Satan" (or "adversary," 4:10), it is clear that the temptations are meant to prevent Jesus from fulfilling God's purposes, which they fail to do (4:11).

One statement made by the devil may surprise the implied audience. He offers Jesus "all the kingdoms of the world and their glory" (4:8–9), implying that he has authority over those kingdoms. Since the devil is known to be a liar (cf. John 8:44),[88] the implied audience may initially wonder if this implied claim is false. For a few reasons, however, we should expect this to be viewed as a true claim. First, Jesus does not respond by correcting the devil's implicit claim of authority. Second, the claim is consistent with biblical language that views the devil (i.e., Satan) as having such authority (2 Cor 4:4; Luke 4:6; cf. Jub. 15:30–34; 1 En. 69:6–7). Finally, the authority of the devil over the nations could explain why, prior to Jesus' death and resurrection, his ministry was restricted

---

86. Kingsbury's view is that transcendent beings witnessed the coming of the Holy Spirit and the heavenly voice at Jesus' baptism (3:16–17; *Matthew as Story*, 51). It is not clear, nor is it essential to the narrative, that this is the case. In Job, Satan's knowledge was the result of his "roaming on the earth" (Job 1:7).

87. The exercise of these powers presents no problem in Matthew's story world, although some scholars propose alternative explanations that do not require a supernatural element (e.g., France, *Matthew*, 131–32).

88. In addition, in Wis 2:24 and LAE 14–16, the devil/Satan is understood to be behind the serpent's deception of Eve (Gen 3:1–5).

to Jews (Matt 10:5–6; 15:24) and would only later include the "nations" or "gentiles" (28:19; cf. 24:14). Therefore, Matthew's implied audience understands the devil to possess authority over the kingdoms of the gentiles.[89]

The devil seems to know that part of Jesus' purpose is to take back for God—and from the devil—the gentile kingdoms (cf. "son of Abraham," 1:1). Rather than lose his authority and be left with nothing, the devil offers to trade these kingdoms to Jesus in exchange for his worship. Since Jesus' only other means of acquiring these kingdoms requires his death, the devil's offer is a real temptation. It would allow Jesus to gain the world's kingdoms while avoiding a painful death. Despite the shrewdness of the offer (cf. 26:39, 42), the devil fails to obtain the worship of God's Messiah (4:11), showing him to be weak compared to God's Son and his opposition to be futile.[90]

The characterization of the devil contributes to the characterization of Jesus, both as a foil and as a powerful, but weaker, opponent. Despite the devil's cunning and power, Jesus is submissive, faithful, and obedient in resisting temptation.[91] Jesus is also shown to be the faithful interpreter of God's word, in contrast to the devil, who misuses scripture. The characterization of the devil contributes to the characterization of the Jewish leaders who also "tempt" Jesus (16:1; 19:3; 22:18, 35). When they oppose Jesus, the Jewish leaders not only follow the example of Herod, but they also—and more significantly—follow the example of Satan.[92] Finally, his characterization contributes to the setting of Matthew's narrative. Satan's claim to possess authority over the kingdoms of the world shows that Jesus enters a situation in which the vast majority of the world is under Satan's authority and needs to be rescued from it. Although this theme does not dominate the narrative, it does point to the universal significance of Jesus' death and resurrection (cf. 28:18–19).[93] When Jesus claims "all authority in heaven and on earth" (28:18) after his resurrection, the implied audience understands that Jesus, who had already triumphed over the devil in this scene, has won a climactic victory over him.

---

89. Carter, "Save His People," 390; Bauer, "Kingship," 315.

90. Kingsbury, *Matthew as Story*, 56; Garland, *Reading Matthew*, 39–40.

91. Garland, *Reading Matthew*, 32, 39–40; Luz, *Matthew 1–7*, 150.

92. Kingsbury, "Developing Conflict," 66; Cf. W. D. Davies and Allison, *Saint Matthew*, 1:355.

93. France, *Matthew*, 1113; Carter, "Save His People," 390.

Angels[94]

Angels are mentioned in Matt 4:11, but the implied audience is told only that they "came and served" Jesus (including by feeding him, as implied by διακονέω) after his temptation.[95] From the OT, the implied audience knows that angels are supernatural beings who perform the Lord's will (Ps 103:20; cf. Ps 91:11, which the devil quotes in Matt 4:6), primarily as messengers, but also in military activity (see above). Their ministry to Jesus in 4:11 tells us that these angels are aligned with the will of God. This ministry tells us more, however, about Jesus. It affirms God's favorable disposition toward his Son Jesus, since it can be inferred that the angels were sent by God to serve Jesus.[96] Their service also tells us about Jesus' status; if angels are subservient to Jesus, then Jesus must be greater than angels. The effect of the angels, then, is to point to the exalted status of Jesus.[97]

The Guards at the Tomb

Another group of characters encountered by the implied audience are those who were guarding (οἱ τηροῦντες) Jesus' tomb during the time leading up to his resurrection (28:4).[98] Pilate permitted the chief priests and Pharisees to set a guard outside the tomb. This was to prevent Jesus' disciples from stealing his body and deceiving the people with a false resurrection claim (27:62–66). The use of the Latin loanword κουστωδία (27:65) indicates that this guard was composed of Roman soldiers (cf. 28:12, στρατιώταις), reminding the audience of the theme of foreign oppression introduced in the prologue (1:11, 17; 2:1–18, 22–23). The

---

94. These angels seem to be distinct from the "angel of the Lord" and are therefore treated separately here. Cf. Viljoen, "Matthean characterisation," 1.

95. For "serving" having the sense of "feeding," see W. D. Davies and Allison, *Saint Matthew*, 1:374; Gundry, *Matthew*, 59.

96. M. Davies, *Matthew*, 45. Edwards notes that the angels' service highlights the "cosmic implications" of the temptation scene, but he does not explain what those implications are (*Matthew's Story of Jesus*, 17–18). Cf. Viljoen, "Matthean characterisation," 3.

97. Cf. Viljoen, "Matthean Characterisation," 3.

98. Although the same participle is used here and in 27:54 (τηροῦντες), nothing requires the implied audience to conclude that these guards must be the same as those who had guarded Jesus while he hung on the cross. Therefore, our interpretation does not depend on understanding the two uses to refer to a single group.

implied audience still lives under Roman rule and knows that the disciples would have been no match for these elite soldiers.

It is not, however, Jesus' disciples whom the guards encounter. Instead, it is the angel of the Lord, whose appearance causes them to shake with fear and become like "the dead" (28:4). The implied audience knows that the fearful response of these ordinarily courageous soldiers is evidence of the angel's glory. Although they have become like dead men, the guards are aware of what is taking place, since they later report "all that had happened" (28:11).

The guards' willingness to accept a bribe and to spread a false report may give the impression that their character is questionable. Their circumstances, however, are so unique that the implied audience would not conclude that all Roman soldiers should be viewed negatively. Such a negative evaluation would be inconsistent with positive presentations of Roman centurions (8:5–13; 27:54) in Matthew. Their unique circumstances as witnesses to unrepeatable events also prevents the implied audience from identifying with the guards as examples to emulate or avoid. The effect of the characterization of these guards on the implied audience is the result of their contribution to the final negative portrayal of the Jewish leaders.[99] The guards provide a way for the Jewish leaders to learn of Jesus' resurrection so that those leaders, in a response that emphasizes the significance of Jesus' resurrection, are shown as going to great lengths to cover up the truth.

Mary Magdalene and the Other Mary

"Mary Magdalene and the other Mary" (28:1) are two of several women "who had followed Jesus from Galilee" and watched his crucifixion "from a distance" (27:55–56). Previously, "the other Mary" was identified as "the mother of James and Joseph" (27:56). The only Mary in Matthew's narrative who fits this description is the mother of Jesus (13:55). If this does refer to Jesus' mother, this obscure way of referring to her is surprising. Although the Johannine parallel might support this being a reference to Jesus' mother (cf. John 19:25), the implied author prevents the implied audience from confidently identifying her as such, shifting the focus to her role as a disciple. The references to these two women without any

---

99. Luz, *Matthew 21–28*, 586; Edwards, *Matthew's Story of Jesus*, 93; Cf. Heil, *Death and Resurrection*, 103–4.

other explanation suggests that they are known to the implied audience and viewed as reliable witnesses. They had witnessed the crucifixion (27:55–56) and burial of Jesus (27:59–61) and now witness his resurrection (28:1–10).

The first thing the implied audience learns about these women is that they go early Sunday morning "to see the tomb" (28:1). If Matt 28:1 is shorthand for Mark 16:1, the women planned to anoint Jesus' body and did *not* expect him to be raised from the dead.[100] Carter argues that the women went with "insightful anticipation of resurrection."[101] He cites Matthew's tendency to improve Mark's presentation of disciples and the fact that the women, familiar with Jesus' passion predictions and having witnessed their partial fulfillment (16:21; 17:22–23; 20:17–19) expect to witness the resurrection too. He also argues that the fact that Jesus' enemies had regarded his predictions highly enough to act on them (27:62–66) makes it reasonable to expect at least some of his disciples to expect his resurrection.[102]

In response to Carter's argument, the following points may be made. First, Matthew's statement of the women's purpose ("to see the tomb," 28:1) is an improvement over Mark's even if they did not anticipate the resurrection. In Mark, the women do not expect Jesus to be raised, but Matthew's neutral presentation (e.g., they came in devotion, not knowing what they would see) is an improvement over the unbelief of Mark 16:1. Second, the resurrection of Jesus is very different from his crucifixion. Nothing miraculous was required for Jesus to die or to predict his death, given the Jewish leaders' opposition (cf. Matt 12:14). Although the women did witness the earthquake associated with Jesus' death (27:51, 54),[103] it was not part of Jesus' prediction and would not necessarily lead them to anticipate his resurrection. Finally, one cannot say with confidence that Jesus' enemies regarded his teachings highly. They knew that he had predicted his resurrection (16:21; 17:22–23; 20:17–19). Their response, however, was intended to prevent his disciples from stealing his body and falsely claiming that he had been raised. They did not anticipate Jesus'

---

100. The omission of the women's purpose as stated in Mark 16:1 may be due to either (1) Jesus having already been anointed for burial in Matthew (26:6–12, although this also appears in Mark 14:3–8) or (2) Matthew's tendency to present disciples more positively (cf. Luz, "Disciples," 101–2).

101. Carter, "To See the Tomb," 201–2; cf. Hauerwas, *Matthew*, 244.

102. Carter, "To See the Tomb," 204–5.

103. Carter ("To See the Tomb," 204) says that the earthquake led the women to anticipate the resurrection.

resurrection, so their response is not evidence that Jesus' disciples anticipated it. Since there is risk in being publicly identified with Jesus (27:56, 58, 69–74), the implied audience understands the women's willingness to assume that risk (by going to the tomb) as a sign of their devotion to Jesus.

Part of the characterization of these women comes through the words of the angel of the Lord to them (28:5–7). His command, "As for you, do not fear" (μὴ φοβεῖσθε ὑμεῖς, 28:5), indicates that, like the guards at the tomb (28:4), the women's instinctive response to the angel is fear. Reverent fear of the Lord or an angel is appropriate (cf. Deut 10:12); fear that the Lord's angel is a danger to the faithful is not (cf. Dan 10:7–12; Ezek 2:1–6; Rev 1:17). The command to "fear not" is typical of OT and early Jewish theophanies or angelophanies and adds an apocalyptic element to the resurrection narrative (cf. Gen 26:24; Exod 20:20; Judg 6:23; Dan 10:12, 19; Tob 12:16–17; 1 En. 14:13—15:1; 2 En. 1:6–10). This apocalyptic element leads the implied audience to expect to hear divine revelation regarding eschatological salvation.[104] The emphatic ὑμεῖς distinguishes the women from the guards. They have reason to "not fear" that the guards lack.[105] Grammatically, this reason could be that they were looking for Jesus (28:5). Their positive disposition toward Jesus should free them from fear, since the angel of the Lord is no threat to those loyal to him. Given the climactic nature of the resurrection announcement, however, 28:5 (i.e., that Jesus had been crucified; cf. 26:56) is better understood as the reason for their inclination toward fear. The reason they should not fear, then, is found in 28:6 (i.e., that Jesus has been raised). Because he has been raised (28:6), they have no reason to fear any longer.

The women are invited to see the empty tomb (28:6). This is apparently to overcome the difficulty of believing that Jesus has been raised. The women are then sent to announce the resurrection and deliver important instructions to Jesus' disciples (28:7). Despite their culture's low view of women as witnesses,[106] these women are sent as witnesses and have the honor of being the first disciples to proclaim that Jesus has been raised.[107]

The women prove to be faithful and obedient disciples by leaving "quickly" to obey the angel's command (28:8). They leave with "fear,"

104. J. J. Collins, *Apocalypse*, 9.
105. France, *Matthew*, 1100; Morris, *Matthew*, 737.
106. Cf. Josephus, *Ant.* 4.8.15.
107. W. D. Davies and Allison, *Saint Matthew*, 3:662; France, *Matthew*, 1098.

not in disobedience (cf. 28:5), but understandably still coming to grips with the angel's announcement. The women also leave with "great joy" (28:8). As the magi felt great joy (χαρὰν μεγάλην) when they were about to meet the newborn king of the Jews, so the women feel great joy (χαρᾶς μεγάλης) when they learn that the Messiah, who appeared to be defeated by his opponents, has been raised from the dead and was not defeated after all.

The women encounter Jesus himself in Matt 28:9–10. They respond by approaching him and worshiping him (28:9). Their worship is an appropriate believing response and is consistent with other positive responses to him (e.g., 2:11; 14:33; 28:17). That they approach him *before* he tells them not to fear (28:10) indicates that they were not afraid of him. Jesus is not rebuking an inappropriate fear but greeting them in a way that is typical in theophanies.[108] Jesus repeats the angel's command for the women to instruct the disciples to meet him in Galilee (28:10). The arrival of the eleven at the designated mountain (28:16) will confirm the women's obedience to this command.

The characterization of "Mary Magdalene and the other Mary" contributes to the narrative's effect on the implied audience in two ways. First, since the Great Commission (28:16–20) forms the conclusion to Matthew's Gospel, the women as characters prepare for that conclusion. They are the link between the resurrection and the Great Commission, explaining how those who had fled in fear (27:56) could personally receive the resurrected Messiah's commission. Second, the women are characters with whom the implied audience can identify and whose example should be followed. In this way, although they do not appear in the prologue, they may be grouped with characters in the prologue (e.g., Joseph, magi, John the Baptist) who respond positively to Jesus.[109] These women appear as ordinary disciples with no special status. If "the other Mary" is Jesus' mother, it is a fact that appears to be deemphasized to facilitate the implied audience's identification with these women. Their exemplary response to Jesus consisting of faith, worship, joy, obedience, and witness to the resurrection is understood by the implied audience as

---

108. "Do not fear" appears in contexts when those receiving the vision are described as responding in fear and in contexts when they are not. In some cases, the heavenly being also invites them to "approach" (1 En. 15:1), which the women here do even before being invited.

109. Significantly, both the women and the magi worship Jesus and experience "great joy" (2:10–11; 28:8–9).

the way that they should respond to the risen Jesus.[110] In addition, the command to the women to "not fear" is heard by the implied audience as a command—and an encouragement—to them.

The Eleven Disciples

Like the two Marys, the eleven disciples do not appear in Matthew's prologue but may be grouped with others who respond positively to Jesus. The implied audience brings to the resurrection narrative a prior knowledge of the disciples. They know that the disciples had been personally called by Jesus (10:1), had received special authority (10:1) and special teaching from him regarding his identity (16:13–21), and that their response had been a mixture of faith and unbelief (e.g., 8:23–27; 14:25–33; 16:22–23).[111] The implied audience's most recent memories of the eleven disciples are negative. They had all abandoned Jesus at the time of his arrest (26:56), and Peter had denied him three times (26:69–74). The implied audience does not yet know how the disciples would be restored and Jesus' investment in them would prove to be not in vain.

Before the eleven disciples appear in Matthew's resurrection narrative, Jesus refers to them as "brothers" (28:10). The implied audience thereby knows that the risen Jesus has already forgiven them.[112] Further evidence that forgiveness has already occurred is found in Matt 28:18–20, where Jesus commissions the eleven without mentioning their abandonment or other failings. There is a surprising silence regarding their failings, leading the implied audience to infer that the death and resurrection of Jesus made those failings irrelevant, even if the disciples, at least as of 28:17, have not understood this. Jesus' final promise to be with them "even to the end of the age" (28:20) indicates that any problem created by their failings was no longer a concern. They were assured of the Messiah's permanent presence (cf. 2 Sam 7:14–16) and of his help in carrying out his commands.

---

110. M. Davies says of the women that "their role represents the part to be played by every follower of Jesus" (*Matthew*, 204–5). Cf. Longstaff, "From the Birth, 176.

111. Cf. J. K. Brown, who concludes that the disciples are presented (especially in 16:21—20:28) as misunderstanding Jesus' teaching and having "little faith" (*Disciples*, 148).

112. Kingsbury, *Matthew as Story*, 91; Luz, *Matthew 21–28*, 607. Cf. Turner, *Matthew*, 682; Moloney, *Shape*, 109–10.

The way the narrator describes the disciples in Matt 28:16 contributes to their characterization. Their presence on the mountain is evidence of their obedience to the command given through the women (28:7, 10).[113] This obedience is a reversal of their abandonment of Jesus. Even if they were not yet convinced that Jesus had been raised, their obedience is evidence of devotion to him. The reference to the disciples as "the eleven disciples" reminds the implied audience of Judas' betrayal (26:14-16, 47-50) and of the fallibility of every disciple. Even though they are called "disciples," the implied audience knows that they are also apostles (cf. 10:2). It is significant, then, that as they receive this commission, the focus is on their status as disciples rather than as apostles. This allows the implied audience to identify with them—and with that commission—more easily.[114]

The disciples are described as doing two things when the see Jesus: they *all* worship and *some* also doubt (28:17).[115] This doubt (or hesitation) is not to be understood as "unbelief" but as inner conflict or an uncertain, divided mind.[116] Their uncertainty regarding (1) how to respond to the risen Jesus and (2) how he would respond to them after they had abandoned him explains how doubt and worship can coexist in this scene.[117] The doubt of some of the eleven disturbs the implied audience,[118]

---

113. Edwards notes that the disciples' obedience helps to reconstruct a positive view of them (*Narrative Portrait*, 132). Some view the disciples' presence on the mountain as placing them in a Moses or Joshua role (e.g., Allison, *New Moses*, 266). Such a parallel, however, is not obvious and would make it more difficult for the implied audience to identify with the disciples and to hear the commission as addressed to it (cf. Luz, *Matthew 21-28*, 620).

114. Cf. J. K. Brown, *Disciples*, 145.

115. On the relationship between the subjects of "worshiped" and "doubted," see France, who concludes that, since (1) only the eleven are present with Jesus here and (2) οἱ δέ requires a change in subject, those who doubted are a subgroup of the eleven who worshiped (*Matthew*, 1111, n. 14). Cf. Luz, who, conceding that all eleven may doubt, prefers "some doubted" as reflecting more common usage and Matthew's customary usage of οἱ δέ (*Matthew 21-28*, 622-23). Edwards notes that a mixed response is consistent with previous responses of the disciples in Matthew (e.g., 14:28-33; 16:16-23; *Matthew's Story of Jesus*, 93-94; *Narrative Portrait*, 134). Morris considers it impossible that the "hesitators were included among the worshipers," but he does not present arguments to support this view (*Matthew*, 745).

116. Luz, *Matthew 21-28*, 623; W. D. Davies and Allison, *Saint Matthew*, 3:68, n. 23; Ellis, "Some Doubted," 576. Cf. Matt 14:31, where this verb is used to refer to Peter's fear after believing and walking on the water.

117. France, *Matthew*, 1112; Wright, *Resurrection*, 643-44.

118. Carter, *Matthew: Storyteller, Interpreter, Evangelist*, 225.

causing them to wonder how Jesus will respond to their doubt. It is these worshiping, yet doubting, disciples whom Jesus commissions to make disciples and to whom he promises his abiding presence (28:19-20). Their earlier commission to preach and heal (10:1-8) did not authorize them to baptize or teach as this new commission does.[119] Their new commission affirms their potential to continue the disciple-making ministry of Jesus[120]—not an inherent potential, but one that results from Jesus' presence (28:20).[121] The implied audience also learns something about how the always-present Jesus responds to their doubts. The mention of the disciples' doubt assures the implied audience that past faithlessness or present doubts do not exclude one from Jesus' commission or promise.

The effect of the characterization of the eleven disciples on the implied audience results from its ability to identify with those disciples. First, the disciples provide an example for the implied audience to follow. The implied audience should imitate the disciples' obedience, their worship of Jesus, and their willingness to approach him despite their awareness of past sins.[122] Of greater significance is the implied audience's identification with the disciples as the recipients of Jesus' words in this passage. The implied audience, like those among the eleven, consists of disciples who worship Jesus, but who have not always acted in faith and whose faith may be mingled with doubt.[123] Like the eleven, they receive both Jesus' commission to make disciples and his promise to be with them always as they carry out that commission. As a result, the words of Jesus that conclude Matthew's Gospel, though spoken to the Eleven are understood by the implied audience as spoken to it, assuring it of his presence—and of the benefits of his presence—and anticipating its faithful response.[124]

---

119. Heil, *Gospel of Matthew*, 151; Edwards, *Narrative Portrait*, 135.

120. Edwards, *Narrative Portrait*, 135.

121. Cf. J. K. Brown, *Disciples*, 148-49.

122. France, *Matthew*, 1109; Carter, *Matthew: Storyteller, Interpreter, Evangelist*, 226; Heil, *Gospel of Matthew*, 151.

123. Powell observes that most of the disciples' phraseology in Matthew exposes their flaws, allowing the implied audience to identify with them more easily ("Characterization," 169). Cf. Moloney, *Resurrection*, 52; W. D. Davies and Allison, *Saint Matthew*, 3:682.

124. France, *Matthew*, 1109. Edwards concludes that "a disciple . . . is not an ideal individual who meets Jesus' expectations, but one who recognizes Jesus and who will follow him, in a limited fashion, under most conditions" and Jesus' followers are "those who try to meet Jesus' expectations, but who probably will not be able to" (*Narrative Portrait*, 143). Edwards's pessimistic conclusion is overly dependent on the disciples' characterization prior to Jesus' resurrection, failing to account for the changes that

Summary

At the beginning of chapter three, six possible effects of characterization on the implied audience were suggested. To summarize the effects of characterization in Matthew's prologue and resurrection narrative, the effects of the various characters will be grouped under those six headings.

1. Characterization can present positive or negative model responses—along with their corresponding ideological points of view—to be adopted or rejected by the implied audience.

   Several characters respond to Jesus in ways the implied audience should also respond to him. The characterization of Joseph, the magi, John the Baptist, the two Marys at the tomb, and the eleven disciples lead the implied audience to the conclusion that it should respond to Jesus in faith, obedience, worship, and joy. The implied audience should also follow Jesus' example of submission and obedience to God. Negative responses to Jesus are seen in the characterization of Herod and of the Jewish leaders. As a result, the implied audience knows that it must not oppose Jesus or his purposes in an effort to protect one's own status. Because the resurrection of Jesus restores the life he lived before his crucifixion,[125] the implied audience understands that the positive responses to Jesus seen in the prologue (i.e., before his death) continue to be the responses expected in its own time (i.e., after his resurrection; cf. 28:20).

2. Characterization may indirectly produce an effect on the implied audience by advancing the plot or developing a theme.

   Some characters produce little, if any, direct effect on the implied audience. Instead, they contribute to the effect of other characters or events. Mary, Jesus' mother, is not developed as a character, but is necessary for Jesus to be born of a virgin in fulfillment of Isa 7:14 (LXX). The magi contribute to the theme of gentile inclusion, even though they make only a brief appearance. The two Marys provide a necessary link between Jesus' resurrection and the climactic Great Commission scene. Ordinary Jews in the prologue raise questions

---

result from his resurrection and from the promise of his abiding presence.

125. See the discussion above in chapter 3, where it is argued that the resurrection narrative emphasizes the continuity of Jesus' form and appearance before and after his resurrection.

about how Jews would respond to Jesus. The slaughtered infants perform no actions, but they do contribute to the implied audience's understanding of the setting into which Jesus came, of the conflict that would lead to his passion, and of the similarity of his story to that of Moses.

3. Characterization of one character may contribute to the characterization of other characters through testimony or association with the other character, or by serving as a foil.

Several characters contribute to the negative characterization of the Jewish leaders. Joseph's righteousness contrasts with and highlights the flawed righteousness of the Jewish leaders. The magi's enthusiastic response to the birth of the Messiah sharply contrasts with the apathetic response of the Jewish leaders and the violent response of Herod. John the Baptist directly condemns the Pharisees and Sadducees. The devil's opposition to and testing of Jesus provides an example that the Jewish leaders will later be seen to follow. The guards at the tomb, who believe that Jesus (at least) may have been raised, highlight the Jewish leaders' final, defiant response to Jesus. Even ordinary Jews, whose initial response is neutral or positive, stand in contrast to their leaders, whose characterization is wholly negative, and who are shown to be responsible for influencing ordinary Jews' responses to Jesus (Matt 27:20; 28:15).

Several characters also contribute to the characterization of Jesus. God, John the Baptist, the Holy Spirit, the angel of the Lord, and other angels all contribute to the implied audience's understanding of Jesus as of divine origin and purpose and as having exalted status. Herod's characterization contributes to the characterization of Jesus, both by showing that Jesus is a legitimate threat to earthly authorities and by serving as a foil. Herod's violent and selfish rule sharply contrasts with the way Jesus will rule. The Jewish leaders are also foils to Jesus, rejecting the truth out of self-interest while Jesus embraces the truth even when it is costly to him. Finally, the devil's characterization contributes to that of Jesus when, despite his power and cunning, he fails in his efforts to tempt Jesus, thereby showing Jesus' superiority to him. When Jesus is raised, the implied audience's understanding of the resurrection is informed by the contributions of these characters, who establish expectations and hopes regarding Jesus and who highlight the gracious ways in which he will exercise his authority.

4. Characterization may guide the implied audience in evaluating people contemporary to them who can be identified with characters in the narrative.

   The one character in Matthew's story world who is also part of the implied audience's world is Jesus. The characterization of Jesus as worthy of faith, submission, worship, and obedience shows the implied audience that Jesus is also worthy of its faith, submission, worship, and obedience. The Jewish leaders' persistent opposition to Jesus in Matthew's narrative leads the implied audience to expect Jewish leaders in its own world to oppose Jesus. As a result, the implied audience should not trust Jewish leaders, especially when they teach about Jesus. Finally, the faithful responses to Jesus of several Jews in Matthew's narrative lead the implied audience to expect some Jewish people in its context to respond in faith to him. The resurrection of Jesus brings him into the implied audience's own time and makes contemporary responses to him relevant.

5. Characterization can increase or clarify the significance of actions due to the significance of the person performing or receiving the action.

   The Jewish leaders' opposition to Jesus takes on greater significance because of both their own characterization and that of Jesus. Since Jesus is the promised Messiah and Son of God, the Jewish leaders' opposition to him is understood by the implied audience as opposition to God and his eternal purposes. Moreover, since the Jewish leaders possess authority and influence over other Jews—and a corresponding responsibility for their well-being—their opposition to Jesus is understood as an egregious neglect of their responsibility (cf. 21:43; 23:13).

   The words and actions of reliable witnesses like the angel of the Lord, the Holy Spirit, John the Baptist, and God take on greater significance because they are spoken or performed by divine beings or a spokesman for God. For example, God's actions to direct the circumstances of Jesus' birth and to protect him from Herod demonstrate that Jesus is vital to God's plan. No human's actions to protect another could have such significance.

The characterization of Jesus as Messiah, royal son of David, son of Abraham, Son of God, and eschatological judge all add significance to his actions. We would see this more frequently if our analysis included the whole of Matthew, since the vast majority of his actions are found between the prologue and resurrection narrative. We can, however, see it even in the portions of Matthew's Gospel that we are analyzing. Jesus' deliverance from Herod's plot means the survival of the Messiah, which has implications that exceed those of the survival of an ordinary child. His submission to John's baptism demonstrates a surprising humility for a king or the Son of God. His victory over the devil is won as the public Messiah, giving his obedience a significance for others that a private individual's obedience would not. Jesus' resurrection is not simply the raising of a healer or teacher. The narrative—especially the prologue—makes clear that Jesus is the messianic king. His resurrection, therefore, ensures that the "kingdom of heaven" will be established.

6. Characterization establishes expectations associated with a character, and subsequent events confirm, threaten, or undermine those expectations.

Jesus is obviously the central character in Matthew's Gospel. His characterization as God's promised Messiah establishes expectations for the reestablishment of an eternal Davidic kingdom. Therefore, when Herod attempts to destroy Jesus, the implied audience views it not only as a threat to Jesus as an individual, but also to the reestablishment of the promised kingdom. Conversely, Jesus' successful flight to Egypt is understood as the preservation of that kingdom hope. When John the Baptist preaches, "Repent, for the kingdom of heaven is at hand" (3:2), the implied audience understands this kingdom hope to be confirmed. The devil's temptation of Jesus is also understood in light of this kingdom hope. A king who gives in to temptation, who is not fully submissive to God and his word, cannot be expected to establish the promised kingdom. His victory, however, strengthens the hope that Jesus will overcome all obstacles and reestablish the kingdom. Jesus' death would have meant the end of his work—not merely of his teaching and healing, but especially of his future work in establishing and reigning over God's kingdom. His resurrection, therefore, is understood by the implied audience as the restoration of that kingdom hope and the guarantee of its fulfillment.

On the other hand, the Jewish leaders, by virtue of their office, are expected to lead the people in a faithful response to God's work and to his Messiah. These leaders are expected to exemplify righteousness and obedience. The narrative, however, undermines this expectation at nearly every point, showing that these leaders are unworthy of their people's trust.

The events that make up the plot of Matthew's Gospel cannot be understood apart from the characters who perform or who are affected by the actions that make up those events. Neither can these events be understood apart from the settings in which they take place. Therefore, now that we have analyzed the characters in Matthew's prologue and resurrection narrative, we will proceed in the next chapter to analyze the settings found in these portions of that Gospel.

5

Settings

INTRODUCTION

Although narrative critics routinely acknowledge setting as an important element in the construction of narratives,[1] settings receive far less attention in narrative-critical studies than characterization and plot receive. Few narrative-critical studies focus primarily on setting,[2] and such studies generally lack a careful consideration of how each setting found within a narrative affects the implied audience.[3] The lack of careful attention to setting is also demonstrated when narrative critics refer to places or times as settings when they are not actually proper settings in which events in the narrative take place.[4]

---

1. Powell, *What Is Narrative Criticism?*, 69–75; Kingsbury, *Matthew as Story*, 28–30; Resseguie, *Narrative Criticism*, 87–88, 94–114; Pennington, *Reading the Gospels*, 173–76.

2. One such study is Skinner, *Locating Paul*.

3. For example, Edwards's *Matthew's Story of Jesus* does not contain the word "setting." When Kingsbury discusses many of the settings found in Matthew, most of his observations are derived from events that occur in those settings; the influence of those settings on the implied audience's understanding of those events is rarely mentioned (*Matthew as Story*, 28–30). In other words, he implies that the significance of a setting is derived from events that occur in it and that settings do not contribute to the significance of events.

4. For example, Powell mentions Jesus' reference to "winter" in Mark 13:18 (*What Is Narrative Criticism?*, 73), and Carter mentions "Ramah" in Matt 2:18 and "heaven and earth" in 28:18 as settings, although they are not settings of events in the narrative (*Matthew: Storyteller, Interpret, Evangelist*, 154, 162).

Settings are temporal, geographical, or circumstantial (e.g., social, historical, political) and can be factual, metaphorical, imagined, or symbolic.[5] Some settings appear not to exert any effect on the implied audience (e.g., the house in Matt 2:11). Nevertheless, whenever a setting is explicitly mentioned, the narrative critic should consider its role in the narrative.[6] This consideration should include circumstantial settings that are not explicitly mentioned but are implied by statements or events that take place in the narrative. For example, Matt 4:1–11 shows the implied audience that subsequent events take place in the circumstantial setting of the devil's active opposition to Jesus, even though this is not stated explicitly as other settings are. This chapter will consider the settings found in Matthew's prologue and resurrection narrative with the goal of understanding their effect on the implied audience—especially on its understanding of Jesus' resurrection.

How Setting Affects the Implied Audience's Response

Narrative critics have identified seven possible effects of setting on the implied audience's understanding of a narrative.

1. A setting can facilitate certain actions within the narrative.[7]

    In some cases, a setting merely makes possible the plot's actions and does not otherwise influence the implied audience's understanding of those actions. Such settings make actions in the narrative intelligible and prevent the implied audience from experiencing

---

5. Powell, *What Is Narrative Criticism?*, 70; Kingsbury, *Matthew as Story*, 28; Marguerat et al., *How to Read*, 84; Carter, *Matthew: Storyteller, Interpreter, Evangelist*, 154.

6. Carter, *Matthew: Storyteller, Interpreter, Evangelist*, 154. Occasionally, a setting is brought in from source material and creates an apparent inconsistency in the narrative (e.g., Matt 12:46 taken from Mark 3:31, which implies a different setting than that of Matt 12:38–45). In such cases, since the implied audience expects the narrative to function as a unified whole, it will harmonize or otherwise account for the apparent inconsistency in order to make sense of the narrative as it has received it (see Powell, *What Is Narrative Criticism?*, 92; Rhoads et al., *Mark as Story*, 3rd ed., 5–6). For example, it may imagine a setting in which both crowds (12:46) and "scribes and Pharisees" (12:38) are present or assume that intervening events are not included in the narrative.

7. Skinner, *Locating Paul*, 49; Powell, *What Is Narrative Criticism?*, 70; Kingsbury, *Matthew as Story*, 28; Resseguie, *Narrative Criticism*, 88; Rhoads et al., *Mark as Story*, 2nd ed., 63.

unnecessary surprise or confusion.[8] Some narrative critics consider it unusual for a setting to do nothing but facilitate the narrative's action,[9] but the desire to assign additional significance to a setting can produce symbolic interpretations of settings that the implied audience would not expect.[10] An example of a setting that facilitates action is the house where the magi worship Jesus (2:11); the house adds no significance to the actions that take place in it.

2. A setting can introduce certain expectations into a narrative.[11]

While the first possible effect of a setting is to establish in the mind of the implied audience which actions are possible, this effect is to establish which actions are likely. The actions that take place within such a setting will either conform to or violate those expectations. When the implied audience's expectations are not realized—and especially when actions are contrary to expectations—it is not simply surprised; it becomes more aware of the significance of those actions. Understandably, these actions then contribute to the plot's conflict or tension. An example of a setting with expectations associated with it is Jerusalem (2:1). The implied audience expects Jerusalem to be a place where the King of the Jews is enthusiastically welcomed. That expectation is violated, however, by the opposition of Herod (2:7–8, 16–18) and the apathy of the chief priests and scribes (2:4–6).

---

8. Chatman refers to some settings as "minimally necessary" (*Story and Discourse*, 143). Cf. Carter, *Matthew: Storyteller, Interpreter, Evangelist*, 154.

9. Resseguie, *Narrative Criticism*, 88; Rhoads et al., *Mark as Story*, 2nd ed., 63.

10. For example, Resseguie explains rivers as boundaries that have the potential to serve as "metaphorical thresholds." Thus, he understands the Jordan River setting of John's baptism to symbolize "the abandonment of past ways and the acceptance of a new future" (*Narrative Criticism*, 95). Since, however, those baptized are not said to cross the Jordan, it is doubtful that the implied audience shares this symbolic understanding. What Resseguie sees as symbolized by the river is seen more clearly in the people's repentance (Matt 3:2) and confession (3:6).

11. Skinner, *Locating Paul*, 49–50; Marquerat et al., *How to Read*, 77; Carter, *Matthew: Storyteller, Interpreter, Evangelist*, 155; Powell, *What Is Narrative Criticism?*, 70; Resseguie, *Narrative Criticism*, 88; Rhoads et al., *Mark as Story*, 2nd ed., 63. Some of these scholars refer to a setting's contribution to the "mood" of a narrative. We include "mood" under the heading of "expectations," since mood may be associated with general expectations.

3. Repetition of settings can establish patterns that relate events to one another.[12]

Such a pattern can establish an archetype that may inform the implied audience's understanding of an event. A repeated pattern can also establish a meaningful contrast between different settings and the actions that take place within them. For example, the repetition of mountain settings in Matthew is viewed by Rogers as relating those scenes to develop the theme of Jesus' superiority to Moses.[13]

4. Movements through settings can establish patterns of events or anticipate plot developments.[14]

When similar events occur in different settings, the implied audience comes to view such events as typical and expected. Changes in setting that show progress in a particular direction can indicate to the implied audience that a series of events is moving toward a climax. In Matthew, while in Caesarea Philippi in northern Galilee, Jesus first tells his disciples that he must go to Jerusalem to suffer, be killed, and be raised (16:13, 21). The changes in setting to Capernaum (17:24), Judea beyond the Jordan (19:1), and Jericho (20:29) show movement toward Jerusalem and lead the implied audience to expect Jesus to experience the climactic events he predicted.

5. A setting can contribute to characterization.[15]

The presence of a character in a particular geographical setting can lead the implied audience to assume that character to possess traits that are typical of those found in such settings. Similarly, a setting can influence the implied audience's understanding of a character's actions, thereby contributing to his or her perception of that character. For example, the secret setting of Herod's meeting with the magi—implied by the dative λάθρᾳ ("in secret," 2:7)—indicates that Herod was trying to prevent others from knowing about the meeting, showing Herod to be a character with evil or selfish motives.

---

12. Skinner, *Locating Paul*, 51.
13. Rogers, "Great Commission," 397–98.
14. Skinner, *Locating Paul*, 53.
15. Carter, *Matthew: Storyteller, Interpreter, Evangelist*, 154; Marguerat et al., *How to Read*, 78; Powell, *What Is Narrative Criticism?*, 70; Resseguie, *Narrative Criticism*, 88.

6. An individual setting can contribute to a narrative's plot or conflict.[16]

Settings can inform the implied audience of the circumstances in which actions take place and, therefore, shed light on the significance of those actions. The circumstances indicated by the setting may explain the necessity of an action, potential obstacles to an action, the purpose or goal of an action, or the effects or consequences of an action. In some cases, the implied audience is unable to understand an action apart from the setting in which it occurs. For example, in Matt 2:22–23, the circumstantial setting is that Archelaus, the son of Herod, is ruling over Judea (2:22). This explains the necessity of the holy family settling in Nazareth (2:23). In addition, it sheds light on the consequences of them settling in Nazareth: Judea is left under the oppressive authority of a foreign government's appointed ruler, unchallenged—for a time—by the Messiah.

7. Multiple settings can relate to each other to form oppositions that enhance the plot.[17]

Two settings can be contrasted in a way that highlights their differences. Such a contrast can influence the implied audience's understanding of one or both. In Matt 2:13–23, Israel and Egypt are set in opposition to one another in a way that highlights the irony that, for the Messiah of the Jews, Egypt is a place of safety while Judea—the land of his people—is a place of danger.

To summarize, setting affects the implied audience's response in seven ways.

1. A setting can facilitate certain actions within the narrative.
2. A setting can raise certain expectations.
3. Repetition of settings can establish patterns that relate events to one another.
4. Movements through settings can establish patterns of events or anticipate plot developments.
5. A setting can contribute to characterization.
6. An individual setting can contribute to a narrative's plot or conflict.

---

16. Resseguie, *Narrative Criticism*, 88; Powell, *What Is Narrative Criticism?*, 70; Rhoads et al., *Mark as Story*, 2nd ed., 63.

17. Skinner, *Locating Paul*, 52; Powell, *What Is Narrative Criticism?*, 71.

7. Multiple settings can relate to each other to form oppositions that enhance the plot.

The remainder of this chapter will consist of a systematic analysis of the settings found in Matthew's prologue and resurrection narrative. This analysis will include all settings that are explicitly mentioned, as well as some that are implied or produced within the narrative. The goal of this analysis is to discern the effects of these settings on the implied audience's understanding of the events that take place within them and, ultimately, its understanding of Jesus' resurrection in Matthew.

The Circumstances into which Jesus the Messiah is Born (1:2–17)

At first glance, the genealogy in Matt 1:2–17 may appear only to prove the claim that Jesus the Messiah is the son of David and of Abraham (1:1). Upon closer examination, however, it is clear that it does something more. The clearest evidence that this is so is the presence of people and of an event that are not essential to the genealogy.[18] These "extra" people are the brothers of Judah (1:2), Zerah (1:3), Tamar (1:3), Rahab (1:5), Ruth (1:5), "the (wife) of Uriah" (i.e., Bathsheba, 1:6), and the brothers of Jeconiah (1:11). The event is the deportation to Babylon (1:11–12). None of these lend support to the claim made in 1:1.

John Nolland argues that Matthew's genealogy is an annotated genealogy that follows the pattern established by the genealogies in Genesis.[19] Annotated genealogies, he argues, serve as "compressed tellings of the history that stands behind them."[20] The inclusion of "extra" names in Matthew's genealogy reminds the implied audience of Israel's history, including high points, such as the call of and covenant with Abraham (1:2), the enthronement of "David the king" (1:6), and Josiah's reforms (1:10). It also reminds them of Israel's low points, such as the conspiracy of "Judah and his brothers" against Joseph (1:2), Judah's solicitation of his daughter-in-law while she posed as a prostitute (1:3), David's adultery with Bathsheba and murder of Uriah (1:6), and the "deportation to Babylon" (1:11–12). The list of fifteen kings from David through Jeconiah

---

18. W. D. Davies and Allison, *Saint Matthew*, 1:169; Luz, *Matthew 1–7*, 83.

19. Nolland, "Genealogical Annotation," 116.

20. Nolland, "Genealogical Annotation," 121. Cf. Bauer, "Genealogy," 146; W. D. Davies and Allison, *Saint Matthew*, 1:169.

(1:6-11) reminds the implied audience of the sinfulness of kings who failed to rule righteously,[21] which resulted in the exile (1:11-12; cf. 2 Kgs 24:3). It is telling that the only event included from Israel's history is "the deportation to Babylon" and that it is mentioned three times (Matt 1:11, 12, 17). The implied audience is not led to focus on the high points of Israel's history, but on its failures and their consequences. The names in the genealogy from the deportation through Joseph (1:12-16) are not the names of kings, further reinforcing the impression that the exile had not completely ended because there has been no Davidic king since.[22]

The genealogy at the beginning of Matthew's Gospel tells the implied audience about the circumstances into which Jesus the Messiah was born. God had made a covenant with the people of Israel, promising to bless them and, through them, the nations (1:1-2). The people of Israel, and especially its kings, had failed to keep that covenant (1:2-11). As a result, God sent the people into exile (1:11-12), and aspects of that exile continued into the time of Jesus' birth (1:12-16). The people of Israel were not experiencing the blessings that God had promised them. Therefore, the Davidic dynasty needed to be restored, and the kingdom needed a king more righteous than those who had gone before. These circumstances are part of Matthew's setting.[23] Through them, the implied

---

21. Of these fifteen kings, the OT presents eight in a positive light (e.g., they "did right in the eyes of the Lord")—David (1 Kgs 9:4; 15:5; but note the mention of Uriah's wife here), Solomon (2 Chr 1:1, but note the negative portrayal at the end of his life in 1 Kgs 11:1-13), Asa (1 Kgs 15:11), Jehoshaphat (1 Kgs 22:43), Uzziah (2 Kgs 15:3), Jotham (2 Kgs 15:34), Hezekiah (2 Kgs 18:3), and Josiah (2 Kgs 22:2). The remaining seven are presented negatively (e.g., they "did not do what was right in the eyes of the Lord")—Rehoboam (2 Chr 12:14), Abijah (1 Kgs 15:3), Joram (2 Kgs 8:18), Ahaz (2 Kgs 16:2), Manasseh (2 Kgs 21:2), Amon (2 Kgs 21:20), and Jeconiah (2 Kgs 24:9). The "telescoping" of this genealogy (i.e., the omission of Ahaziah, Joash, Amaziah, and Jehoiakim) results in there never being more than two consecutive good or bad kings, producing a "roller coaster" effect in the implied audience's experience of the genealogy.

22. Cf. Piotrowski, "After the Deportation," 195; Mello, *Matthieu*, 63. The concept of continuing exile is often associated with the scholarship of Wright (see, for example, his *People of God*, 268). Critiques of Wright on this point often focus on his historical claim that most Second Temple Jews saw themselves as living in continued exile (e.g., Mason, "Wright on Paul," 432-52; Jones, "Disputed Questions," 401-5)—a claim that goes beyond our claim that Matthew's point of view is that the exile has not ended. Casey's critique is more relevant, since it includes statements of Jesus in Matthew (23:21; "Critical Review," 99-100). Casey's critique, however, is largely a response to Wright's claim that the end of the exile is marked by the restored presence of God (*People of God*, 268), a claim that we do not make, as we see the reestablishment of the kingdom under a Davidic king as more central to Matthew's understanding of return from exile.

23. Piotrowski, "After the Deportation," 200.

audience understands Israel's problems and the historical pattern of previous kings that Jesus the Messiah must break. As the implied audience encounters the narrative, it understands the significance of Jesus' words and works in light of these circumstances. In particular, when Jesus is raised, the implied audience understands that his resurrection guarantees the establishment of God's kingdom under a righteous king, the end of the exile, and the blessings of Abraham to Jews and gentiles.

During the Betrothal of Mary to Joseph (1:18)

Matthew 1:18 provides the circumstantial and temporal setting of Jesus' conception. Mary was "found" with child "after she had been betrothed to Joseph" but "before they came together." This setting explains why it was necessary that Jesus' conception be "by the Holy Spirit" (1:18) and prepares for later statements about him being God's Son (e.g., 2:15; 3:17). These circumstances also provide a context in which Joseph's plan to divorce Mary quietly—a plan which leads to God's intervention (1:19–21)—is intelligible.

The setting found in Matt 1:18 prepares and provides an explanation for the statement in 1:23 that the circumstances of Jesus' birth fulfill Isa 7:14 LXX, since a "virgin" (παρθένος) would bear a son. This setting does not lead the implied audience to an understanding of Jesus and of his birth that cannot be reached through other, more direct statements (e.g., 1:23; 2:15; 3:17). Therefore, we conclude that this particular setting does not influence the implied audience's understanding of any particular event. It simply provides an explanation for certain actions and statements that come later (1:19–21; 2:15; 3:17).

"In a Dream" (1:20; 2:12, 13, 19, 22)

The phrase "in a dream" (κατ' ὄναρ) occurs in Matthew's prologue five times (1:20; 2:12, 13, 19, 22). In all five cases, it provides the setting of some instruction or warning to human characters in the narrative. In the OT, dreams are often the context of divine communication (e.g., Gen 20:3; 31:11; 1 Kgs 3:5; Dan 7:1; cf. Num 12:6),[24] so the implied audience

---

24. France, *Matthew*, 52; W. D. Davies and Allison, *Saint Matthew*, 1:207; Luz, *Matthew 1–7*, 95; Gundry, *Matthew*, 22. The LXX typically uses ὕπνος or ἐνύπνιον, rather than ὄναρ as in Matthew. On dreams as vehicles of divine communication, see Oepke,

understands that these, too, are acts of divine communication. In three of these cases, the communication is said to take place through the "angel of the Lord" (1:20; 2:13, 19). In the other two, however, the implied audience is told only that the magi (2:12) or Joseph (2:22) are "warned" in a dream (cf. Jer 33:2; 43:2, 4). When the communication comes from the angel of the Lord, the setting "in a dream" merely provides a context in which that communication can take place. When the angel of the Lord is not mentioned (or is not involved), however, this setting is what leads the implied audience to understand the communication as also coming from God. As a result, the information contained in these communications is understood to be true and reliable.

After Jesus was Born in Bethlehem of Judea (2:1)

In Matt 2:1, one part of the setting of the magi's visit is provided— "after Jesus was born in Bethlehem of Judea." It would be improper to view "Bethlehem of Judea" as a geographical setting for Matt 2:1–8 in a narrative-critical sense because the events described take place in Jerusalem. This phrase indicates the timing and circumstances in which those events occur, not their location. The function of this setting is to provide a context in which the events that follow are intelligible. It explains why the magi visit Jerusalem and why Herod attempts to destroy Jesus. This temporal-circumstantial setting does not make an independent contribution to the significance of these events. The events take place because Jesus, the Messiah, had been born.

In the Days of Herod the King (2:1)

In Matt 2:1, the phrase "in the days of Herod the king" provides both temporal and circumstantial aspects of the setting. Temporally, it is obvious that the events that follow could only happen "in the days of the Herod the king," so that this setting provides a logical context for certain events. Circumstantially, this setting makes a more significant contribution to the implied audience's understanding of the narrative. The king is Herod, who was appointed by Rome and not by Yahweh. When Jesus the Messiah is born, the people of Israel live under the authority of a foreign

---

"ὄναρ," 229–30; and Hanson, "Dreams and Visions," 1400. Cf. Josephus, *Ant.* 11.8.4.

government.²⁵ They are subject to Herod's will and do not enjoy life under a Davidic king as God had promised (2 Sam 7:12–13). This is consistent with the previously introduced circumstantial setting of continuing exile (Matt 1:11–12).

The implied audience's prior knowledge of Herod, along with the following narrative (2:2–18), contributes to its understanding of this setting.²⁶ Herod's actions result in the "weeping and great mourning" (2:18) of God's people. This setting is significant both for this pericope and for the Gospel as a whole. The implied audience understands that Jesus is born at a time and place when God's people are under the oppressive rule of a foreign government's appointed ruler who can—and does—perform brutal acts of injustice against his people with impunity. This is—and will continue to be—the lot of God's people until God intervenes. This is one thing from which the Messiah will save them (1:21). Since they have not yet been saved from this when Jesus dies, it is a salvation that is made possible by Jesus' resurrection.

JERUSALEM (2:1)

One additional setting found in Matt 2:1 is "Jerusalem." Jerusalem is where the magi arrive and inquire about the location of the newborn King of the Jews (2:2). At the capital of the land of the Jews, this is where one would expect the magi to begin their search. Jerusalem is also a setting with associated expectations. It is the "holy city" of God's people, the "center of religious, social, and political power."²⁷ It is where God's king ought to be ruling in safety and where the eschatological Messiah ought to be enthusiastically welcomed by his people (cf. 21:8–9). These expectations, however, are undermined by the mention of Herod's rule (2:1), which is a threat to Jesus' safety (2:13–18), and by the actual response of the people there. The implied audience is surprised that the chief priests and scribes receive the news of the Messiah's birth unenthusiastically and make no effort to investigate the magi's claim (2:4–6). Jerusalem will appear again as a setting in Matthew (21:10—28:15), with the repetition

---

25. Mello, *Matthieu*, 71.
26. Luz, *Matthew 1–7*, 112.
27. Carter, *Matthew: Storyteller, Interpreter, Evangelist*, 160. Cf. Turner, *Matthew*, 79.

contributing to the theme of the Jewish leaders' response to Jesus, which culminates in the resurrection narrative (28:11–15).

The House (2:11)

In Matt 2:11, the magi find Jesus in a house in Jerusalem. They enter the house, which serves as the setting for their worship and giving of gifts to Jesus. The implied audience knows from the context (2:8) that this house is in Bethlehem. In Matt 2:11, however, there is no special emphasis on Bethlehem. The magi simply enter "the house." That they encounter Jesus in a house does not add any significance to their worship. The significance lies in their actions rather than in the house in which they are performed.

During the Night (2:14)

After Joseph is instructed in a dream to take Jesus and Mary and flee to Egypt (2:13), the temporal setting of their departure is given as "during the night" (νυκτός; 2:14). Although it is not made explicit that they departed the same night as the dream, the implied audience is led to that conclusion by the lack of any intervening narrative.[28] The immediate departure of the holy family and the protection afforded by night's darkness convey a sense of urgency to the implied audience. In addition, the immediacy of Joseph's obedience contributes to his positive characterization.[29] Although the angel does not explicitly command them to depart that night, the setting of their departure shows that Joseph understood "Get up and take" (2:13) to mean that the threat to Jesus was real and immediate.[30] The implied audience has no reason to question Joseph's understanding and, therefore, accepts it as accurate.

Because νυκτός breaks the pattern of the close parallelism between the angel's words (2:13) and the description of Joseph's actions (2:14–15), Soares-Prabhu argues that it is included in order to evoke the exodus, which takes place at night according to various Jewish sources.[31] Although Jesus' flight to Egypt does not neatly parallel the story of Moses or the exodus (e.g., Jesus flees to, rather than from, Egypt), it is possible

---

28. Thus, the NASB's "while it was still night." Cf. Lagrange, *Matthieu*, 32.
29. Gundry, *Matthew*, 33; Bonnard, *Matthieu*, 28.
30. W. D. Davies and Allison, *Saint Matthew*, 1:261; France, *Matthew*, 79.
31. Soares-Prabhu, "Jesus in Egypt," 236–38.

that νυκτός is one of several elements in this narrative (along with a ruler threatening a child's life, the similar wording of Matt 2:20 and Exod 4:19, and the quotation in Matt 2:15) that generally bring to mind the exodus and contribute to the characterization of Jesus as the ideal Israel and a new Moses.[32]

Egypt (2:19)

Although Egypt is mentioned in Matt 2:13-15, it is the setting of an event only in 2:19-21. While in Egypt, Joseph is again instructed by the angel of the Lord in a dream (2:19). He is to take Jesus and Mary back to Israel (2:20), which he does (2:21).[33] Many commentators point out that Egypt's significance is that it is a traditional place of refuge (e.g., Gen 12:10; 46:3-7; Num 11:5; 1 Kgs 11:40; 2 Kgs 25:26; Jer 41:16-18; Josephus, *Ant.* 12.9.7).[34] This leads the implied audience to understand the command to leave Egypt as a command to leave a place of refuge and safety. At first, the implied audience may expect the command to mean that Israel is now a safe place and that refuge is no longer necessary (2:19-20). They will discover, however, that the return from Egypt to Israel is a return to a place of danger (2:22)—an ironic contrast between the two locations. The flight to Egypt also makes possible the fulfillment statement in 2:15—"out of Egypt I called my son" (Hos 11:1). Finally, the mention of Egypt contributes to the characterization of Jesus as the new Moses and the ideal Israel, as it recalls Israel's exodus which Jesus recapitulates, leading the implied audience to expect Jesus to accomplish a new exodus.[35]

---

32. Allison argues that characterization of Jesus as ideal Israel and a new Moses are not mutually exclusive (*New Moses*, 142). The same textual features can contribute to both conceptions.

33. The entire journey, from their departure from their home in Egypt to their arrival in Israel, is summed up in the single aorist verb εἰσῆλθεν, though the implied reader correctly understands Egypt only as the setting of their departure.

34. Kingsbury, *Matthew as Story*, 28-29; Stock, *Method and Message*, 37; Garland, *Reading Matthew*, 30; France, *Matthew*, 79; Luz, *Matthew 1-7*, 120; R. E. Brown, *Birth of the Messiah*, 203; Lagrange, *Matthieu*, 31; Gnilka, *Das Matthäusevangelium*, 50.

35. Gundry, *Matthew*, 33; Léon-Dufour, *Matthieu*, 27.

After Herod Died (2:19)

The temporal and circumstantial setting of the holy family's return from Egypt to Israel—"after Herod died"—is indicated in 2:19. While a return to Israel is possible while Herod is alive, it is more logical after his death. In fact, the angel identifies the death of Herod (and of others; 2:20) as the reason for the command to return. As a circumstantial setting, "after Herod died" leads the implied audience to expect Israel to be a safe place for the young Messiah and his family. That expectation is undermined, however, in 2:22, where it learns that Jesus is still in danger. The continuation of danger "after Herod died" helps the implied audience to understand that the death of an evil king is not an adequate solution to Israel's problems.

Israel (2:21)

In Matt 2:21, Israel is mentioned as the setting for the events of 2:22–23. Joseph has brought his family back to Israel, which should be a place of safety, especially after Herod's death (2:19). This leads the implied audience to expect safety for Jesus the Messiah. It is surprised, however, to learn that Israel is not safe because Archelaus, the most violent of Herod's sons,[36] is reigning over Judea—the province in which both Jerusalem and Bethlehem are located. The surprise is reinforced when it appears that even God did not anticipate this danger,[37] since Joseph is directed elsewhere only *after* he himself sees Archelaus as a danger (2:22). This setting affects the implied audience's understanding of the plot, emphasizing the theme of continued exile and raising questions about when and how Israel will be freed from foreign oppression.[38]

---

36. Lagrange, *Matthieu*, 37.

37. Although this may be theologically problematic, we contend that it is good narrative analysis.

38. It would be possible to discuss "under the reign of Archelaus" as a separate, circumstantial setting. Since, however, it is not introduced as a narrative setting (i.e., it is the content of what Joseph hears within the narrative, rather than a narrative setting supplied by the implied author), and since that discussion would not add to the discussion of Israel as a setting, we will not include it as a separate section. Archelaus's reign is also included in our discussion of the phrase "in those days" found in Matt 3:1. The locations of Galilee and Nazareth are mentioned in Matt 2:22–23. They are not the settings in which any of the events in the narrative take place, so they will not be discussed here. The holy family's move to Nazareth, however, will be discussed in the chapter on plot.

"In Those Days" (3:1)

In Matt 3:1, the implied audience is told that the temporal and circumstantial setting of John the Baptist's ministry is "in those days." There is a gap of 25–30 years between 2:23 and 3:1 (cf. Luke 3:23). Therefore, some scholars discount "in those days" as being adopted from Mark 1:9 (where it refers to the time of John the Baptist's ministry),[39] while others view it as a term with eschatological connotations.[40] Narrative criticism, however, encourages us to consider the meaning of this phrase within Matthew's story world.

In the literary context of 3:1, "in those days" is most naturally understood to refer to the time period described in the two preceding chapters, along with the accompanying circumstances. The implied audience may be aware that that there is a significant time difference between 2:23 and 3:1. But "in those days" downplays the significance of that time difference and establishes continuity between the circumstances of 2:23 and those of 3:1.[41] The implied audience understands that, despite the passage of time and a change in the name of the ruler over the Jews,[42] little, if anything, has actually changed. God's people continue to live under the oppressive authority of a foreign power (i.e., in a form of exile; cf. 2:1–18, 22–23), without a Davidic king (cf. 1:1), and in need of salvation (cf. 1:21). Their own leaders (i.e., chief priests and scribes; cf. 2:4–6) remain apathetic to the plans and purposes of God. In addition, the land of Israel continues

---

39. W. D. Davies and Allison, *Saint Matthew*, 1:288.

40. Hagner, *Matthew 1–13*, 47; Garland, *Reading Matthew*, 33; W. D. Davies and Allison, *Saint Matthew*, 1:287–88; Gnilka, *Das Matthäusevangelium*, 1:65. Cf. Bonnard, *Matthieu*, 31. Mello is wrong in claiming that, in the OT, "in those days" only refers to the future (*Matthieu*, 83). Some scholars treat "those days" as equivalent to "that day" in places like Zech 12:3–4 and Isa 10:20, although this jump is not necessarily warranted. Although "in those days" does occur in the OT in eschatological contexts (e.g., Jer 3:16, 18; Joel 2:29; 3:1; Zech 8:23), it occurs more often with reference to past or present events in the narrative (e.g., Gen 6:4; Exod 2:11; Judg 1:6; 1 Sam 3:1), which is how it is used here.

41. Cf. Luz, *Matthew 1–7*, 134. Gundry explicitly rejects the eschatological interpretation of the phrase, taking it to refer to "the time of Jesus' residence in Nazareth" (*Matthew*, 41). He does not, however, note the circumstances of that time that could affect the implied audience. France sees "in those days" as connecting 3:1 to chapter 2, but he narrows that connection to the fulfillment theme in that chapter (i.e., 2:15, 17, 23, *Matthew*, 99).

42. History tells us that Archelaus ruled for nine years (Josephus, *J.W.* 2.7.3), so there was a different ruler at that time. The implied author, however, treats the change in leadership as inconsequential by not mentioning it.

to be a dangerous place for the Messiah who was born to rule over it and its people (cf. 2:22-23).

The implied audience's understanding of John the Baptist's ministry is affected by the temporal setting of his ministry. John's announcement that "the kingdom of heaven is at hand" (3:2) is understood to mean that God's reign—through his Messiah—would soon be established and that God's people would be saved from foreign oppression. When the people of Jerusalem and Judea go out to John (3:5-6) while the Jewish leaders are, at best, apathetic, the implied audience understands that God's work to establish his kingdom will take place apart from and in spite of, rather than through, those leaders. John's warning about a "coming wrath" (3:7; cf. 3:10-12) is understood to mean that God's kingdom will be established in conjunction with the destruction of God's enemies (cf. 7:19; 13:30, 40-42; 21:41; 22:13, 44; 24:37-51)—not just of gentiles (e.g., rulers like Herod and Archelaus), but also of Jews who fail to repent. All of this also affects the implied audience's understanding of Jesus' resurrection; since the kingdom does not come with wrath before his death, his resurrection ensures that it can and will still come.

The Wilderness of Judea (3:1)

Matthew 3:1 also places John the Baptist's ministry in "the wilderness of Judea." This wilderness lies to the east of Jerusalem and to the north of the Dead Sea.[43] Although this area was uninhabited, it was not entirely remote, being less than a day's journey from Jerusalem or Jericho. Commentators note a number of associations with the wilderness. It is associated with eschatological expectation as the place where God's people prepare for his coming.[44] It can be viewed as a place of danger,[45] as well as a place of testing.[46] This wilderness is dangerous, not simply because it is wilderness, but because it is in Judea, which 2:22 shows to be a dangerous

---

43. Cf. W. D. Davies and Allison, *Saint Matthew*, 1:290.

44. Kingsbury, *Matthew as Story*, 29; W. D. Davies and Allison, *Saint Matthew*, 1:291; France, *Matthew*, 100; Hagner, *Matthew 1-13*, 47; Garland, *Reading Matthew*, 33; Stock, *Method and Message*, 44.

45. Luz, *Matthew 1-7*, 134; Pregeant, *Matthew*, 28; Garland, *Reading Matthew*, 37; Turner, *Matthew*, 126.

46. Kingsbury, *Matthew as Story*, 29; Resseguie, *Narrative Criticism*, 95-96; Stock, *Method and Message*, 44; Garland, *Reading Matthew*, 37; Turner, *Matthew*, 106. Cf. Luz, *Matthew 1-7*, 134.

and hostile place,[47] despite being David's territory which should be loyal to his royal descendant.[48] Matthew's qualifier "of Judea" prevents the implied audience from easily associating this setting with Israel's testing in a different wilderness (cf. Deut 8:2).

It is the association of the wilderness with eschatological expectation that is most significant in this pericope. This is shown by the fulfillment quotation in Matt 3:3. The wilderness setting allows John, who preaches in the wilderness, to be the prophesied one "crying in the wilderness" (cf. Isa 40:3), a point the implied author makes explicit. This is a sign to the implied audience that eschatological salvation is to be expected. The setting in the wilderness of Judea also facilitates the plot by making it possible for "Jerusalem and all Judea and all the district around the Jordan" to go to John for baptism (Matt 3:5–6). Finally, the placement of these events in a setting other than Jerusalem suggests that the holy city and its temple may lose their validity.[49] The implied audience understands that, as God works to establish his kingdom, he does so without regard for the institutions thought by his people to be essential. It begins to wonder what this will mean for the city and its temple (cf. 24:2).

THE JORDAN RIVER (3:6, 13)

Although John's preaching is set generally "in the wilderness of Judea" (3:1), the setting of his baptizing is identified more specifically as "the Jordan River" (3:6).[50] Some suggest that the Jordan River symbolizes a "threshold experience," due to its previous role in Israel's entry into the promised land (cf. Josh 3:17).[51] Since those being baptized, however, are not said to cross the Jordan themselves, it is not clear that the implied audience should detect such a symbolic significance. In fact, the Jordan River appears frequently in the OT.[52] It served as a physical boundary and was crossed often for various reasons (1 Sam 13:7; 2 Sam 17:24), even after the conquest of the promised land. It was where Elisha received

---

47. W. D. Davies and Allison, *Saint Matthew*, 1:291.
48. Gundry, *Matthew*, 42.
49. Gnilka, *Das Matthäusevangelium*, 1:65.
50. Cf. Lagrange, *Matthieu*, 46.
51. Rhoads and Michie, *Mark as Story*, 65. Cf. W. D. Davies and Allison, *Saint Matthew*, 1:300.
52. See W. D. Davies and Allison's discussion of associations with the Jordan River found in ancient texts (*Saint Matthew*, 1:300).

Elijah's mantle and a double portion of the spirit that was upon him (2 Kgs 2:6–13), an event one may be tempted to associate with the baptism of Jesus (upon whom the Spirit comes; Matt 3:16) by John (who resembles Elijah; 3:4). The Jordan was also the place where Naaman dipped (ἐβαπτίσατο) himself in order to be cleansed from leprosy (2 Kgs 5:14 LXX). Since John's baptism scene does not conform perfectly to any of these OT narratives, it is best to view the "Jordan" here as contributing to the general sense of connection between Matthew's story world and Israel's history. Given John's location in the "wilderness of Judea," the Jordan is also an appropriate location for his baptism.

"Then" (4:1)

Matthew 4:1 identifies the temporal setting of Jesus' temptation by using the word "then" (τότε). In this context, "then" refers to the time immediately following Jesus' baptism and the accompanying events[53]—the coming of the Holy Spirit upon Jesus (3:16) and the voice from heaven calling Jesus God's "beloved son" (3:17). This temporal setting suggests a logical relationship between Jesus' baptism and his temptation: The Holy Spirit comes upon Jesus and then, as the first order of business, leads him into the wilderness to be tempted. In addition, two of the devil's temptations are based on Jesus' being "the Son of God" (4:3, 6), which Jesus was called in the verse preceding the temptation scene.

The temporal relationship between the two events helps the implied audience to avoid a misinterpretation of Jesus' temptation. Out of context, this temptation could be viewed as a form of discipline or as some kind of trial that could lead to Jesus' approval. Since God's unconditional approval had already been reported to the implied audience, and since Jesus' temptation occurs immediately afterward, it understands that this temptation is not in conflict with God's approval of and pleasure in Jesus. Whatever the purpose of Jesus' temptation may be, it is not the means by which Jesus gains his Father's approval.

The Wilderness of Temptation (4:1)

Matthew 4:1 also provides the geographical setting of Jesus' temptation as "the wilderness" (τὴν ἔρημον). The context leads the implied audience

---

53. Akin, "Discourse Analysis," 84.

to understand it with additional specificity. Since it occurs immediately following Jesus' baptism in the Jordan in the wilderness of Judea, this scene takes place in a more remote location away from the wilderness of Judea.[54] Since Jesus is "led up" into the wilderness, it is understood as a more mountainous area where food and people are scarce.[55] The scarcity of food, along with the danger associated with the wilderness—demons were thought to dwell there[56]—make it an ideal setting for such a temptation.[57]

The wilderness setting of Jesus' temptation also leads the implied audience to view Jesus as repeating Israel's history.[58] If Jesus were tempted elsewhere, it would have little reason to view Jesus as repeating Israel's history, but this is precisely what is suggested by the combination of the wilderness setting and the motif of temptation (or testing).[59] Therefore, this setting contributes to Jesus' characterization as the true and faithful Israel. The implied audience learns that Jesus remained faithful and obedient when he was tested in the wilderness, which is in contrast to Israel's disobedience in the desert when it responded to testing with their own test of God (cf. Exod 17:2).

After Jesus had Fasted Forty Days and Forty Nights (4:2)

In Matt 4:2, the setting of the first temptation (4:3) is "after he (Jesus) had fasted forty days and forty nights."[60] While this information leads the implied audience to think of Jesus as being like Moses (Exod 34:28) and possibly Elijah (1 Kgs 19:8),[61] it also contributes to its understanding of the first temptation. The observation at the end of the verse—that Jesus

---

54. Akin, "Discourse Analysis," 84.

55. France, *Matthew*, 129; Gundry, *Matthew*, 54.

56. W. D. Davies and Allison, *Saint Matthew*, 1:354; Luz, *Matthew 1–7*, 134; Turner, *Matthew*, 126; Garland, *Reading Matthew*, 37; Pregeant, *Matthew*, 28.

57. Hagner, *Matthew 1–13*, 63.

58. W. D. Davies and Allison, *Saint Matthew*, 1:354; M. Davies, *Matthew*, 44; J. K. Brown, *Matthew*, 35. Cf. Turner, *Matthew*, 106.

59. Although Israel is said to have been "tested" in the wilderness (e.g., Exod 16:4) and Jesus is "tempted," forms of the same word—πειράζω—are used in both cases. Context calls for different English words.

60. Luz, *Matthew 1–7*, 151; M. Davies, *Matthew*, 44.

61. Mello, *Matthieu*, 94–95; Allison, *New Moses*, 166.

was hungry—may seem unnecessary.[62] Nevertheless, given the implied audience's knowledge of Jesus from outside the narrative (i.e., as members of a community that worships Jesus as divine), it may not think of Jesus as being capable of hunger. It is told, therefore, that Jesus *was* hungry after fasting for forty days, just like anyone else would be. This setting adds significance to the first temptation. If Jesus had not fasted, the temptation to turn stones into bread (4:3) would appear to be a temptation only to show off his power—the devil does not mention *eating* the bread—rather than a temptation to satisfy his hunger apart from his Father's will.[63] The implied audience understands that Jesus feels extreme hunger, making his prioritization of God's word over food all the more impressive.

THE PINNACLE OF THE JERUSALEM TEMPLE (4:5)

The second temptation of Jesus is set in "the holy city" (i.e., Jerusalem; cf. 27:53) at the "pinnacle of the temple" (4:5). At first, the highest point of the temple may appear as simply a logical location for the devil's temptation of Jesus—"throw yourself down" (4:6)—because a fall from such a height would certainly be fatal.[64] Since, however, there would be sufficiently high places in the mountainous wilderness (cf. 4:8) from which Jesus could jump, the implied audience should look for additional significance in the temple setting.[65] It has been proposed that the additional significance is that it would make Jesus' compliance a public display,[66] although nothing in the context of Matthew 4, Psalm 91 (quoted by the devil), or Deuteronomy 6 (quoted by Jesus) points to such a view. Alternatively, on the basis of Ezekiel 47, it has been proposed that this setting evokes the expectation for eschatological miracles to take place at the temple.[67] There is no similarity, though, between this temptation and the miracles in Ezekiel 47. It has also been suggested that the temple's significance may be reflected by the rabbinic view that the pinnacle of the temple was the highest point in the world.[68] It does not, however, make

---

62. Cf. Turner, *Matthew*, 127.
63. W. D. Davies and Allison, *Saint Matthew*, 1:362; Morris, *Matthew*, 73.
64. France, *Matthew*, 132.
65. Gundry, *Matthew*, 56.
66. Gundry, *Matthew*, 56.
67. Schweizer, *Good News*, 63.
68. W. D. Davies and Allison, *Saint Matthew*, 1:365.

it more of a test for Jesus, since it would be wrong for him to take such a leap from any height.

The significance of the temple setting for this temptation seems to be understood best in light of the temple's intended function. The implied audience knows that the temple is the dwelling place of God and the place where he is to be worshiped (Deut 12:2–12). Therefore, to leap from the pinnacle of the temple is to test God in the location where he dwells, effectively challenging him "to his face." In addition, it turns the place built for the worship of God into a place for testing him—an arrogant misuse of the temple. In these ways, the temple setting of the second temptation adds to the implied audience's understanding of that temptation by emphasizing the ways in which the test would offend God, explaining why Jesus views it as testing God (Matt 4:7) and why he rejects the command of the devil.[69]

A Very High Mountain (4:8)

The third and final temptation is set on "a very high mountain" (Matt 4:8). From this "very high mountain," the devil shows Jesus "all the kingdoms of the world and their glory," and offers them in exchange for Jesus' worship (4:9). Although there is no real place from which one can see "all the kingdoms of the world," this is no problem in Matthew's story world. Either such a place exists in the story world, or—more likely—the implied audience understands this to be a visionary experience.[70] A high mountain is as appropriate a place as can be imagined from which to see these kingdoms. Therefore, this setting at least makes this sight "possible" in the narrative. Since, however, a mountain is not necessary for this offer to be made (cf. Luke 4:5), we should ask if the mountain setting makes any other contribution to the implied audience's understanding of this pericope.

Several commentators suggest that the mountain setting here contributes to the characterization of Jesus as the new Moses.[71] While we

---

69. When the temple becomes the setting of events later in the narrative (21:12–17), the implied audience will be invited to consider any possible connection between that pericope and this one.

70. Cf. Gnilka, *Das Matthäusevangelium*, 1:85; Morris, *Matthew*, 77; France, *Matthew*, 134; Turner, *Matthew*, 129; M. Davies, *Matthew*, 45.

71. Rogers, "Great Commission," 387–92; Gnilka, *Das Matthäusevangelium*, 1:85; Schweizer, *Good News*, 64; Hagner, *Matthew 1–13*, 68; Gundry, *Matthew*, 57; Stock,

may balk at the idea of Jesus being portrayed as both the ideal Israel and the new Moses in the same pericope, we must remember that the overall presentation of Jesus is cumulative. Therefore, contributions to both of these aspects of his characterization can occur together. Without denying the clear allusion to Israel's experience in the wilderness, a strong case can also be made for seeing this mountain setting, along with the vision of kingdoms to be possessed (cf. Deut 34:1–4), as contributing to the implied audience's understanding of Jesus as the new Moses.[72]

It is apparent that mountains are important in Matthew, since they are the settings for several important events (4:8; 5:1; 15:29; 17:1; 24:3; 28:16).[73] The mountain motif appears to relate at least some of these events to one another, although there are competing theories as to what theme(s) the related scenes are meant to highlight.[74] Given that this temptation does not occur on a mountain in Luke 4:5–8, the implied author appears to have intentionally created a connection between the temptation of Jesus and the resurrection narrative (4:8–10; 28:16–20).[75] The mountain motif, "worship" (4:9; 28:17), sonship language (4:3, 6; 28:19), and the concept of authority (4:8; 28:18) relate these two scenes and invite the implied audience to consider the latter in light of the former. After Jesus' resurrection, the implied audience will see that Jesus obtains something greater than what the devil offers him, that he obtains it through sacrifice rather than through forbidden worship, and that he obtains it from God rather than from the devil.[76]

Method and Message, 54; Brossier, "Les évangiles," 24; Mello, *Matthieu*, 97.

72. Allison, *New Moses*, 166–72.

73. Cf. Rogers, "Great Commission," 387; Turner, *Matthew*, 688; Garland, *Reading Matthew*, 265.

74. For example, Rogers argues that the mountain scenes bring together the Moses and Son of God motifs in order to show that Jesus is greater than Moses ("Great Commission," 387–92, 397–98), while Donaldson argues that the mountain scenes highlight Jesus' sonship and the fulfillment of the hopes associated with Zion, rather than with Sinai (*Jesus on the Mountain*, 199–200).

75. Cf. Luz, *Matthew 1–7*, 1:148.

76. Cf. Donaldson, *Jesus on the Mountain*, 194; W. D. Davies and Allison, *Saint Matthew*, 1:369; Luz, *Matthew 21–28*, 621; France, *Matthew*, 1113.

After the Sabbath, at the Dawning of the First Day of the Week (28:1)

The temporal setting of the discovery of the empty tomb is provided in Matt 28:1. Although there is debate over the time reference of ὀψὲ σαββάτων—since the normal meaning of ὀψέ is "late" (thus, "late on the Sabbath," or late Saturday afternoon)[77]—we follow the majority of commentators who understand it to mean "after the Sabbath" (i.e., Sunday morning).[78] Prior to the resurrection, the first day of the week had no special significance other than marking the end of the Sabbath, allowing normal activities to resume and the women to visit the tomb.[79]

The implied audience knows that, since Jesus died and was buried on Friday afternoon (cf. 27:62), the "first day of the week" is the third day since Jesus' death.[80] One possible significance of the third day after death is that it was when a person's death could be confirmed; it was thought that anyone buried alive by mistake would awaken by the third day, so that a tomb would be watched up to that time to confirm the death (cf. 27:64).[81] With the stone covering the tomb's entrance, however, it is unlikely that the women would have been able to confirm Jesus' death.[82] In Matthew's story world, the significance of the third day is found in Jesus' predictions of his resurrection (16:21; 17:22–23; 20:18–19; cf. 27:63). Jesus had specifically related the timing of his resurrection to the timing of Jonah's emergence from the "belly of the sea monster" (12:40), referring to his future resurrection as "the sign of Jonah" (12:39; 16:4). This makes

---

77. For this view, see Gundry, *Matthew*, 585–86; Schweizer, *Good News*, 523; and Reeves, *Resurrection Narrative*, 54–55.

78. W. D. Davies and Allison, *Saint Matthew*, 3:663–64; Luz, *Matthew 21–28*, 594–95; France, *Matthew*, 1099; Turner, *Matthew*, 680; Morris, *Matthew*, 734; Bonnard, *Matthieu*, 413. The implied audience would not expect the timing of Jesus' resurrection to be changed from what they know from the tradition (cf. Mark 16:1; Luke 24:1; John 20:1). Therefore, they will accept the more obscure use of ὀψέ. In addition, the women's purpose—"to see the tomb" (Matt 28:1)—is more fitting for Sunday morning, when the sun was rising, than for Saturday evening, after it had become dark (cf. W. D. Davies and Allison, *Saint Matthew*, 3:663; Morris, *Matthew*, 734).

79. The notion that the Sabbath would have prevented the women from doing the "work" of anointing Jesus' body (cf. Exod 20:10) is not relevant in Matthew, since the anointing is not mentioned. The implied audience likely understands the prohibition against travel on the Sabbath (cf. Exod 16:29) as prohibiting the women from visiting the tomb until after the Sabbath.

80. Moloney, *Resurrection*, 44; Gnilka, *Das Matthäusevangelium*, 2:493.

81. Longstaff, "Women," 281. Cf. Gnilka, *Das Matthäusevangelium*, 2:493.

82. France, *Matthew*, 1099, n. 24.

his resurrection a sign to the scribes and Pharisees (12:38) by which he is authenticated as God's messenger, although that sign will not lead to their repentance (12:41). The indirect, but apparent, identification of the day of Jesus' resurrection as the third day leads the implied audience to understand that Jesus' resurrection took place on the day that he had predicted. The resurrection itself is a demonstration of God's power and sovereignty. That the resurrection takes place as it was predicted is an even more convincing demonstration, proving God's ability to finish all that he had purposed to do in Jesus.[83]

The Sealed and Secured Grave of Jesus (28:1; cf. 27:59–66)

The geographical setting of the discovery of the empty tomb and the resurrection announcement is given in Matt 28:1, which the implied audience understands in the context of 27:59–66. Matthew 28:1 says that the women "came to look at the grave." The grave had been hewn out of the rock and covered with a large stone (27:60). It was then secured by a guard (κουστωδία; 27:65–66) consisting of multiple soldiers (cf. 28:11).

This setting makes multiple contributions to the implied audience's understanding. First, it makes the narrative intelligible by providing an appropriate setting for the resurrection, since it is where Jesus was buried. Second, it makes plausible the subsequent narrative about the Jewish leaders' bribery and falsified explanation of the empty tomb (28:11–15). Third, it is a setting which leads the implied audience to reject as implausible the claim that the disciples stole Jesus' body (28:13), a claim that continued to be spread into its own time (28:15). This setting leads the implied audience to the conclusion that the best explanation for the empty tomb is the divinely-wrought resurrection of Jesus (cf. 28:6).

Jerusalem (28:11)

The geographical setting of the guards' interaction with the chief priests and elders is "the city" (28:11). The implied audience knows that "the city" is Jerusalem (cf. 21:10; 27:53). As mentioned above, Jerusalem is where the Messiah ought to be enthusiastically welcomed by his people.

---

83. Quarles points out that this fulfillment is stressed by the use of καθώς (*Matthew*, 539).

That, however, has not been the case up to this point (cf. 2:4–6; 23:37).[84] The implied audience may wonder whether the death of Jesus (27:50), the signs accompanying his death (27:51–53), and the report of the empty tomb (28:11) will result in a change of heart in Jerusalem. The only attitude toward Jesus in Jerusalem that the implied audience learns about after his resurrection, however, is that of the chief priests and elders. Theirs is an attitude of resolute opposition to the extent that they even justify bribery and false witness (28:12–13). The implied audience understands that Jerusalem has become the opposite of what it was intended to be (cf. 5:35),[85] explaining the destruction that would later come upon it (cf. 23:38; 24:2, 15–21).

THE APPOINTED MOUNTAIN IN GALILEE (28:16)

The setting of the final scene of Matthew's Gospel is a mountain in Galilee—a mountain that Jesus had chosen for his meeting with the disciples (28:16). There are three important aspects of this setting. First, since it was the mountain "appointed" for the disciples (cf. 28:7, 10; cf. 26:32), it shows the obedience of the disciples.[86] They went where Jesus told them to go. This contributes to their positive characterization, since they had previously abandoned Jesus out of fear (26:56).

Second, this scene takes place on a "mountain." The mountain setting produces multiple effects on the implied audience. It contributes to the implied audience's understanding of Jesus as a new, but greater, Moses.[87] Like Moses, Jesus appears on a mountain, but with a greater authority, calling the implied audience to pledge its obedience to Jesus, rather than to Moses or to anyone sitting in "Moses' seat" (cf. 23:2–3). In addition, the mountain setting, along with the motifs of worship and authority, connect this scene with the third temptation (4:8–10).[88] On

---

84. The "crowds" of 21:9, 11, who respond positively to Jesus, are understood as those who accompany Jesus as he enters Jerusalem and, therefore, as distinct from "all the city" in 21:10.

85. Cf. Turner, *Matthew*, 79.

86. Gundry, *Matthew*, 594.

87. Rogers, "Great Commission," 397–98; Gundry, *Matthew*, 54, 593–94; W. D. Davies and Allison, *Saint Matthew*, 3:423–24; Moloney, *Resurrection*, 51; Allison, *New Moses*, 262–66.

88. Luz, *Matthew 21–28*, 621; W. D. Davies and Allison, *Saint Matthew*, 1:369; Garland, *Reading Matthew*, 40; Donaldson, *Jesus on the Mountain*, 194.

that mountain, Jesus was offered authority over "all the kingdoms of the world" (4:8–9), but only if he bowed his knee to the devil (4:9). Here, however, he possesses an even greater authority—"all authority in heaven and on earth" (28:18)—having conquered the devil. The implied audience, therefore, understands Jesus' resurrection as playing a role in his victory over the devil and in his acquisition of kingly authority. Furthermore, mountains are often places of divine revelation.[89] This characteristic was important in other mountain scenes in Matthew (though not necessarily in 4:8–10), and this mountain setting relates this scene to those.[90] The implied audience understands that, in this final mountain scene, Jesus gives the climactic revelation in Matthew's Gospel. His claim of universal authority (28:18), his commissioning of his disciples to a universal disciple-making mission (28:19–20), and his promise of eternal presence and assistance (28:20) are possible only because he has been raised from the dead.

Third, this mountain is in "Galilee." The implied audience is aware of Galilee's significance in Matthew's narrative. It is where Jesus and his family had initially settled when Archelaus's reign was viewed as a threat (2:22).[91] It is also the place to which Jesus withdrew after John's arrest (4:12).[92] It is the home of at least some gentiles (4:15), even if it is still predominantly Jewish.[93] It is the setting for most of Jesus' public ministry, establishing a continuity between the earthly and resurrected Christ.[94] It is the place where Jesus originally commissioned the twelve to ministry (10:1–42), making it an appropriate place to recommission them. Now that he had suffered the ultimate rejection in Jerusalem—crucifixion at the will of the Jewish leaders and the crowds (27:20–23)—he returns to Galilee and calls his disciples to meet him there.[95] As Jesus stands on a mountain in Galilee claiming all authority in heaven and on earth (28:18; cf. Dan 7:14), the implied audience understands that Jesus has

---

89. Luz, *Matthew 21–28*, 621–22; W. D. Davies and Allison, *Saint Matthew*, 3:422–23; Garland, *Reading Matthew*, 265; Hagner, *Matthew 1–13*, 883; Stock, *Method and Message*, 439; Powell, *What Is Narrative Criticism?*, 75; Carter, *Matthew: Storyteller, Interpreter, Evangelist*, 157–58; Rogers, "Great Commission," 387.

90. Gundry, *Matthew*, 594; Turner, *Matthew*, 688; Donaldson, *Jesus on the Mountain*, 193–94.

91. Luz, *Matthew*, 3:621.

92. Luz, *Matthew*, 3:621.

93. Turner, *Matthew*, 688; Hagner, *Matthew 1–13*, 883; Freyne, *Galilee*, 170–71.

94. Bonnard, *Matthieu*, 417.

95. Luz, *Matthew 21–28*, 621; Stock, *Method and Message*, 439.

received not only the authority over the gentile kingdoms that the devil had possessed (Matt 4:8–9), but also authority over God's kingdom that the Jewish leaders had possessed (21:43; cf. 23:13). From "Galilee of the gentiles," and not from Jerusalem, the son of Abraham sends his followers to invite the nations—gentiles and Jews—to receive the blessings that belong to disciples of the kingdom (cf. 13:52), and the son of David sends his followers to proclaim the gospel of the kingdom (cf. 24:14).[96] Therefore, the implied audience understands that Jerusalem, its leaders, and its institutions are no longer central to God's plan and purposes.[97] From that time on, the people of God are those who follow his Messiah, who has promised to be with them forever (28:20).

Summary

The effects on the implied audience of the settings discussed above will now be summarized under the headings of the seven possible types of effects described at the beginning of this chapter.

1. A setting can facilitate certain actions within the narrative.

    The betrothal period of Mary and Joseph (1:18) makes necessary Jesus' conception by the Holy Spirit (1:20) and Joseph's plan to divorce Mary quietly (1:19). The time after Jesus' birth (2:1) is an appropriate time for the magi's visit (2:1), and his birth is the logical antecedent of Herod's attempt to destroy him (2:7–18). Herod's actions as king (2:3–18) are only possible "in the days of Herod the king" (2:1). Jerusalem (2:1) is the fitting site for the magi's visit (2:1). Egypt (2:19) makes possible the fulfillment quotation in 2:15. Herod's death (2:19) is a logical occasion for the holy family's return to Israel (2:20–21). The setting of John's ministry in the wilderness of Judea (3:1) both enables the fulfillment quotation in 3:3 and explains the crowds' access to him (3:5). The Jordan River (3:6) is a logical place of baptism in that wilderness. Jesus' being led by the Spirit into the wilderness (4:1) logically follows the coming of the Spirit on him after his baptism (3:16), and the devil's challenge— "if you are the Son of God" (4:3, 6)—makes more sense after God,

---

96. Freyne, *Galilee*, 267. Cf. Léon-Dufour, *Matthieu*, 28; Heil, *Death and Resurrection*, 12–14.

97. Cf. Luz, *Matthew 21–28*, 621; Garland, *Reading Matthew*, 263–64; Gnilka, *Das Matthäusevangelium*, 2:506; Rhoads and Michie, *Mark as Story*, 71.

from heaven, calls Jesus his Son (3:17). The end of a forty-day fast in the wilderness (4:1–2) is an appropriate time for Jesus to be tempted to turn stones into bread (4:2–3). Jesus' grave (28:1) is the logical setting for the announcement of his resurrection (28:6). The secured grave (28:1; cf. 27:65–66) allows for the guards' report of the empty tomb (28:11). In these ways, many of the settings have made possible the events that make up the plot without giving them any special significance.

2. A setting can have certain expectations associated with it.

The circumstantial setting of continued exile (1:11–12, 17) creates an expectation of a "return" from exile by means of the reestablishment of the Davidic kingdom (cf. 1:1). The dream setting (1:20; 2:12, 13, 19, 22) indicates that divine communication is taking place. Jerusalem (2:1) is a place where the implied audience expects the Messiah to be enthusiastically welcomed. The temporal setting "after Herod died" (2:19) creates an expectation of safety for the child Jesus, as does the geographical setting of Israel (2:21). Egypt (2:19), since Jesus departed from it, contributes to the expectation of a new exodus. The wilderness setting (3:1) is associated with the expectation of eschatological salvation, and the mountain setting at the end of the Gospel (28:16) creates an expectation of divine revelation. These settings lead the implied audience to expect certain things, some of which are realized, while others, significantly, are not.

3. Repetition of settings can establish patterns that relate events to one another.

In Matthew's prologue and resurrection narrative, the setting of Jerusalem appears at the beginning and the end (2:1; 28:11), relating the Jewish leaders' initial and final responses to Jesus the Messiah and highlighting a progression from apathy to resolute opposition. The first and last mountain scenes in Matthew (4:8–10; 28:16–20) form a connection between Jesus' temptation to obtain "all the kingdoms of the world" by worshiping the devil and his actually obtaining them—and more—through his death and resurrection.

4. Movements through settings can establish patterns of events or anticipate plot developments.

This effect on the implied audience does not seem to occur in Matthew's prologue or resurrection narrative.[98] The implied audience might understand the Messiah's beginning and end in Galilee (2:22; 28:16)—with a period in Jerusalem in between—as highlighting that his ministry in Jerusalem was largely ineffective due to the opposition of the Jewish leaders. Such an understanding, however, would be largely dependent on material that falls between the prologue and the resurrection narrative.

5. A setting can contribute to characterization.

The setting of Jerusalem (2:1; 28:11) contributes to the implied audience's negative assessment of the Jewish leaders located there. The nighttime setting of Joseph's flight with his family (2:14) contributes to the positive view of him as immediately obeying the angel's command. The wilderness setting of Jesus' temptation (4:1) contributes to the implied audience's view of him as the ideal Israel. The disciples' arrival at the "appointed mountain" (28:16) shows that, after Jesus' resurrection, they are obedient and devoted to the Lord. Finally, Jesus' appearance on that mountain (28:16) contributes to his characterization as the new and greater Moses.

6. An individual setting can contribute to a narrative's plot or conflict.

The circumstances suggested by Matthew's genealogy (1:2-17) shape the implied audience's understanding of what the Messiah would need to do for his people. The Jerusalem setting (2:1) makes the apathetic response to Jesus' birth more disturbing. The nighttime flight to Egypt (2:13-14) shows the immediacy and reality of the threat Herod posed to Jesus. That Archelaus was a threat after Herod's death (2:19-22) shows that the kind of danger and oppression associated with Herod will not simply end with the death of such a ruler. The carrying forward of the circumstances outlined in the first two chapters—foreign oppression and failed leadership—into chapter 3 by the phrase "in those days" (3:1) informs the implied audience's understanding of the significance of John's

---

98. W. D. Davies and Allison do suggest that the progression of settings in the temptation narrative from a low place to a very high place (wilderness, pinnacle of temple, very high mountain) corresponds to the heightening tension of the scene (*Saint Matthew*, 1:352). It is not clear, however, that this progression makes the heightening of the tension more apparent than is it already made by the content of the temptations.

announcement of the kingdom (3:2; i.e., it would overcome oppressive and apathetic leadership) and of the people's going out to John (3:5–6; i.e., as an alternative to their leaders in Jerusalem). It also helps the implied audience to understand Jesus' resurrection as being what enables him to overcome those human obstacles to God's reign. The temporal setting of Jesus' temptation is immediately after his baptism (cf. "then," 4:1), which shows that the temptation should not reflect negatively on Jesus. The temple setting of the second temptation (4:5) shows it to be a temptation to misuse the temple. The setting of Jesus' resurrection on the morning after the Sabbath (28:1) shows the sovereignty of God in fulfilling Jesus' predictions of his resurrection "on the third day" (16:21; 17:23; 20:19). The setting of Jesus' resurrection at a sealed and secured grave (28:1; cf. 27:65–66) contributes to the implied audience's understanding that they should reject as false—and impossible—the lie invented by the Jewish leaders (28:13). The mountain setting of the Great Commission (28:16–20) leads it to understand that Commission as a climactic revelation from God. Finally, that Commission's setting in Galilee (28:16) shows that Jerusalem and its leaders have lost their significant role in God's plan to grow his kingdom (cf. 21:43; 24:2). In each of these cases, events take on added significance because of the settings in which they occur.

7. Multiple settings can relate to each other to form oppositions that enhance the plot.

The settings of Egypt (2:19) and Israel (2:21), though only mentioned briefly in Matthew's prologue, highlight the irony that the Messiah is safe in Egypt, but in danger in Israel. Jerusalem (2:1; 28:11) and Galilee (28:16; cf. 28:7, 10) are also set in opposition to one another. Jerusalem, where God's temple and the Jewish leaders are, is replaced by Galilee of the gentiles (cf. 4:15) as the place from which the Messiah sends his followers to make disciples of his kingdom.

In all of these ways, the settings of Matthew's prologue and resurrection narrative play a role in the narrative's effect on the implied audience. For the purposes of understanding the significance of Jesus' resurrection, the settings especially play a role in (1) showing the circumstances into which Jesus was born and which he would need to overcome in order to establish the messianic kingdom, (2) connecting the temptation of 4:8–9 with Jesus' possession of "all authority" after his resurrection (28:18), (3) showing the extreme opposition (and untrustworthiness) of the Jewish leaders, and (4) demonstrating the sovereignty of God in raising Jesus as predicted. This final point strongly suggests to the implied audience that, as a result of Jesus' resurrection, God can and will fulfill everything that had been prophesied of and predicted by Jesus.

Now that the settings of Matthew's prologue and resurrection narrative have been analyzed, the next chapter will analyze the events that make up their plot with the goal of understanding their effect on the implied audience.

6

Plot

Introduction

Our analysis of characters and settings has prepared for the analysis of the actions performed by those characters in those settings. These actions contribute to the plot which, as discussed in chapter 1, is more than the accumulation of the actions performed within a narrative. It is the particular arrangement of these actions—including speech, thoughts, feelings, and perceptions[1]—that constitutes the plot and contributes to the narrative's effect on the implied audience.[2] Like characterization, plot has received considerable attention from narrative critics.[3] Since the actions that form the plot are performed by characters, plot and characterization are effectively inseparable,[4] although they may be distinguished for the purpose of analysis.[5]

1. Powell, *What Is Narrative Criticism?*, 35.
2. Chatman, *Story and Discourse*, 43.
3. Plot has been the focus of attempts to resolve the debate over Matthew's structure (Matera, "Plot," 233–53; Carter, "Kernels and Narrative Blocks," 463–81). Some studies identify conflict as the key to understanding the plot (Kingsbury, "Developing Conflict," 57–73; Branden, *Satanic Conflict*; Cf. Rhoads and Michie, *Mark as Story*, 73). Other narrative studies of Matthew that highlight plot are Heil, *Death and Resurrection*, and Howell, *Inclusive Story*.
4. Resseguie, *Narrative Criticism*, 198.
5. Our final synthesis will attempt to integrate the analysis of plot and character. Generally speaking, characterization affects the implied audience's understanding of the character's actions and, therefore, of the plot. This is because expectations come to

How Plot Affects the Implied Audience's Response

The goal of narrative criticism is to understand the effect of a narrative on the implied audience. Despite the significant attention that narrative critics have given to plot, it is difficult to find a comprehensive discussion of the ways that plot can affect the implied audience. Therefore, we will start with a list—derived from various narrative-critical works—of a plot's possible effects on the implied audience.

1. The plot exerts an emotional or aesthetic effect on the implied audience.

    The emotional or aesthetic effect of plot is the effect that is mentioned most often in narrative-critical works.[6] Resseguie suggests that such effects can increase the implied audience's interest in the narrative or help persuade it to adopt the narrative's point of view.[7] Whether the implied audience simply appreciates the plot's artistic quality or is emotionally affected by it, such artistry attracts the implied audience's attention to that part of the narrative.[8] Similarly, the implied audience's emotional response to a character or to an action—whether positive or negative—can powerfully shape its evaluation of that character or action.

2. Repetition of similar events emphasizes the importance or typical nature of such events in the mind of the implied audience.

    Repetition is another way that events in a narrative's plot are emphasized.[9] Such repetition can also draw the implied audience's at-

---

be associated with a character as he or she is presented.

6. Resseguie, *Narrative Criticism*, 202, 208; Matera, "Plot," 236; Marguerat et al., *How to Read*, 42; Rhoads and Michie, *Mark as Story*, 1, 95; Morgan, "Emplotment," 80, 88; Powell, *What Is Narrative Criticism?*, 36. In addition to "affective" or "aesthetic," some use the synonyms "emotional" or "artistic" to describe these effects. Such effects, due to their ability to facilitate persuasion, are also considered by rhetorical critics (cf. Witherington, *New Testament Rhetoric*, 16).

7. Resseguie, *Narrative Criticism*, 202, 208.

8. Heil notes that the artistic design of Matt 26:1—28:20 emphasizes the contrast between positive and negative responses to Jesus (*Death and Resurrection*, 1, 107–8). Matthew's infancy narrative includes similar contrasting responses (Carter, *Matthew and the Margins*, 73).

9. Anderson, "Double and Triple Stories," 72; Powell, *What Is Narrative Criticism?*, 39–40; Marguerat et al., *How to Read*, 127; Bauer, "Structure," 13.

tention to variations between repeated (or similar) events.[10] While the significance of these variations is not always apparent,[11] they may allow for the emphasis of some important feature. The implied audience's recognition of the emphasis created by repetition can affect it in ways similar to the affective or aesthetic effects discussed above.

3. The plot can contribute to the presentation of a character.

We have already seen that a character's actions, as well as those of others, can "show" the implied audience what that character is like.[12] Plot can also show the development of a character over time or the relationship between a character's actions and the resulting circumstances. The implied audience's understanding of a character, then, leads to its acceptance of the narrative's evaluative point of view regarding the character, as well as to its imitation or rejection of that character's beliefs and actions.[13] Since they have already been discussed in chapters 3 and 4, most of the contributions of plot to characterization relevant to our analysis will not be included in this chapter.

4. The plot creates expectations in the implied audience that influence its understanding of later events.

Resseguie points to the way in which the primacy effect—the effect of the material that comes first in the plot—"creates expectations" that can be "fulfilled, modified, or even shattered by what comes later."[14] The implied audience is especially aware of occasions when its expectations are not fulfilled (i.e., are modified or shattered). Its quest to understand why those expectations are not fulfilled will lead to a particular evaluation of characters, their actions, or their beliefs. When these expectations *are* fulfilled, the implied audience

---

10. Anderson, "Double and Triple Stories," 85.
11. Anderson's examples of variation within repeated events only raise questions ("Double and Triple Stories," 85).
12. See, for example, Powell, *What Is Narrative Criticism?*, 52–53.
13. Marguerat et al., *How to Read*, 56; Howell, *Inclusive Story*, 248; Rhoads and Michie, *Mark as Story*, 139–40.
14. Resseguie, *Narrative Criticism*, 209–10.

experiences a pleasing aesthetic effect, and its preliminary point of view is further strengthened.[15]

5. Causal relationships established by the plot lead the implied audience to view such relationships as part of the narrative's point of view.

The causal relationship between events is what transforms a series of events into a plot.[16] Chatman argues that the implied audience expects a causal relationship between events in a narrative so much that it will infer causation even when it is not made explicit.[17] These causal relationships lead the implied audience to an understanding of the narrative's point of view since they show "how things work" in the story world.[18] Since, in the case of Matthew, the implied author expects the implied audience to accept the narrative's point of view as pertinent to its own world, the causal relationships between events in the plot are understood as a guide for its own actions.[19]

6. Speech may be understood as addressing the implied audience.[20]

The implied audience will sometimes understand a character's speech—which is part of the plot—as addressed to it.[21] This understanding may be indirect, as the implied audience identifies with the audience within the narrative (e.g., the disciples).[22] In addition,

---

15. Some commentators refer to an event as preparing the implied audience for a similar event that occurs later. I include such preparation under this heading, as it results in an aesthetic effect and, by fulfilling expectations, emphasizes certain ideas and themes (e.g., Kingsbury, "Developing Conflict," 72; Heil, *Death and Resurrection*, 7–19).

16. Powell, *What Is Narrative Criticism?*, 40–42; Resseguie, *Narrative Criticism*, 199–201; Kingsbury, *Matthew as Story*, 3. Cf. Forster, *Aspects of the Novel*, 86.

17. Chatman, *Story and Discourse*, 45–46. Cf. Carter, *Matthew: Storyteller, Interpreter, Evangelist*, 132.

18. Cf. Morgan, who indicates that "plot can be viewed as an exploration of ideological or theological values in narrative form" ("Plot Analysis," 91).

19. Marguerat et al., *How to Read*, 147–48.

20. This is part of the concept of "transparency" to the time and situation of the implied audience (Luz, *Matthew 1–7*, 11–12, 42).

21. Powell, *What Is Narrative Criticism?*, 50; Kingsbury, *Matthew as Story*, 109–11; M. Davies, *Matthew*, 23. Cf. W. D. Davies and Allison, *Saint Matthew*, 3:688–89, and Kupp, *Matthew's Emmanuel*, 236, who explain why Matt 28:18–20 may be heard as directly addressing the implied audience.

22. Cf. Carter, *Matthew: Storyteller, Interpreter, Evangelist*, 226.

a narrative may sometimes be understood as addressing the implied audience more directly, such as when words like "whoever" or "everyone" extend the relevance of Jesus' words beyond the audience within the narrative.[23] Kingsbury notes a number of places in Matthew where Jesus' words seem to hold little relevance for the audience within the narrative (5:11; 6:16–18; 7:15–23; 10:18, 22, 41–42; 13:1–52; 18:15–20; 24:1—25:46), suggesting that, in these places, Jesus may be "speaking past" the audience within the narrative to the implied audience.[24]

7. The outcome of a narrative's plot usually highlights its main point.

Pennington observes that "the main point of a passage is usually found in the climax and resolution and/or the following action/interpretation."[25] He even says that understanding how to find the main point in this way is "the most important thing we gain from doing narrative analysis."[26] Pennington applies his principle to individual pericopes, but it also seems appropriate to apply it to a work as a whole. Marguerat and Bourquin add that each plot is primarily a "resolution plot" or a "revelation plot."[27] Combining their approach with Pennington's, we can ask what the outcome of a pericope or of a narrative *reveals* to the implied audience or how its *resolution* affects the implied audience. The effect of the resolution is especially seen in the establishment of any causal relationships, which then contribute to the implied audience's point of view or response.

8. Gaps in the plot invite the implied audience to supply information in accordance with its own knowledge or to ask how the plot will turn out.

A plot may include unresolved conflict, uncertainty regarding the causal relationship between actions, or other gaps that must be filled

---

23. Kingsbury, *Matthew as Story*, 111; M. Davies, *Matthew*, 23.

24. Kingsbury, *Matthew as Story*, 107–9. See also Luz, who, because he does not view the five great discourses in Matthew as advancing the plot, concludes that they are addressed to its readers (*Matthew 1–7*, 12–13).

25. Pennington, *Reading the Gospels*, 176.

26. Pennington, *Reading the Gospels*, 176.

27. Marguerat et al., *How to Read*, 56.

in by the implied audience.[28] These gaps are filled in on the basis of the implied audience's own experience or its existing knowledge or point of view.[29] When narrative critics can be reasonably confident regarding the way in which the implied audience would fill in some gap, they can consider the effect of this gap-filling experience. Possible effects of this experience include a feeling of tension or concern, which attracts the implied audience's attention, and a consideration of how it should act in a similar situation.[30] In addition, when it is not clear how a gap should be filled, the audience is led to ask what might happen as the plot unfolds.

To sum up, eight possible effects of plot on the implied audience have been identified. These will be considered in the following analysis of the plot of Matthew's prologue (1:1—4:11) with the goal understanding the plot's effect on the implied audience's interpretation of the significance of Jesus' resurrection. These eight effects are:

1. The plot exerts an emotional or aesthetic effect on the implied audience.
2. Repetition of similar events emphasizes the importance or typical nature of such events in the mind of the implied audience.
3. The plot can contribute to the presentation of a character.
4. The plot creates expectations in the implied audience that influence its understanding of later events.
5. Causal relationships established by the plot lead the implied audience to view such relationships as part of the narrative's point of view.
6. Speech may be understood as addressing the implied audience.
7. The outcome of a narrative's plot usually highlights its main point.
8. Gaps in the plot invite the implied audience to supply information in accordance with its own knowledge or to ask how the plot will turn out.

---

28. Powell, *What Is Narrative Criticism?*, 44; Edwards, *Matthew's Story of Jesus*, 10; Marguerat at al., *How to Read*, 129; Chatman, *Story and Discourse*, 45–46.

29. Cf. Powell, *What Is Narrative Criticism?*, 44.

30. Cf. Edwards, *Matthew's Story of Jesus*, 10; Powell, *What Is Narrative Criticism?*, 44.

Jesus' Genealogy (1:1–17)

Although Matt 1:1–17 contains a series of aorist verbs (ἐγέννησεν, ἐγεννήθη), it is not understood by the implied audience to narrate events that make up Matthew's plot. Rather, it contributes to the implied audience's understanding of who Jesus is (by tracing his lineage) and of the circumstances into which he was born (by recalling the history of Israel— and particularly of the line of David—leading up to the birth of the one who would reestablish the Davidic throne). Therefore, its contributions are discussed above under characterization and setting.[31]

The Conception and Birth of Jesus (1:18–25)

In Matt 1:18–25, the implied audience is given more information about an event mentioned at the end of the genealogy—the birth of Jesus by Joseph's wife, Mary (1:16). This pericope begins the plot. Jesus is conceived by the Holy Spirit in Mary's womb (1:18). Joseph plans to send her away (or "divorce her"; ἀπολῦσαι) quietly (1:19). Therefore, God intervenes to ensure that Joseph takes Mary as his wife (1:20, 24) and Jesus as his legally adopted son (1:21, 25).

Many commentators mention that Matt 1:18–25 answers a question raised by 1:16: How is Jesus a descendant of David if Joseph did not beget him?[32] The answer is that Jesus is born to Joseph's wife (1:20, 24) and that Joseph, a "son of David" (1:20), legally adopts him. The implied audience understands that Jesus, though not Joseph's biological son, is legally his son as the result of Joseph's marriage to Mary prior to Jesus' birth (1:24–25) and/or of his naming of Jesus (1:21).[33] In this way, Jesus is also

---

31. See, for example, Carter, who states that the "genealogy provides the interpretive framework which shapes the understanding of the rest of the story" (*Matthew and the Margins*, 55).

32. Talbert, *Matthew*, 33; Bauer, "Genealogy," 154; Garland, *Reading Matthew*, 20–21; Gundry, *Matthew*, 19–20; Luz, *Matthew 1–7*, 97; Gnilka, *Das Matthäusevangelium*, 1:15.

33. Levin argues that such an understanding of adoption was derived from Roman practice, rather than from any Jewish custom ("Adoption," 431–34). Bockmuehl also argues against the assumption of such a practice in Judaism, preferring to explain Jesus' status as a son of David as the result of Mary's ancestry ("Son of David," 491–92). Regardless of the historical background, in Matthew's story world, Jesus' status as a son of David is presented as coming through Joseph and as the result of Joseph's actions in Matt 1:24–25.

a son of David and can be *the* son of David (1:1).[34] The implied audience therefore understands that Jesus has a rightful claim to David's throne.

As the first events in Matthew's Gospel are narrated, God is presented as the cause of those events.[35] The conception of Jesus is "by the Holy Spirit" (1:18). His birth alone, however, does not make him a descendant of David. Jesus would not be in David's line if Joseph had ended his betrothal to Mary (1:19). God ensures that Jesus obtains this status by sending his angel to convince Joseph to take the pregnant Mary as his wife (1:20). As a result, both Jesus' human existence and his status as a son of David are results of God's activity.[36] The implied audience understands that, as God's promises to David and to Abraham are fulfilled, they are fulfilled not by natural means, but through God's supernatural involvement. This becomes part of the narrative's point of view, which is emphasized throughout the infancy narrative by fulfillment quotations citing the OT (1:23; 2:6, 15, 18; cf. 2:23; 3:3; 4:15–16).[37]

This passage, of course, also contributes to the characterization of Jesus. Jesus "will save his people from their sins" (1:21) and will be at least a sign—if not the means—of God's restored presence with them (1:23).[38] These two aspects of Jesus' characterization supplement the titles found in 1:1. Jesus' establishment of his messianic kingdom will involve salvation from sin and the restoration of God's presence. When understood against their background in the OT (cf. Ps 25:18–22; 79:1–13; Isa 7:14–16; 8:3–4), these statements lead the implied audience to expect Jesus to deliver his people from the oppression of their enemies.[39] Therefore, the implied audience expects Jesus to establish an earthly kingdom and not merely a heavenly one.[40] Since this physical kingdom is not yet established when Jesus dies, his resurrection will make it possible to complete that work.

At the end of Matthew 1, the implied audience expects Jesus, the promised Messiah of Israel, to reestablish the kingdom and to sit on

---

34. Morris, *Matthew*, 32; Léon-Dufour, *Matthieu*, 22.

35. Carter, *Matthew: Storyteller, Interpreter, Evangelist*, 141; Carter, *Matthew and the Margins*, 66; M. Davies, *Matthew*, 35.

36. Léon-Dufour, *Matthieu*, 22.

37. Brossier, "Les évangiles," 21. Cf. Pennington, *Reading the Gospels*, 178; R. E. Brown, *Birth of the Messiah*, 98; Gundry, *Matthew*, 14; France, *Matthew*, 40; Luz, *Matthew 1–7*, 97.

38. Cf. Bockmuehl, "Being Emmanuel," 2.

39. See the discussion above in chapter 3 on the characterization of Jesus.

40. Contra W. D. Davies and Allison, *Saint Matthew* 1:210; M. Davies, *Matthew*, 32; Kingsbury, *Matthew as Story*, 48.

David's throne. As the narrative unfolds, it will see whether his path to the throne is smooth or is filled with obstacles and opposition.

Herod's Response to the Messiah's Birth (2:1–18)

The events of Matt 2:1–18 develop the plot that began in 1:18–25. They are some of the effects of the birth of Jesus as indicated by the phrase "after Jesus was born" (2:1) and by the magi's stated purpose of seeking the newborn king of the Jews (2:2).[41] While the magi, the "chief priests and scribes," and Herod all perform actions in this pericope, the actions of Herod, who is present throughout, are most central to the plot.[42] The magi present an exemplary response to Jesus (2:10–11) and foreshadow the inclusion of gentiles in the plan of God (28:19),[43] but they quickly disappear from the scene. The apparently apathetic response of the "chief priests and scribes" (2:4) to Jesus' birth surprises the implied audience and raises questions about how they will ultimately respond to Jesus. Herod's attempt to destroy Jesus, however, moves the plot forward into its next section.

The implied audience knows that Jesus is the protagonist in the story and, therefore, has a negative emotional response to the immediate threat to his life (2:13).[44] Hearing this pericope in the context of the preceding one, it understands that there is more at stake here than the well-being of the protagonist. The hope of God's people to experience salvation from sins (1:21), the restored presence of God (1:23), freedom from foreign oppression (1:12, 17),[45] and the reestablishment of God's kingdom (1:1) is bound up with Jesus. Any threat to him is a threat to that hope. The implied audience understands that if Herod is successful in destroying Jesus, that hope would be destroyed along with him.

This also sheds light on God's intervention to protect Jesus from Herod (2:13). God's warning to Joseph to flee to Egypt was more than just the gracious preservation of his own Son (cf. 1:20; 2:15), but the gracious

---

41. Cf. Matera, "Plot," 246; Lagrange, *Matthieu*, 19.

42. Léon-Dufour, *Matthieu*, 23.

43. W. D. Davies and Allison, *Saint Matthew*, 1:253; Luz, *Matthew 1–7*, 115; Carter, *Matthew and the Margins*, 82; Léon-Dufour, *Matthieu*, 24; Turner, *Matthew*, 76.

44. Cf. W. D. Davies and Allison, *Saint Matthew*, 1:258.

45. Cf. Carter, *Matthew and the Margins*, 73.

preservation of the kingdom hopes of his people.[46] Because Jesus survives, their hope survives—but only through God's intervention.

The outcome of this pericope shows the implied audience how the plot has been developed to this point. Although the long-ago promised Messiah (1:1; 2:4), the King of the Jews (2:2), has been born (1:25; 2:1), a foreign empire's appointed ruler has threatened his life (2:13) and forced his flight into a foreign land (2:14–15). His people are left in mourning (2:18) under the heavy hand of that ruler while the Messiah—their hope of salvation (1:21)—is a refugee far from their land (2:14–15). While this development suggests to the implied audience that Jesus will have to overcome much opposition on his path to the throne,[47] it also offers glimmers of hope. There is a proleptic reference to Herod's death and Jesus' return from Egypt (2:15).[48] Even the quote from Jer 31:15 in Matt 2:18, which refers to "weeping and great mourning," comes from a context (Jer 31:16–17) that includes promises of return from exile, hope, and the return of those children who "are no more."[49]

Our analysis of this pericope's role in the overall plot development may be distinguished from other literary analyses of it. For example, Brown states that Matthew 2 is necessary in order to make the infancy narrative the "gospel in miniature" with "passion and rejection, as well as success."[50] Garland, whose commentary claims a literary approach, focuses on the way that Jesus' movements in this chapter "conform to a messianic pattern directed by God."[51] These interpretations of the pericope appear to treat it as independent of its literary context or, at least, to explain its significance without reference to that context.[52]

---

46. Carter, *Matthew and the Margins*, 89.

47. M. Davies, *Matthew*, 37; Morris, *Matthew*, 33; Cf. Brossier, "Les évangiles," 22.

48. Morris, *Matthew*, 47.

49. Carter, *Matthew and the Margins*, 87; Morris, *Matthew*, 46; Turner, *Matthew*, 95. This note of hope seems to be ignored by those who interpret it as foreshadowing God's judgment of Jerusalem (Cf. Gnilka, *Das Matthäusevangelium*, 1:52–53; Gundry, *Matthew*, 35).

50. R. E. Brown, *Birth of the Messiah*, 183; Cf. Mello, *Matthieu*, 77.

51. Garland, *Reading Matthew*, 13, 28–29.

52. The insights of Brown and Garland, as well as observations about Mosaic parallels found here (cf. W. D. Davies and Allison, *Saint Matthew*, 1:253–54; Talbert, *Matthew*, 37–39), are important for interpretation. Narrative criticism's unique contribution, however, includes disciplined attention to the relationships between pericopes as they develop the plot. That is the focus of this chapter.

The Messiah's Return from Egypt (2:19-23)

Jesus' return from Egypt and settlement in Nazareth are briefly narrated in Matt 2:19-23. Léon-Dufour views this pericope, along with the rest of Matthew 2, as doing nothing but explaining why Jesus was known as a Nazarene despite having been born in Judea.[53] A narrative-critical reading, however, should explain how it further develops the plot of the narrative. That this pericope is related to the previous one is indicated by the reference in 2:19 to Herod's death, which was anticipated in 2:15, as well as by the conjunction δέ.

Because Herod had attempted to have Jesus killed, the implied audience is not surprised that Herod's death leads to an opportunity for Jesus to return from Egypt to Israel (2:20-21). Since Herod's opposition was the great obstacle introduced almost immediately following Jesus' birth, there is hope that his death means the end of significant threats to Jesus' life and mission. That hope is short-lived when Herod's son Archelaus is introduced as still posing a threat to Jesus (2:22).[54] The suspicion that this is a real danger—and not just Joseph's perception—is confirmed when Joseph is warned in a dream (by God) about the danger (2:22). Although the specific content of the warning and any instructions associated with it are not reported in the narrative, Joseph's pattern of obedience (1:24; 2:14, 21) leads the implied audience to infer that he was instructed to leave Israel and settle instead in Nazareth of Galilee.[55]

The introduction of an ongoing threat to Jesus produces an emotional response in the implied audience. There is a sense of disappointment in knowing that there would be no easy path to the throne for Jesus. The repeated motif of a foreign power's ruler posing a threat to Jesus strengthens this effect and produces a negative perception of such rulers (and of foreign rule). It suggests that part of the narrative's point of view is that any foreign ruler claiming authority over Israel and its people is a threat to Jesus and his purposes.[56] Jesus must somehow overcome the authority of the Roman Empire in order to reestablish the kingdom. The implied audience, consisting of Christian believers, knows that Jesus

---

53. Léon-Dufour, *Matthieu*, 23.

54. Mello, *Matthieu*, 79.

55. Cf. Turner, who views this as only a warning and the move to Nazareth as "Joseph's responsible decision making" (*Matthew*, 97).

56. Cf. Carter, *Matthew and the Margins*, 73.

will succeed through his death and resurrection. This pericope helps it to understand and appreciate what Jesus overcame through those great acts.

The outcome of this narrative shows how the plot has developed to this point. Although the king who threatened Jesus' life has died, it is not safe for the Messiah to live in Judea among the people he came to save. He is forced to live elsewhere while his people live under the oppressive rule of Archelaus. There will be many obstacles for Jesus to overcome in order to save his people and establish the promised kingdom. The reference to the elusive prophetic statement—"He shall be called a Nazarene" (2:23)—however, reminds the implied audience that even Jesus' settlement in Nazareth conforms to God's plan, bringing hope that he will accomplish all that he has promised.

The Ministry of John the Baptist (3:1–12)

The account of John the Baptist's ministry in Matt 3:1–12 has only minimal continuity with the events preceding it. It introduces new characters and does not directly build on previous events. Although the events of Matthew 3 take place about a generation after the events of chapter 2 (cf. Luke 3:23), the phrase "in those days" (3:1) indicates that they occur under the same circumstances that were in place at the end of chapter 2.[57]

The characters introduced in this pericope—John the Baptist, ordinary Jews, and the Pharisees and Sadducees—are discussed above in chapter 4. All are essentially new to the narrative, although the Pharisees and Sadducees contribute to the overall characterization of Jewish religious leaders that began in 2:4–6. As a group, the Jewish religious leaders initially appear to be apathetic in response to the news of the Messiah's birth. That characterization is further developed here as John's words to them portray them more negatively (3:7–10). As the narrative unfolds, their actions will further develop their characterization.

Certain elements of this pericope contribute to the development of the plot that began in the first two chapters of Matthew. The content of John's preaching—"Repent, for the kingdom of heaven is at hand" (3:2)—contains the first explicit use of kingdom ($\beta\alpha\sigma\iota\lambda\varepsilon\iota\alpha$) language in Matthew. It reinforces the implied audience's inference that Jesus, as Messiah and son of David (1:1), intends to establish God's kingdom and

---

57. See the discussion above where "in those days" is considered part of the setting of this pericope.

that the kingdom's fate is tied to Jesus' fate.[58] This kingdom expectation is also supported by references to "coming wrath" (3:7) and fiery judgment (3:10–12). The establishment of the kingdom is associated with eschatological judgment—an association that will be developed and emphasized throughout the Gospel (5:20; 7:21; 8:11–12; 13:41–43; 25:31–46).

This pericope further develops the characterization and mission of Jesus. In addition to Messiah, he is also eschatological judge (4:12).[59] Given the variety of messianic expectations at that time (see discussion above), some may not have expected the Messiah to be the eschatological judge. It is significant, then, that his role in judgment is made explicit here. The reference to burning chaff in 3:12 is a metaphor for judgment and is reminiscent of Mal 4:1 (3:19 LXX), where the Lord promises to burn like chaff "all the arrogant and those who do evil." The context of Malachi 4 is suggested to the implied reader by John's similarity to Elijah (Matt 3:22; cf. Mal 4:5). The context of the exodus is also suggested by references to Egypt (Matt 2:13–15) and the Jordan River (3:5), and by the threat to Jesus' life, which is similar to the threat to Moses' life (Exod 1:22). Exodus 15:7 contains another reference to burning chaff (cf. Matt 3:12) in the context of celebrating God's overthrow of Pharaoh and his army (Exod 15:4).

These references to judgment using the language of burning chaff hint at the way Jesus might eventually overcome opposing earthly powers such as those seen in Matthew 2. He may violently destroy them with fire as part of the eschatological judgment when he fully establishes his kingdom. The plot does not require this understanding. The implied audience, though, hearing this pericope in the context of what came before and seeking to relate the narratives, understands that this is one possible solution to the obstacles that Jesus faces. At this point in the narrative, it remains to be seen exactly how Jesus will overcome other kingdoms and establish his rule (cf. 4:8–10).

The Baptism of Jesus (3:13–17)

The pericope containing the baptism of Jesus (3:13–17) was important in our analysis of Jesus' characterization. It was noted there that Jesus'

---

58. I.e., the nearness of the kingdom is due to the nearness of the king.

59. Luz, *Matthew 1–7*, 139; Carter, *Matthew: Storyteller, Interpreter, Evangelist*, 141; Bauer, "Genealogy," 155. Cf. M. Davies, *Matthew*, 42; Schweizer, *Good News*, 51.

submission to baptism demonstrates his humility and commitment to righteousness, contrasting him with other characters in the narrative (2:13–18; 3:7–8; 5:20). The coming of the Spirit upon Jesus (3:16) is his anointing with power for his mission and reign (cf. Isa 61:1ff; 2 Sam 5:3).[60] God's declaration from heaven (Matt 3:17) affirms Jesus as the messianic Son of God (cf. Ps 2:7) and suggests that a unique, filial relationship exists between them.[61]

This pericope, though brief, also contributes to the development of Matthew's plot.[62] The last time the implied audience had heard of Jesus, he had settled with his family in Galilee (2:22–23)—rather than in Judea (2:22)—to avoid the threat posed by Archelaus. When Jesus comes "from Galilee" (3:13) to Judea (cf. 3:1), then, it suggests an element of risk that the implied audience senses. He is no longer in hiding, avoiding a potential conflict with Rome's appointed ruler. There is no indication that Jesus emerges from hiding because he is ready to overthrow Roman rule and establish his kingdom. Nevertheless, there are elements of kingdom hope in God's response to Jesus' baptism. The Spirit's coming upon Jesus and the mention of God's pleasure evoke Isa 42:1, which promises that God's Servant "will bring forth justice to the nations." Jesus' own actions, however, do not conform to the image of a king who is about to engage in a military campaign. To the surprise of the implied audience, he does not come with an army, but in humility and submission.[63]

Although Matt 3:11 highlights ways that Jesus is different from John (cf. 11:18–19), Jesus' submission to John's baptism (3:15) identifies him with John and with John's repentance movement and message (cf. 3:2, 6, 8).[64] Since John had criticized the Pharisees and Sadducees (3:7–10), Jesus' identification with John leads the implied audience to expect conflict

---

60. Cf. Talbert, *Matthew*, 57, 59; Turner, *Matthew*, 120.

61. Talbert, *Matthew*, 59. Cf. Kingsbury, *Matthew as Story*, 52.

62. Outlines of Matthew that emphasize the way in which 1:1—4:16 present the characters of Jesus and the Jewish leaders (e.g., Kingsbury, *Matthew as Story*, 57–58) implicitly deemphasize the development of the plot in this section.

63. Luz, *Matthew 1–7*, 144; Léon-Dufour, *Matthieu*, 41.

64. Kingsbury suggests that Jesus, through his baptism, identifies himself with sinful humankind (*Matthew as Story*, 51). The immediately following narrative (Jesus' temptation in 4:1–11), however, highlights Jesus' sinlessness. It seems better here to view Jesus as identifying with the movement of repentance toward God. Carter's interpretation of Jesus' baptism—that it signals his consent to carry out his mission of saving people from their sins and the manifestation of God's presence (*Matthew and the Margins*, 105)—attempts to interpret Jesus' baptism in the overall context of Matthew to this point, but it appears to neglect the nearest context of John's baptism (3:1–12).

between Jesus and the Jewish leaders. The movement with which Jesus identifies does not have as its focus the overthrow of the foreign power that exercises authority over the people, but repentance toward the God who is sovereign over every power and who often used foreign powers to discipline his people (ex. Judg 2:11–15). Because "the kingdom of heaven has come near" (3:2; cf. 4:17), it is necessary to repent so that, when the kingdom arrives in its fullness, one will not be excluded from it. Such a movement of repentance is necessary if the Messiah's people (cf. 1:21) will be included when he establishes his kingdom.

While the implied audience may not be surprised that repentance is necessary preparation for the coming kingdom, nothing in the narrative has led it to expect the Messiah himself to become the primary prophetic messenger of the call to repentance. Up to this point, everything in the narrative has prepared the implied audience to expect Jesus to act as a king (1:1, 17; 2:2–6). Jesus' identification with John's baptism, however, is the start of a very different way of relating to people. John comes in the mold of Elijah the prophet (3:4; cf. 11:14). Then Jesus identifies with John, not only by submitting to his baptism (3:15), but also by preaching the same message that John preaches (4:17; cf. 3:2).[65] It is no wonder that, later on, some will think that Jesus is John the Baptist (14:2; 16:14) or some other prophet (16:14).

In Matthew's narrative, the baptism of Jesus marks his first appearance to the public. He appears, at least initially, more as a prophet than as a king. For the implied audience, which has the benefit of knowing Matthew 1–2, this is a bit of a plot twist. It should begin wonder how Jesus, acting like a prophet, will be able to establish the promised kingdom. If it expects Jesus, through preaching and teaching, to gather an army to challenge the foreign powers, that expectation will soon be subverted by Jesus' teaching about gentleness, mercy, peacemaking, and joy when persecuted (5:2–12). Nevertheless, since Jesus' baptism follows immediately after both the promise of his eschatological judgment (3:12) and John's expression of his need to be baptized by Jesus (3:14; cf. 3:11), expectation of Jesus' future judgment is not undermined. He is becoming a prophet of the judgment that he himself will execute (e.g., 13:41–43). Nor does this

65. Redaction criticism, by focusing on the way that Matthew uses his Markan source material, could argue that Matthew identifies John with Jesus by making John preach the same message that Jesus preaches (Mark 1:15)—something that does not occur in Mark (cf. 1:4, 7–8). Narrative criticism, however, in focusing on the implied audience's experience of the narrative, observes that Jesus preaches (Matt 4:17) what was first preached by John (3:2).

undermine the expectation that Jesus will reign as the messianic king, which God's own words—"This is my beloved son" (3:17)—reinforce. Jesus' path to the throne will be more complicated than the implied audience may have initially thought, but he will still end up on his throne (cf. 25:31).

Since it holds significance for the plot as it develops later, one other aspect of Jesus' characterization here is worth repeating. God's declaration that Jesus is his beloved Son (3:17) completely aligns Jesus with his heavenly Father. From this point on, the implied audience knows that anyone who opposes Jesus is also opposed to God himself.[66]

The Temptation of Jesus (4:1–11)

In Matt 4:1–11, Jesus is led into the wilderness by the Holy Spirit to be tempted by the devil (4:1). After Jesus fasts for forty days (4:2), the temptations begin. The devil tempts him to turn stones into bread (4:3), to test God by forcing an angelic rescue with a jump from the pinnacle of the temple (4:6), and to acquire "all the kingdoms of the world and their glory" (4:8) from the devil by worshiping him (4:9). Each time, Jesus refuses the temptation and quotes from Deuteronomy (Matt 4:4, 7, 10; cf. Deut 8:3; 6:16; 6:13). Following the third temptation, Jesus commands the devil to "Go" (ὕπαγε, 4:10), after which the devil leaves him (ἀφίησιν, 4:11) and angels serve him (διηκόνουν, 4:11).[67] To appreciate this pericope's contribution to the plot's development, one must carefully consider its relationship to the events that precede it.

The first verse of this pericope informs the implied audience that Jesus was led by the Holy Spirit into the wilderness in order to be tempted by the devil (4:1). Just two verses earlier, the Spirit had "come upon" Jesus at his baptism (3:16). Before seeing the Spirit operative in Jesus' public ministry (cf. 12:28), the implied audience sees him bring about Jesus' encounter with the devil. The context in which the temptation takes place (i.e., 3:16–17) prevents the implied audience from viewing it as a type of discipline or a way for God to evaluate Jesus. There is no doubt or fear

---

66. Cf. France, *Matthew*, 124.

67. Kingsbury states that Jesus here "withstands the enticements of Satan and therefore vanquishes him" (*Matthew as Story*, 55–56). See also Morris, *Matthew*, 78. We should note, however, that references to Satan's (or the devil's) activity later in the Gospel (12:26; 13:38–39; 25:41) lead the implied audience to expect Satan to be vanquished sometime in the future rather than viewing him as having already been vanquished.

from God's perspective regarding the outcome of the encounter.[68] God initiates it in order to demonstrate Jesus' obedience and superiority to the devil, to bring to light the conflict between them, and to prepare for its ultimate resolution.[69] The temptation is part of God's plan and not a dramatic turn of events requiring divine intervention (cf. 2:13–15).

In Matt 3:15, Jesus spoke for the first time in Matthew's story. His words there—"in this way it is fitting for us to fulfill all righteousness"—are a claim of devotion to God's righteous standards. Up to this point, Jesus has only *claimed* such a commitment. One way, therefore, that 4:1–11 develops the plot is by demonstrating the validity of Jesus' claim that he is committed to "all righteousness." Jesus demonstrates a knowledge of and commitment to the scriptures (4:4, 7, 10) which determine his response to the devil's temptations.[70] The demonstration of this commitment produces an affective response in the implied audience, which is far more impressed by a demonstration than by a mere claim. Jesus' demonstrated commitment to righteousness distinguishes him from Herod (2:13–18) and from the Jewish leaders (3:7–10). In the context of Matthew's narrative, since Jesus is introduced as the messianic king, it also distinguishes him from the many disobedient kings in Israel's past (1:6–11). Since the rule of those kings had resulted in the Babylonian exile (1:11), Jesus' extreme commitment to righteousness explains why he can—and brings hope that he will—succeed in establishing God's kingdom when others had failed.

The temptation narrative also develops the implied audience's understanding of the way in which Jesus will express his divine sonship.[71] Immediately before the temptation narrative, God declares that Jesus is his "beloved Son" (3:17).[72] The devil then bases his first two temptations on Jesus' being God's Son ("If you are the Son of God," 4:3, 6). The devil tempts Jesus to express his divine sonship in miraculous, self-serving acts like turning stones into bread (4:3) and forcing his own angelic rescue (4:6).[73] Jesus, however, refuses to assert his sonship in such ways. Rather than serving himself and powerfully displaying his status, he expresses

---

68. Cf. Morris, *Matthew*, 70.
69. Cf. Kingsbury, *Matthew as Story*, 58.
70. Carter, *Matthew and the Margins*, 106.
71. Talbert, *Matthew*, 60; Turner, *Matthew*, 127–28.
72. Schweizer, *Good News*, 58.
73. Schweizer, *Good News*, 62.

his sonship in humble obedience.[74] After all, although he is the Son of God, he is still a son and does not seek to escape his Father's authority. As the narrative develops, the implied audience will not be surprised when Jesus continues to live in humble obedience, even in the face of extreme opposition, and even while dying on the cross (cf. "If you are the Son of God, come down from the cross," 27:40).[75]

The introduction of the devil ("the tempter," 4:3; "Satan," 4:10) also develops the plot. In the first three chapters of Matthew, the external obstacles to God's people experiencing his promises are earthly ones—foreign oppressors (1:11; 2:1, 13–18, 22) and their own unrighteous leaders (1:6–11; 3:7–10). Now the implied audience learns that there is also a significant spiritual obstacle that must be overcome—the devil himself.[76] The devil's opposition to Israel is only briefly mentioned in the OT (1 Chr 21:1 LXX; cf. Zech 3:1–2 LXX), so it is not necessarily assumed by the implied audience.[77] It is significant, therefore, that his opposition is made explicit in this pericope. Although the devil's efforts here are directed against Jesus and not directly against the people of Israel, the implied audience already understands that the people's destiny is tied to Jesus and to the success of his mission (cf. 1:21).[78] Because of this understanding, and because the devil's activity later will be directed at the people (4:24; 8:16,

---

74. Kingsbury, *Matthew as Story*, 57.

75. Cf. M. Davies, who refers to Jesus' impending crucifixion not "as a tragic accident but as Jesus' faithful expression of sonship in refusing to meet the evil of violence with violence" (*Matthew*, 46). While she is correct in viewing Jesus' obedience as an expression of his sonship, her focus on nonviolence as the reason it is not a "tragic accident" seems to ignore the significance of his death as an atonement for sins (26:28; cf. 20:28).

76. Carter, *Matthew: Storyteller, Interpreter, Evangelist*, 141; Kingsbury, *Matthew as Story*, 56; Lagrange, *Matthieu*, 63; Schweizer, *Good News*, 64. Carter focuses on Satan's control of the Roman Empire and all other empires (*Matthew and the Margins*, 106–7). This control may be inferred from Matthew, but it is not made explicit. Carter's focus leads to his understanding of Jesus as coming to overcome earthly powers on behalf of the marginalized in general, while Matthew's focus is on Jesus' significance for Israel and, only as an outworking of that significance (i.e., as "son of Abraham"), for the gentiles.

77. Although intertestamental writings develop the concept of a cosmic conflict between evil spiritual forces and God, Matthew's implied audience cannot be assumed to possess a highly developed idea of Satan such as that seen in the lesser-known *Testament of Job* (e.g., 1:12; 2:4). Whether in Job or the *Testament of Job*, Satan's actions toward Job, an individual, are not necessarily understood as affecting Israel.

78. Powell, *What Is Narrative Criticism?*, 49.

28–32; 9:32–33; 12:22; 13:19, 38–39; 15:22; 17:14–18),[79] this is an important introduction to the spiritual opposition that Jesus must overcome in order to establish God's kingdom for the blessing of his people. After his death and resurrection, Jesus will have decisively overcome all opposition to his mission and to his people's experience of his promised blessings.

The devil's opposition to Jesus also develops the plot by showing the implied audience that the devil stands to lose something if Jesus succeeds in his mission.[80] Otherwise, the devil would have no motive to tempt Jesus. What the devil stands to lose is the subject of the third temptation—"all the kingdoms of the world and their glory" (4:8). When the characterization of the devil (i.e., Satan) was discussed above, it was argued that his implicit claim of authority over these kingdoms (cf. Luke 4:6, where the claim is explicit) is a legitimate claim. He appears to know that Jesus, as the son of David *and* the son of Abraham (1:1), had come to take from him authority over "all the kingdoms of the world."[81] Therefore, he offers Jesus those kingdoms in exchange for Jesus' worship.[82] Jesus' response shows that this would have made him subservient to the devil ("You shall worship the Lord your God and *serve* him only," 4:10). It would not have been a mere feigning of worship (i.e., bowing in homage) that the devil could have used to his advantage in some way. Had Jesus accepted the devil's offer, he would have obtained authority over the world's kingdoms, but the devil—and not the God of Israel—would have had authority over Jesus.

From the temptation narrative, the implied audience learns that if Jesus succeeds in his mission, the devil will lose the authority that he possessed over the world's kingdoms. It also shows that Jesus will succeed.[83] At the end of the narrative, when Jesus claims "all authority in heaven and

---

79. W. D. Davies and Allison, *Saint Matthew*, 1:403; Powell, *What Is Narrative Criticism?*, 48.

80. Léon-Dufour, *Matthieu*, 59.

81. In a future study, I hope to test the hypothesis that, in response to the events at Babel (Gen 11:1–9), God divided the world into nations, giving the devil authority over all but the future nation of Israel, which was chosen through Abraham immediately after this division (Gen 12:1–3). If this hypothesis is true, then it can be said that Jesus came to take back from the devil authority over the gentile nations and that he possessed authority over Israel even before his death and resurrection. This would explain the expansion of "disciple-making jurisdiction" from only Israel before his death (Matt 10:6; 15:24) to "all nations" (28:19) after his death and resurrection.

82. Gnilka, *Das Matthäusevangelium*, 1:90. Cf. Léon-Dufour, *Matthieu*, 53.

83. Heil, *Gospel of Matthew*, 16; Garland, *Reading Matthew*, 40; Kingsbury, *Matthew as Story*, 58; Léon-Dufour, *Matthieu*, 52.

on earth" (28:18), it is clear that Jesus has obtained that authority—not by becoming subservient to the devil, but through his humble obedience to his Father. A theological explanation of the way that Jesus, apparently by virtue of his death and resurrection, has obtained that authority from the devil is not provided in the narrative. This is no surprise, however, since such theological reflection is not germane to narrative works. Other NT writings attempt to explain *how* and *why* Jesus' death and resurrection resulted in this transfer of authority (Rom 1:3-4; Eph 2:11-16; Col 1:13; 2:14-15; Rev 5:9-10). What Matthew's narrative does is to make clear that this transfer has indeed taken place.

Summary of Matthew's Plot as It Is Developed in 1:1—4:11

After a long history detailed in the OT and recalled by the genealogy in Matt 1:1-17—a history that included promises to Israel that had not yet been fulfilled—God intervenes in history to bring about the miraculous conception of his promised Messiah (1:18, 20) and to place him in the line of David (1:19-25). His birth will ultimately lead to both salvation from sin (1:21) and the restoration of God's presence (1:22-23) which, understood against the OT background, includes the reestablishment of a sovereign, Davidic kingdom.

Herod responds to the report of Jesus' birth (2:2) by attempting to destroy him (2:13, 16), which would also result in the destruction of the kingdom hopes of God's people. God intervenes to preserve the life of his Messiah (2:13-15) while Herod's massacre of innocent children illustrates the misery of God's people under foreign oppression (2:16-18). When Herod dies, it appears safe for Jesus to return to Israel (2:19-21). The rule of Herod's son Archelaus, however, presents an ongoing danger to Jesus that forces his family to settle instead in Galilee (2:22-23) away from God's people and land, but nevertheless in conformity with God's plan (2:23).

The ministry of John the Baptist (3:1-12) proclaims the nearness of God's kingdom (3:2), confirming the kingdom expectations created by the presentation of Jesus as Messiah in chapters 1 and 2. John's words also associate Jesus' eschatological judgment (3:7, 10-12) with those kingdom expectations. Jesus' arrival at the site of John's baptism (3:13) marks his emergence from hiding and his willingness to assume the risks of public activity. His submission to John's baptism (3:15) identifies him with the repentance movement and message of John (cf. 3:2; 4:17), which is not focused on foreign oppression that must be overthrown, but on God (3:2, 6, 13), who has often used foreign oppression to discipline his people, and who threatens something far worse in the future (3:7). When Jesus demonstrates his commitment to righteousness by submitting to baptism (3:15), he receives a royal anointing with the Spirit (3:16) and a royal title ("my beloved Son," 3:17). Nothing that he does, however, is overtly messianic, with the result that he initially appears more like a prophet than a king (cf. 14:2; 16:14). The Father's declaration of Jesus' sonship (3:17) also aligns Jesus and his Father, so that all future responses to Jesus—positive or negative—are also responses to God.

The temptation of Jesus by the devil (4:1–11) reveals that there is spiritual opposition to Jesus and his mission in addition to the earthly opposition encountered earlier (2:13–23). It also reveals that the devil will lose his authority over the kingdoms of the world if Jesus is successful in his mission (4:8; cf. 28:18). Jesus refuses to obtain that authority from the devil by becoming subservient to him (4:9), ensuring that he would obtain it instead through humble obedience to God. His divine sonship is expressed in this humble obedience rather than in self-serving acts of power (4:3–7). Jesus' responses to the devil's temptations (4: 4, 7, 10) demonstrate his commitment to righteousness and his superiority to previous kings in Israel's history (1:6–11), which will enable him to succeed in establishing the promised kingdom.

The overall trajectory of Matt 1:1—4:11—a trajectory that the implied audience expects will continue throughout the narrative—is one in which the divinely wrought and appointed Messiah will fulfill God's promises to Israel and for the nations by reestablishing God's promised kingdom. He will do this despite the opposition of foreign earthly powers and of the devil, and despite the apathy and sin of the Jewish leaders. This is the "primacy effect" established by Matthew's prologue. As the plot develops, the implied audience expects to learn how Jesus will successfully overcome those obstacles and establish that kingdom. They also expect to learn how those other than foreign rulers and the devil (i.e., Jewish leaders and ordinary Jews) will respond to Jesus. Assuming that this trajectory is not altered in Matt 4:12—27:66, this primacy effect will make a significant contribution to the context in which the implied audience will understand Jesus' resurrection (28:6).

The Influence of the Prologue's Plot on the Significance of Jesus' Resurrection

Eight possible effects of plot on the implied audience were discussed at the beginning of this chapter. Those effects and their contributions to the implied audience's understanding of the significance of Jesus' resurrection are:

1. The plot exerts an emotional or aesthetic effect on the implied audience.

    The implied audience has reacted negatively to the threats to Jesus' life and mission (2:8, 16–18, 22–23). It has been impressed by Jesus' humility and devotion to righteousness (3:13–15; 4:1–10) and desires to see him experience victory over those who oppose him.

2. Repetition of similar events emphasizes the importance or typical nature of such events in the mind of the implied audience.

    When Herod's son Archelaus is presented as a threat to Jesus (2:22–23), it repeats a motif first encountered in 2:16–18, where a foreign government's ruler poses a threat to his life. This repetition leads the implied audience to see foreign powers in general as threats and focuses its attention on the need for Jesus to gain authority over these powers (cf. 28:18).

3. The plot can contribute to the presentation of a character.

    The statements made to Joseph about Jesus contribute to the implied audience's understanding of Jesus' mission, since he will "save his people from their sins" (1:21) and be called "Immanuel" (1:23). The implied audience also learns that Jesus is the eschatological judge (3:11–12) in addition to being the Davidic king (1:1), so they expect that he will both reestablish the promised kingdom and carry out the final judgment.

4. The plot creates expectations in the implied audience that influence its understanding of later events.

    The opposition to Jesus encountered from both earthly (2:16–18, 22–23) and spiritual (4:1–10) powers leads the implied audience to the understanding that Jesus must overcome earthly and spiritual opposition to succeed in his mission. They also understand that success in his mission will come at the expense of earthly authorities and of the devil.

5. Causal relationships established by the plot lead the implied audience to view such relationships as part of the narrative's point of view.

   God is the cause of Jesus' birth (1:18, 20), his adoption into the line of David (1:20, 24), his survival of Herod's assassination attempt (2:13–15), and his temptation by the devil (4:1–11). The initiative of God in all of these events establishes for the implied audience that, through Jesus, God is actively working to keep the promises that he had made to his people.

6. Speech may be understood as addressing the implied audience.

   This effect is not present in Matthew's prologue unless, perhaps, God's voice from heaven at Jesus' baptism (3:17) should be understood as addressing the implied audience.

7. The outcome of a narrative's plot usually highlights its main point.

   Multiple pericopes end in ways that emphasize God's initiative in Jesus' life (1:24–25; 2:13–15, 22–23; 3:17; 4:11). In addition, the implied audience encounters a pericope that ends in death and mourning (2:18), highlighting the circumstances in which God's people are destined to live until his Messiah reestablishes his kingdom, and from which the Messiah will save them.

8. Gaps in the plot invite the implied audience to supply information in accordance with its own knowledge or to ask how the plot will turn out.

   As Matthew's prologue unfolds, the combination of expectations and obstacles leads the implied audience to ask certain questions that it hopes will be answered before the end of the narrative. What will be the relationship between Jesus' victory over foreign oppression and his eschatological judgment? How will Jesus, who does not initially act like a king, manage to establish the promised kingdom? How will Jesus obtain authority over the world's kingdoms from the devil without becoming subservient to him?

The primary effect of the plot of Matthew's prologue on the implied audience's understanding of Jesus' resurrection is the result of the expectations that it establishes. The primacy effect established there is to establish the implied audience's expectation that Jesus will establish the kingdom that God had promised to his people. The death of Jesus, therefore, is not understood *primarily* as a gracious sacrifice for the sins of individuals—though it is also that (20:28)—but as the ultimate, and apparently effective, attempt of the Roman and Jewish authorities to destroy Jesus (27:20–26; cf. 2:8, 13, 16, 22). Similarly, since this plot and these expectations are established long before the introduction of conflict between Jesus and the Jewish authorities over his identity, the resurrection is not understood *primarily* in terms of how it vindicates Jesus following his condemnation by those authorities. Since Matthew's prologue associates kingdom hopes with the life and person of Jesus the Messiah, the restoration of his life after his death results in the restoration of those hopes. Therefore, the implied audience understands the resurrection of Jesus in terms of the benefit it brings to those who trust him to fulfill the expectations that were established at the beginning of the Gospel; Jesus can and will reestablish and reign over that kingdom, and his people will live and participate in the kingdom (cf. 7:21; 8:11; 13:41–43; 18:3–4; 25:34). This is why the female disciples have "great joy" (28:8), why the Jewish leaders desperately try to explain the empty tomb some other way (28:11–15), why the eleven remaining disciples, who had previously deserted him (26:56; cf. 26:69–75), have the courage to meet him in Galilee to receive his commission to make disciples (28:16–20), and why he can be with them always (28:20) to ensure their success.

In the next chapter, we will conclude our narrative-critical analysis by considering the narrative's point of view. That point of view is largely the result of the cumulative effects of the characters, settings, and plot that have been analyzed in chapters 3 through 6.

7

Point of View

Introduction

The final aspect of this narrative-critical study is point of view. Point of view has been described as having multiple "planes"—phraseological, spatial, temporal, psychological, and ideological (or evaluative).[1] Four of these planes are more helpful for describing how the narrative works (i.e., how the story is told) than for understanding its effect on the implied audience.[2] The ideological (or evaluative) point of view, however, is central to the narrative critic's goal of understanding the narrative's effect.[3] It, therefore, will be the focus of this chapter.

---

1. Carter, *Matthew: Storyteller, Interpreter, Evangelist*, 106; Kingsbury, *Matthew as Story*, 33–37.

2. For example, Edwards's observation that the narrator of Matthew is "reticent-omniscient" is an explanation of the way the story is told (*Matthew's Story of Jesus*, 10; cf. W. D. Davies and Allison, *Saint Matthew*, 1:205). Cf. Kingsbury, *Matthew as Story*, 35–36; Powell, *What Is Narrative Criticism?*, 23–24.

3. Ideological point of view can be described as the foundation or sum of the other planes of point of view (Carter, *Matthew: Storyteller, Interpreter, Evangelist*, 106; Van Aarde, "Ideological/Theological Perspective," 35; Cf. Marguerat, "Le point de vue," 94, 97). The terms "ideological point of view" and "evaluative point of view" are used somewhat synonymously in narrative-critical discussions (cf. Kingsbury, *Matthew as Story*, 33). This is because the ideology presented by a narrative typically "entails rendering some judgment" based on that "conception of reality" (Kingsbury, *Matthew as Story* 34). Because an ideology is the foundation of any such judgment, and because the narrative may not always provide an occasion for making such a judgment, the term "ideological point of view" is preferred and will be used in this discussion.

The effect on the implied audience of a narrative's ideological point of view is more straightforward than the effects of character, setting, or plot are. As a result of its encounter with the narrative, the implied audience is expected to embrace (or adopt or appropriate) the implied author's ideological point of view.[4] Because the implied audience is assumed to share some aspects of Matthew's ideological point of view (e.g., belief in miracles, authority of the OT, existence of angels),[5] those aspects of the point of view do not result from an encounter with the narrative. The effect of the narrative's ideological point of view is rather the result of implicit and explicit ideas that are developed within the narrative and that the implied audience is expected to embrace by the end of the narrative.[6]

Because the main character and protagonist in Matthew's Gospel is Jesus, the Son of God (3:17), many have pointed out that the ideological points of view of God, Jesus, and the implied author are the same, producing a single, normative point of view.[7] It should be noted, however, that there is a distinction in principle between God or Jesus as characters in Matthew's narrative and God or Jesus outside of that story world. This does not mean that there are inconsistencies between the two, but the distinction does allow us to view the implied author as emphasizing some particular aspect(s) of their point of view without concluding that he rejects other aspects.

In this chapter, the conclusions of a few prominent narrative critics regarding Matthew's ideological point of view will be briefly discussed and critiqued. Then, observations related to ideological point of view from earlier chapters of this study will be rehearsed, albeit with minimal

---

4. Kingsbury, *Matthew as Story*, 34; Kingsbury, "Figure of Jesus," 21–22; Reeves, *Resurrection Narrative*, 23; Resseguie, *Narrative Criticism*, 167, 173; cf. Rhoads et al., *Mark as Story*, 3rd ed., 44–46; Anderson, *Matthew's Narrative Web*, 74; Marguerat, "Le point de vue," 107.

5. Powell, *What Is Narrative Criticism?*, 24–25; M. Davies, *Matthew*, 20, 33, 203; Turner, *Matthew*, 71, 80; Schweizer, *Good News*, 34.

6. It may be difficult to determine which ideas are assumed by the implied author and which are not, both because (1) the implied author has embraced all of them prior to composing the narrative, and (2) the believing audience likely has some prior understanding of or belief in elements of the narrative that may not presented as though a prior understanding is assumed. For discussions on the way that ideological point of view has shaped the composition of Matthew's narrative, see Dreyer, "Names of Jesus," 86; Van Aarde, "Plot Mediated," 65; and Van Aarde, "Ideological/Theological Perspective," 34–35.

7. Carter, "Narrative/Literary Approaches," 19–20; Reeves, *Resurrection Narrative*, 24; Anderson, *Matthew's Narrative Web*, 56; Howell, *Inclusive Story*, 174; Marguerat, "Le point de vue," 94.

commentary. Finally, we will present the ideological point of view regarding Jesus' resurrection that Matthew's implied audience is expected to embrace as a result of the preparation provided by the prologue's ideological point of view.

Narrative Critics on Matthew's Ideological Point of View

Since point of view is of special interest only, for the most part, to narrative critics, it is not surprising that analyses employing other methodologies do not attempt to articulate Matthew's ideological point of view. It *is* surprising, however, that some important narrative-critical studies of Matthew contain no reference to ideological point of view in their conclusions.[8] In this section, the conclusions of four narrative critics who *do* discuss Matthew's ideological point of view will be analyzed.

Keith Howard Reeves[9]

In his conclusion, Reeves refers to ideological point of view only with reference to the resolution of the conflict between Jesus and his disciples.[10] According to Reeves, "Jesus teaches that the essence of discipleship involves suffering and servanthood, but the disciples are concerned about status, wealth, and power."[11] This conflict is resolved when Jesus appears to the disciples (28:17), who "recognize 'on his person' that the purpose of his ministry was death on the cross (16:21). In turn, they come to appropriate Jesus' point of view concerning the nature of discipleship (16:21; 20:28)."[12]

Reeves's conclusion regarding the effect of Jesus' resurrection on the disciples is debatable. Nothing in the narrative portrays the disciples as

---

8. E.g., Edwards, *Matthew's Story of Jesus*; Garland, *Reading Matthew*.

9. Reeves, *Resurrection Narrative*.

10. Reeves does not use the adjective "ideological" here to describe "point of view" (*Resurrection Narrative*, 85). Since, however, he discusses a point of view regarding a concept, and therefore a particular way of thinking about it, we consider it an ideological point of view. Reeves does also refer to the Jewish religious leaders' point of view that "Jesus is a blasphemer" (*Resurrection Narrative*, 86). Because that point of view is not shared by the narrator, it is not considered here.

11. Reeves, *Resurrection Narrative*, 85.

12. Reeves, *Resurrection Narrative*, 86.

necessarily experiencing a change in the way they think about the essence of discipleship. They had better opportunities to understand the cost of discipleship—Jesus' teaching (16:21; 17:22–23; 20:18–19) and his arrest and trial (26:47—27:32). The disciples, who are presented in Matthew as understanding Jesus' teaching (14:33; 16:12; 17:23; cf. 13:11),[13] demonstrate this understanding by their flight from Jesus (26:56) and by Peter's denial (26:69–75); they appear, however, unwilling to follow Jesus and risk paying the cost of discipleship. Jesus' resurrection gives the impression that he has a purpose beyond, or other than, death. A more accurate point of view regarding Jesus' resurrection, then, is that instead of changing the disciples' thinking about the essence of discipleship, it changes their belief about Jesus' ability to make suffering and servanthood worth the cost involved (cf. 16:27).[14]

Jack Dean Kingsbury[15]

Kingsbury's discussion of point of view in Matthew has two main thrusts. One thrust is the same as the one found in Reeves's work—that Jesus' resurrection appearance resolves the conflict between them and Jesus.[16] The critique of Reeves above will, therefore, suffice as a critique of this thrust in Kingsbury's work.

Kingsbury's other thrust is a christological one. He argues that "Matthew's Christology is preeminently a Son-of-God Christology."[17] Although he claims that Matthew (as narrator) aligns his evaluative point of view with that of Jesus and God,[18] Kingsbury subordinates all other points of view to that of God as found in 3:17 (cf. 16:16; 27:54).[19] Practically, his insistence on making this one point of view dominant downplays the potential for the differing emphases of the aligned points of view (i.e., those of God, Jesus, and Matthew) to complement one another

---

13. See, for example, Carter, *Telling Tales*, 134–35.

14. Reeves's interpretation follows that of his teacher, Kingsbury, whose views are discussed below. Despite coming later, Reeves's work is discussed first to highlight the advantages of Kingsbury's approach.

15. Kingsbury, *Matthew as Story*; Kingsbury, "Figure of Jesus."

16. Kingsbury, *Matthew as Story*, 91–92.

17. Kingsbury, "Figure of Jesus," 3.

18. Kingsbury, "Figure of Jesus," 5.

19. Kingsbury, "Figure of Jesus," 5–7, 15.

(e.g., that the role of messianic king is filled by one with a unique, Father-Son relationship to God).

Kingsbury's view was critiqued in chapter three (on characterization). Despite including "Messiah" as part of Matthew's "initial evaluative point of view concerning Jesus' identity,"[20] he minimizes the significance of his messianic identity. He defines Jesus' kingship in terms of suffering obedience and dismisses the idea that Jesus lays claim to the throne of Israel.[21] In doing so, Kingsbury seems to ignore the kingdom expectations associated with the initial evaluative point of view regarding Jesus' identity (1:1, 17; 2:6), as well as Jesus' references to his future reign (16:28; 19:28; 25:31–46; cf. 20:21–23; 21:5–9). The beginning of Matthew's Gospel does not seem to influence Kingsbury's understanding of its conclusion.

David B. Howell[22]

Howell connects Matthew's ideological point of view to the implied audience's response.[23] According to Howell, Matthew's dominant ideological point of view "is found in his conviction that Jesus is the Son of God whose mission and message are to be accepted and obeyed."[24]

Howell's assessment of Matthew's point of view regarding Jesus' identity rightly incorporates multiple aspects—God's Son, Messiah, promise fulfillment, and salvation from sin.[25] He does not, however, elaborate on the expectations associated with Jesus' identity. Therefore, it is not clear how Howell understands Matthew's point of view regarding the way that Jesus fulfills God's promises or saves his people from their sins. His focus on the disciples' response only requires that Jesus be established as having supreme authority.[26]

In very general terms, Howell articulates Matthew's ideological point of view regarding the way one should respond to Jesus: his "mission and message are to be accepted and obeyed."[27] He does not explain

20. Kingsbury, *Matthew as Story*, 48.
21. Kingsbury, *Matthew as Story*, 9.
22. Howell, *Inclusive Story*.
23. Howell, *Inclusive Story*, 161, 174, 179, 187.
24. Howell, *Inclusive Story*, 190.
25. Howell, *Inclusive Story*, 249–50.
26. Howell, *Inclusive Story*, 17.
27. Howell, *Inclusive Story*, 162, 190; cf. 250.

what the implied audience understands Jesus' mission and message to be or how it should accept and obey them. Since Howell devotes most of his book to a discussion of Matthew's rhetoric, he does not appear to be concerned about clarifying Matthew's ideological point of view further. As a result, although there is little in his view with which one can disagree, there is also little in the way of specificity when it comes to understanding the conclusion of Matthew's Gospel.

Warren Carter[28]

According to Carter, Matthew 1–3 establishes several aspects of God's point of view.[29] Regarding Jesus, he maintains that "God's will and action bring forth Jesus so that he may carry out God's purposes."[30] Carter refers to Israel's past sins (1:6b, 10), its exile (1:11–12), and Roman oppression, concluding that God's view of the human condition is that they "need to be saved from this exploitative structure and loss of direction and purpose."[31] God's protection of Jesus from Herod demonstrates his point of view that he "is powerful enough to overcome the threats and advance the divine purpose."[32] Carter then understands Jesus' submission to baptism as Jesus "actively embracing the divine will to which he had been commissioned in 1:21–23," allying Jesus and God, and making Jesus "the reliable advocate of God's point of view through the rest of the gospel."[33]

Carter's assessment of the ideological point of view in Matthew 1–3 has much to appreciate, especially his identification of the salvation that Jesus would bring as containing a this-worldly dimension (e.g., from Rome and its oppression). God's ability to overcome all opposition to his divine purpose is an important perspective throughout Matthew which culminates with Jesus' resurrection (28:6) and his promise of his continued presence (28:20). Despite these strengths, Carter's explanation of

---

28. Carter, *Matthew: Storyteller, Interpreter, Evangelist*.

29. The choice to limit the discussion to the establishment of God's point of view is Carter's, apparently because he views the temptation narrative (4:1–11) as maintaining, rather than establishing, that point of view (*Matthew: Storyteller, Interpreter, Evangelist*, 127–28).

30. Carter, *Matthew: Storyteller, Interpreter, Evangelist*, 109.

31. Carter, *Matthew: Storyteller, Interpreter, Evangelist*, 110.

32. Carter, *Matthew: Storyteller, Interpreter, Evangelist*, 113.

33. Carter, *Matthew: Storyteller, Interpreter, Evangelist*, 114.

God's point of view as it is established in Matthew 1–3 could be improved in several ways.

First, Carter's references to "God's purposes" should be replaced with more specific statements that employ kingdom language (cf. 1:1, 16, 17, 21, 23). Second, Carter's explanation of the salvation that Jesus will accomplish shifts from what is explicit in the text—salvation of the Jews from "their" sins and from exile/oppression (1:21; cf. 1:11–12, 17; 2 Kgs 21:10–15; 24:8–16)—to what is not explicit—salvation of all people from all forms of exploitative, oppressive rule.[34] Third, Carter's view of Jesus' baptism—that it aligns him with God and is his acceptance of his commission—reads into the text what is not there and ignores the ways that the text has already aligned Jesus and God (Matt 1:18–25).[35] Finally, Carter's discussion of Matthew's ideological point of view is focused on its first three chapters,[36] so it fails to show how the remaining chapters may develop or nuance that point of view. As an unintended consequence, point of view does not appear to influence Carter's conclusions as he discusses the effects of the narrative on the implied audience. Carter's study could be improved by the integration of his conclusions regarding the narrative's effect on the implied audience and his discussion of its ideological point of view.

Aspects of Ideological Point of View Found in Matthew's Prologue

In chapters 3–6, it was noted that certain characters, settings, and events presented the implied audience with ways of thinking with which they should align themselves. These ways of thinking (i.e., aspects of ideological point of view) are summarized below.

Jesus' Genealogy (1:1–17)

In this first section of the narrative, Matthew's implied audience is provided with an initial ideological point of view regarding Jesus' identity.[37]

---

34. Carter, *Matthew: Storyteller, Interpreter, Evangelist*, 110, 113, 198.
35. Carter, *Matthew: Storyteller, Interpreter, Evangelist*, 114.
36. Carter, *Matthew: Storyteller, Interpreter, Evangelist*, 105–16.
37. Kingsbury (*Matthew as Story*, 48) and Carter ("Narrative/Literary Approaches," 19; *Matthew: Storyteller, Interpreter, Evangelist*, 107) claim that Matthew's genealogy

He is the promised, eschatological Messiah of Israel (1:1, 16, 17) who, having been born in the fullness of time (1:17), will fulfill the promises made to Abraham and David (1:1).[38] This section also provides an ideological point of view regarding the circumstances into which Jesus is born. He is born while Israel, due to the failures of its kings (1:6–11), has not yet experienced a full restoration from exile (1:11, 12, 17) since there is no Davidic king or kingdom at the time. The introduction of Jesus as the Messiah (Χριστός) in this context strongly suggests to the implied audience that Jesus will reestablish the promised Davidic kingdom that had ended with the exile (1:12).

The Conception and Birth of Jesus (1:18–25)

While the genealogy informs the implied audience of Jesus' existence and ancestry, the next section provides them with an ideological point of view regarding the way that Jesus came to be born and to be a descendant of David. Jesus' existence is the result of God's work through his Holy Spirit resulting in his conception (1:18, 20).[39] Likewise, Jesus' placement in David's line is the result of God's intervention through his angel to ensure that Joseph takes Mary as his wife despite her unexpected pregnancy (1:19–20, 24–25).[40] As a result, God is seen as directing the events and circumstances of Jesus' life in order to accomplish his purposes through him.[41]

This section also further develops the ideological point of view regarding Jesus' identity.[42] Jesus "will save his people from their sins" (1:21) and fulfill the Immanuel promise of Isa 7:14 (Matt 1:23). These statements, when understood in the context of the OT, develop the narrative's point of view that Jesus will defeat the foreign powers who, because of Israel's sins, rule over them and that he will reestablish the Davidic

---

points to God's activity throughout Israel's history. Since God is not yet mentioned, however, it seems better to view the emphasis as being on Jesus' identity (cf. 1:1) and the recalling of Israel's history in general rather than on God's activity in particular.

38. Cf. Schweizer, *Good News*, 45.
39. Carter, *Matthew: Storyteller, Interpreter, Evangelist*, 109.
40. Cf. Garland, *Reading Matthew*, 13.
41. Resseguie, *Narrative Criticism*, 183–84.
42. Mello summarizes Matthew 1 as the answer to the question, "Whose son is Jesus?" ("De qui Jésus est-il le Fils?"; *Matthieu*, 58). It seems, though, that chapter 1 tells the implied audience more than this about Jesus' identity, and it also tells it about his mission.

kingdom.⁴³ The fulfillment quotation in 1:23 is the first of five such quotations in Matthew's prologue (cf. 2:6, 15, 18, 23; cf. 3:3) which together establish the ideological point of view that Jesus' life conforms to OT patterns and expectations.⁴⁴

Herod's Response to the Messiah's Birth (2:1–18)

Before any characters in the narrative respond to Jesus or his birth, God's involvement in 1:18–25 aligns Jesus with God and prepares the implied audience to evaluate various responses to Jesus.⁴⁵ This section (2:1–18) presents three responses to the Messiah's birth, providing the implied audience with an ideological point of view regarding the characters who respond in these ways (and regarding others who can be identified with those characters). Herod's violent attempt to destroy Jesus (2:13, 16–18) produces a negative ideological point of view regarding foreign rulers as they oppose Jesus and his rule. The apathetic response of the Jewish leaders (2:4–6) provides an initial—but not yet decisive—negative point of view regarding them. Their responses to Jesus through the rest of Matthew, culminating in 28:11–15, will lead to a much more negative point of view. The magi's worship of Jesus (2:1–2, 9–11) produces a positive point of view regarding those who worship Jesus and a point of view regarding gentiles as capable of proper and worshipful responses to Jesus.⁴⁶

Since Jesus has already been presented as coming to reestablish the kingdom, the opposition of Herod and the apathy of the Jewish leaders

---

43. Syntheses of 1:21 and 1:23 such as "he is to manifest God's saving presence" (Carter, "Narrative/Literary Approaches," 19) are too general to create any specific expectation. Carter sees a more specific expectation beginning at 4:17, where "Jesus now proclaims 'the reign of the heavens is at hand'" ("Narrative/Literary Approaches," 20). These kingdom expectations, however, are found already in chapter 1 in references to the Messiah and the exile, and they are present in the OT backgrounds to 1:21, 23. Views like that of M. Davies (*Matthew*, 32), who says that Jesus would save "the Jewish people not from their military opponents but from their sins," fail to understand the OT perspective that foreign oppression is God's response to his people's sin.

44. Anderson, *Matthew's Narrative Web*, 59; Resseguie, *Narrative Criticism*, 183–84; Garland, *Reading Matthew*, 13. Cf. Luz, *Theology*, 39–40.

45. Cf. Howell, *Inclusive Story*, 187, 200.

46. Turner, *Matthew*, 15. Gnilka says that Matthew 2 shows that Jesus the Messiah's salvation is destined for all peoples while rejecting the Jews for whom it was first intended (*Das Matthäusevangelium*, 1:62). He is correct regarding the universality of salvation, but he goes too far in saying that the Jews were rejected. No final rejection of the Jews appears in Matthew's prologue; there is a warning, but no rejection. Furthermore, the rest of the narrative shows that many Jews do receive that salvation.

introduce obstacles to the mission of Jesus.[47] This establishes for the implied audience the ideological point of view that Jesus' mission necessarily involves the overcoming of opposition.[48] In order to establish the messianic kingdom, Jesus must overcome the opposition of foreign rulers. He must also overcome the apathy of those who should be his strongest supporters (i.e., the chief priests and scribes, 2:4–6), either by bringing about their repentance or by overcoming their opposition.

This section also develops the narrative's ideological point of view regarding Jesus' identity in a way that is consistent with his previous presentation as the messianic king. As such, he is worthy of worship (2:2, 11) and is a threat to other kings (2:3, 13, 16–18). God's intervention to protect Jesus from Herod (2:13–15) strengthens the view, established earlier, that God is directing the circumstances of Jesus' life to ensure his success. It also results in the initial presentation of Jesus as the true or faithful Israel (2:15), adding to the narrative's ideological point of view regarding his identity.[49]

The Messiah's Return from Egypt (2:19–23)

This brief section affirms aspects of the ideological point of view established earlier. God continues to direct the circumstances of Jesus' life (2:19–20, 22). Jesus' life conforms to prophetic expectations (2:23) and OT patterns (2:20; cf. Exod 4:19). The threat to Jesus the Messiah presented by Archelaus (Matt 2:22) strengthens the ideological point of view regarding foreign rulers by showing that Herod's opposition to God's appointed king (2:3, 16–18) is not unique, but is typical of those who possess earthly authority.

---

47. Carter focuses on the way that Matthew 2 illustrates the systemic sin from which Jesus came to save his people, rather than on the specific ways that Herod and the religious leaders threaten the mission of Jesus ("Narrative/Literary Approaches," 19). Cf. Carter, *Matthew: Storyteller, Interpreter Evangelist*, 110–13.

48. Carter, *Matthew: Storyteller, Interpreter, Evangelist*, 113.

49. M. Davies views chapters 3 and 4 as developing the "Jesus-as-Israel" typology (*Matthew*, 41). Such a view can fail to appreciate the way in which the events of chapters 3 and 4 develop the narrative's plot. Cf. Garland, *Reading Matthew*, 13.

The Ministry of John the Baptist (3:1–12)

When John the Baptist's ministry is introduced by the phrase "and in those days" (ἐν δὲ ταῖς ἡμέραις; 3:1),[50] the circumstances of Matthew 1–2—and the narrative's ideological point of view regarding those circumstances—are brought forward into the time of Jesus' adulthood and public ministry. This section reinforces the ideological point of view regarding Jesus' identity as messianic king and his mission to reestablish the kingdom by explicitly referring to "the kingdom of heaven" (3:2). It also adds the role of eschatological judge (3:11–12) to that of messianic king. The initial negative point of view regarding the Jewish leaders (2:4–6) is strengthened by John's sharply critical and threatening words to them (3:7–10). Nevertheless, John's command to "bear fruit worthy of repentance" (3:8) suggests an ideological point of view regarding those leaders that, at this point in the narrative, there is hope for their repentance.

The focus of John's message, which is presented as preparation for the coming of the Lord (3:3), is not on the overthrow of foreign powers, but on the Jews' repentance toward God (3:2, 6) in order to avoid his judgment (3:7, 11–12). This contributes to the narrative's ideological point of view that, despite living under the oppression of foreign authorities, the people's own sins (cf. 1:21) are their greatest problem. Salvation from their enemies (cf. 2:1, 17–18, 22) and, more importantly, from the wrath of God (3:7), will result from the forgiveness that is granted in response to their genuine (cf. 3:8) repentance.[51]

The Baptism of Jesus (3:13–17)

The section containing Jesus' baptism further develops the narrative's ideological point of view regarding Jesus. Jesus' positive virtues of humility, submission to God's authority, and commitment to righteousness (3:13–15) stand in contrast to the negative points of view regarding the Jewish leaders (3:7–10) and, implicitly, the former kings of Israel

---

50. See the discussion of "in those days" in chapter 5 (on settings) above, where we preferred to focus on the role of this phrase within the narrative rather than on its possible evocation of eschatological ideas.

51. Although John's baptism in Matthew is not referred to as a "baptism of repentance for the forgiveness of sins" as in Mark 1:4 and Luke 3:3, the concept of forgiveness may be inferred from the reference to fleeing God's wrath (Matt 3:7). Matthew's redaction of Mark results in an emphasis on John's message of the kingdom.

(1:6–11).⁵² Jesus' anointing by God's Spirit (3:16) shows that Jesus is empowered to carry out God's mission of establishing his kingdom. Furthermore, God's declaration from heaven (3:17) shows that Jesus possesses a unique Father-Son relationship with God, even if the precise nature of that relationship is not explained. Finally, Jesus' alignment with and implicit endorsement of John's message concerning the kingdom and repentance (3:3) indicate that Jesus will establish the kingdom while somehow providing for the forgiveness of those who repent of their sins.

The Temptation of Jesus (4:1–11)

The final section of the prologue develops the narrative's ideological point of view regarding Jesus and opposition to his mission. Regarding opposition, a supernatural dimension is added to the earthly dimension already seen.⁵³ Not only must Jesus overcome foreign rulers and failed Jewish leaders, he must also overcome the devil (4:1–11), who seeks to undermine Jesus' commitment to righteousness and obedience. If the devil succeeds, Jesus will follow in the footsteps of the kings of Israel and Judah who failed to persevere in obedience to God and his word. As a result, Jesus would be unable to establish the promised and hoped-for kingdom. The fact that this encounter is "arranged" by the Holy Spirit (4:1), however, establishes the narrative's point of view that this event does not jeopardize Jesus' mission, but is rather an occasion for Jesus to prove his superiority to the devil and to Israel and its kings. Therefore, an aspect of the ideological point of view is that no form of opposition can prevent Jesus from establishing the kingdom and fulfilling God's promises.⁵⁴

This section also provides an ideological point of view regarding Jesus who, as Messiah, demonstrates (4:4, 7, 10) his earlier claim to be committed to righteousness (3:15).⁵⁵ It shows him as superior to Israel

---

52. Carter indicates that this scene allies Jesus and God, since he views Jesus' submission to baptism as his embracing of God's will and commission (*Matthew: Storyteller, Interpreter, Evangelist*, 114). Such a specific interpretation of Jesus' baptism, however, depends on reading the fulfillment of scripture (1:22; 2:15, 17, 23) into the fulfillment of "all righteousness" (3:15), which is unnecessary (and unexpected). Furthermore, God had already allied himself with Jesus in chapters 1 and 2.

53. Cf. Carter, *Matthew: Storyteller, Interpreter, Evangelist*, 127.

54. Resseguie, *Narrative Criticism*, 183–84; Garland, *Reading Matthew*, 39–40. Mello, writing that nothing can endanger the salvation of God, does well in being more specific than many others about Jesus' mission (*Matthieu*, 80).

55. Cf. Léon-Dufour, *Matthieu*, 53.

and to Moses, who failed tests that resembled the temptations faced by Jesus. From the point of view of Matthew, Jesus should be followed and trusted more than Moses or those who claim to derive their authority from Moses (23:2).[56] Finally, this scene shows that Jesus expresses his sonship (cf. 3:17) not in self-serving ways,[57] but in humble submission to his Father.

Summary

To summarize, the ideological point of view of Matthew's prologue is that Jesus is the promised Messiah who will complete Israel's restoration from exile. He will end the foreign oppression that resulted from his people's sins and will reestablish the Davidic kingdom promised by God for their benefit and for that of gentiles. He is also the true Israel, is greater than Moses and Israel's previous kings, and will serve as eschatological judge. Jesus has been born into circumstances in which God's people are under the oppression of foreign powers, and they—especially their leaders—are in need of repentance. Nevertheless, neither these obstacles nor the opposition of the devil himself will prevent Jesus from living in humble obedience to God and fulfilling God's plans for the reestablishment of the kingdom. What remains to be seen is *how* he will overcome these obstacles and how particular characters will respond to him along the way.

If this is an accurate summary of the ideological point of view presented in Matthew's prologue, then it is also the ideological point of view that the implied audience is expected to embrace and to carry into the remainder of the narrative.[58] Unless the narrative clearly undermines one or more aspects of this initial point of view,[59] when Jesus is raised from the dead (28:6), this point of view will shape the implied audience's understanding of his resurrection.

---

56. Cf. France, *Matthew*, 18; Schweizer, *Good News*, 45.

57. Kingsbury, *Matthew as Story*, 55.

58. Cf. Edwards, *Matthew's Story of Jesus*, 10; Anderson, *Matthew's Narrative Web*, 76; Carter, *Matthew: Storyteller, Interpreter, Evangelist*, 110.

59. A preliminary review of the intervening chapters has not revealed anything that undermines this initial point of view. A more thorough narrative-critical analysis of the effects of 4:12—27:66 on the implied audience is a subject for future study.

Conclusion

The ideological point of view found in Matthew's prologue shapes the implied audience's understanding of the rest of Matthew's narrative. Therefore, as Jesus carries out his public ministry, the increasing opposition that he faces (cf. 9:3, 11, 34; 12:2, 9–14, 24, 38; 15:1–2, 12; 16:1; 19:3–9; 21:15–16, 23–27, 45–46; 22:15–40; 26:3–5, 14–16, 47–50; 27:1–2, 19–23) is understood as a threat to God's plan to establish his promised kingdom under the rule of his Messiah. Since the hopes of Israel—and the blessing for the gentiles (cf. 1:1)—are dependent on the success of God's plan, this opposition is understood to be a direct threat to those hopes. Therefore, when the Jewish leaders, with Pilate's cooperation, succeed in putting Jesus to death (27:1–2, 20–26, 50), the implied audience understands it as the apparent victory of Jesus' opponents and the defeat of God's plans.[60] Jesus appeared to be incapable of reestablishing the kingdom or of saving his people from their sins when he fell victim to foreign powers and the Jewish leaders.

Jesus' resurrection, then, is the restoration of the hopes that are necessarily associated with his role as Messiah (1:1) and eschatological judge (3:11–12). The promised kingdom will indeed be reestablished (i.e., exile would come to an end, 1:11–12, 17). The people will indeed be saved from their sins (1:21), meaning that foreign oppression, to which God had subjected them because of their sins, will be removed. Those who persist in their sin will be subject to God's wrath (3:7–12), while those who repent (3:3) will be greatly rewarded (cf. 3:11–12). Since foreign powers (2:16–18), Jewish leaders (12:14; 27:20–26), the devil (4:1–10), and even death (27:50) have been unable to thwart God's plan through Jesus, the implied audience understands that nothing will ever succeed in preventing God from accomplishing his kingdom purposes through Jesus. The resurrection restores their messianic hopes after their Messiah had died.

The actions of the characters in Matthew's resurrection narrative are consistent with this ideological point of view regarding Jesus' resurrection. In response to the angelic announcement of Jesus' resurrection (28:6), the two Marys depart with "fear and great joy" (28:8). They (28:9)—and later the disciples (28:17)—worship the risen Jesus. The Jewish leaders, knowing they had failed to stop Jesus, engage in bribery and false witness in a desperate attempt to suppress the news of Jesus'

---

60. Cf. Carter, *Matthew: Storyteller, Interpreter, Evangelist*, 151.

resurrection (28:12–14). The disciples, who had deserted Jesus when he fell into the hands of his opponents (26:56), journey to Galilee to see him alive again (28:16). Jesus declares that "all authority in heaven and on earth" (28:18) has been given to him; no longer can the devil or any earthly ruler make a legitimate claim of authority. Then he commissions his disciples to resume the disciple-making work to which he had previously commissioned them (10:1–8), now extending that work beyond Israel to the gentiles (cf. 10:5). As they anticipate the end of the age (28:20) when Jesus will fully establish God's kingdom (13:40–43; 16:28; 24:14; 25:31), Jesus promises his continued presence with them (28:20), ensuring that nothing—no opposition of any kind—will keep his work from being accomplished through them.

8

Conclusions

THE SIGNIFICANCE OF THIS STUDY

This study began with the observation that, despite the emphasis in the NT on the importance of Jesus' resurrection (cf. 1 Cor 15:14, 17), contemporary scholars and preachers often fail to explain his resurrection in a way that reflects this emphasis. As the survey in chapter 1 illustrates, scholarly discussion of Jesus' resurrection in Matthew is no exception to this trend. If this failure is to be remedied, the significance of Jesus' resurrection must be better understood. Narrative criticism, since it attempts to understand each NT narrative work as a literary whole, provides a means of understanding Jesus' resurrection within the literary context(s) in which it appears. The prologue of Matthew (1:1—4:11) is assumed to provide the initial literary context that shapes the implied audience's understanding of the resurrection as the fitting conclusion to that Gospel. Therefore, the goal of this study has been to understand Jesus' resurrection in Matthew's Gospel as the implied audience understands it. This goal has been pursued by means of a sustained, comprehensive, narrative-critical analysis of Matthew's prologue (1:1—4:11).

REVIEW OF CONCLUSIONS OF CHAPTERS 2–7

In chapter 2, seventeen verbal similarities and four conceptual similarities between Matthew's prologue and resurrection narrative were identified.

Criteria were developed and applied in order to support claims that the implied audience is expected to notice these similarities and view them as establishing a relationship between the beginning and end of Matthew's narrative. While some criticize narrative critics for making an *a priori* assumption of literary unity,[1] these similarities legitimize the appropriateness of considering how Matthew's prologue affects the implied audience's understanding of Jesus' resurrection. The implied audience expects the narrative to be unified,[2] and these similarities invite it to carefully reflect on the way(s) in which Matthew's resurrection narrative is related to its prologue. Finally, for an author-oriented narrative critic,[3] the fact that several of these similarities result from redactional activity suggests that the historical author-redactor of Matthew deliberately connected the conclusion of this Gospel to its beginning. Therefore, it appears that Matthew's author expected his audience to recognize and consider the relationship between its prologue and resurrection narrative.

In chapter 3, the characterization of Jesus was analyzed. Jesus is presented in several complementary ways, such as God's Son (2:15; 3:17), ideal Israel (2:15; 4:1–11), and the new and greater Moses (2:13–18; 4:1–11). Most importantly—because it occurs first and is most relevant to the developing narrative—Jesus is the promised, eschatological Messiah of Israel (1:1, 16–18) who, in fulfillment of God's promises to Abraham and David (1:1), will put an end to foreign oppression (2:1; 2:13—3:1; cf. 1:11–12, 17), reestablish God's kingdom (cf. 1:1; 3:2), and complete Israel's return from exile (cf. 1:11–12, 17). He will also carry out God's eschatological judgment (3:11–12). Therefore, the implied audience is expected to view him as worthy of full submission (cf. 3:14), worship (2:2, 11), and obedience (3:15; 4:11; cf. 28:10, 16). Furthermore, it is guided to evaluate positively all who respond to Jesus in such ways (2:2, 10–12; 3:14–15). Conversely, Jesus' characterization leads the implied audience to evaluate negatively all who oppose Jesus or who respond to him in apathy or unbelief (2:1–18; cf. 3:7–10; 28:11–15). Finally, Jesus' characterization leads the implied audience to view opposition to Jesus (2:13–23; 4:1–11) as a threat to the kingdom hopes associated with his messianic identity and to view his resurrection as the overcoming of that opposition and the assurance of those hopes.

1. Ashton, *Studying John*, 158, 165.
2. Powell, *What Is Narrative Criticism?*, 7.
3. Cf. Powell, "Reading Strategy," 26.

In chapter 4, the other characters in Matthew's prologue and resurrection narrative were analyzed. There, it was noted that the implied audience is provided with several examples of proper responses to Jesus—submission, worship, and obedience—by both Jews (1:18-25; 3:13-15) and gentiles (2:2, 10-11). The initial apathy (cf. 2:4-6) and eventual resolute opposition (28:11-15) of the Jewish leaders to Jesus were also observed, with their characterization leading the implied audience to a negative evaluation of Jewish leaders both in Matthew's story world and in the implied audience's own world (cf. 28:15). The testimony of reliable characters (1:20-23; 3:11-12, 16-17) was seen as contributing to the positive characterization of Jesus and as aligning him with God. Finally, the inability of the devil, despite his supernatural abilities, to successfully oppose Jesus (4:1-11) emphasized Jesus' superior power and righteousness (cf. 3:15).

In chapter 5, the settings in Matthew's prologue and resurrection narrative were analyzed. Of greatest significance for our study is the circumstantial setting into which Jesus the Messiah is born. Because his birth follows the sins and failures of Israel and its kings (1:6-11), as well as the resulting exile (1:11-12, 17) that had not fully ended (1:17), the implied audience expects the arrival of God's Messiah to fulfill God's promises to David and Abraham (1:1)—a restored Davidic kingdom and blessing to the nations (Isa 1:24—2:4; 11:1-12; Gen 12:2-3). This would necessarily involve the end of the foreign oppression under which God's people were living at that time (Matt 2:1; 2:13—3:1). The mountain settings in the prologue (4:8) and resurrection narrative (28:16) lead the implied audience to understand that Jesus has obtained the authority offered by the devil (4:9) without becoming subservient to him (4:10), but rather by means of his death and resurrection (28:18).

In chapter 6, the plot of Matthew's prologue was analyzed. We concluded that the prologue's plot establishes for the implied audience the expectation that God's Messiah will fulfill his promises to Israel and for the nations by reestablishing the promised kingdom (1:1; 3:2). Furthermore, the plot demonstrates that Jesus the Messiah will accomplish this in spite of opposition from foreign earthly powers (2:13-22) and of the devil (4:1-11), as well as the apathy and sin of the Jewish leaders (2:4-6; 3:7-10). Elements of the plot also contribute to the implied audience's understanding that Jesus' birth (1:18-25), the circumstances of his life (2:13-23), and the success of his mission (4:1-11) are the result of God's guidance and intervention. This expectation leads the implied audience to view Jesus' death primarily as his apparent defeat at the hands of his enemies and to view his resurrection (28:6) as his victory over his enemies and the assurance that he will reestablish the kingdom and carry out God's eschatological judgment (cf. 3:11–12).

In chapter 7, the ideological point of view of Matthew's prologue was analyzed. Since this point of view is the product of characterization, settings, and plot, this chapter incorporated their contributions to the point of view that the implied audience is expected to appropriate as a result of its experience of Matthew's narrative. The ideological point of view of Matthew's prologue is that Jesus is the promised Messiah (1:1) who will complete Israel's restoration from exile (1:17) by ending foreign oppression (i.e., saving them from their sins and the consequences of those sins; cf. 1:21) and reestablishing the Davidic kingdom that God had promised for their good and for the good of the gentiles (1:1). In doing these things, Jesus would have to overcome the things that threaten the kingdom hopes of his people—the opposition of foreign powers (2:13–22) and of the devil (4:1–11), as well as the apathy (2:4–6; and eventual opposition, cf. 27:20) of the Jewish leaders themselves. The implied audience, therefore, understands Jesus' resurrection as his decisive victory over that opposition— and over death itself –which guarantees that he will succeed in reestablishing the promised kingdom.

Summary of Conclusions

How is Matthew's implied audience expected to understand the significance of Jesus' resurrection in light of the effects of its prologue? It is expected to understand Jesus' resurrection as the overcoming of opposition to his messianic mission to reestablish God's kingdom in fulfillment of God's promises to David and to Abraham.[4] The prologue raises the question, "How will Jesus reestablish God's kingdom in the face of significant opposition from multiple sources?" Jesus' resurrection answers that question. He will do so not by continually avoiding their attacks (cf. 2:13–14) or by assembling a military force, but through the sovereign act of God to raise him to life after he is put to death (28:5–6). Because his life has been restored, he is able complete the work that he had come to do—work that was not finished as of the time of his crucifixion.

4. This expectation is seen in early Judaism, for example, in Pss. Sol. 17:4–6, 21–25; 18:3–9. Cf. T. Sim. 7:1–2; T. Levi 8:14; 4 Ezra 11:36–46; 12:31–32; 4Q252 6. See the discussion in Rogers, "Promises to David," 285–302.

Narrative criticism leads to an understanding of Jesus' resurrection in Matthew that has a different emphasis than those produced by other methodologies. When historical critics focus on the effect of historical events on real people, they conclude that Jesus' resurrection demonstrated to some that Jesus, and not those who condemned him to death, was in the right (i.e., it vindicated him).[5] When they focus on the OT background to the resurrection narrative, historical critics are led to understand Jesus' resurrection as a sign of the arrival of the eschatological kingdom or of Jesus' enthronement (cf. Dan 7:14).[6] For the implied audience in narrative-critical study, however, there is never any doubt as to whether Jesus is in the right. Nor does the OT provide the primary context for understanding the resurrection narrative. It understands the resurrection of Jesus within the context of the story world developed in Matthew's narrative.

Narrative critics allow considerations within the text to determine the questions that must be answered as the narrative unfolds. Ideally, they do not allow the issues or questions raised within the text to be silenced by the many legitimate questions that may be raised by external considerations. By focusing on the way a narrative answers the questions raised within its story world, narrative criticism is able to make a distinctive contribution to scholarly research. In the case of Matthew's prologue, the story world initially developed is one in which Jesus the Messiah comes to reestablish God's kingdom and faces opposition from multiple sources. Our analysis of that context leads to the conclusion that, since Jesus is the promised Messiah, his resurrection is the restoration and guarantee of the messianic kingdom hopes associated with him.[7]

---

5. Bruner, *Matthew 13–28*, 789; Case-Winters, *Matthew*, 338; W. D. Davies and Allison, *Saint Matthew*, 3:673; Gundry, *Matthew*, 585; Hagner, *Matthew 14–28*, 874–75; Hare, *Matthew*, 327; Hauerwas, *Matthew*, 245; Lange, *Matthew*, 548; Luz, *Matthew 21–28*, 597; Patte, *Matthew*, 400; Wilkins, *Matthew*, 939; Wright, *Matthew for Everyone*, 200.

6. Bonnard, *Matthieu*, 416–18; Case-Winters, *Matthew*, 341; W. D. Davies and Allison, *Saint Matthew*, 3:673; Evans, *Matthew*, 483; Filson, *Matthew*, 302; Gnilka, *Das Matthäusevangelium*, 507; Gundry, *Matthew*, 595; Hagner, *Matthew 14–28*, 875; Hare, *Matthew*, 329; Harrington, *Matthew*, 414–16; Hauerwas, *Matthew*, 245; Jones, *Matthew*, 321; Lagrange, *Matthieu*, 544; Lange, *Matthew*, 541; Luz, *Matthew 21–28*, 623–24; Meier, *Vision of Matthew*, 361; Mounce, *Matthew*, 267–68; Osborne, *Resurrection Narratives*, 97; Patte, *Matthew*, 400; Schniewind, *Matthäus*, 276; Schweizer, *Matthäus*, 348; Wilkins, *Matthew*, 933.

7. Of the fifty-five sources reviewed for chapter 1, only three narrative-critical works made mention of Jesus' future return to rule or judge in their explanations of Jesus' resurrection (M. Davies, *Matthew*, 206; Kingsbury, *Matthew as Story*, 93; Turner,

Implications for Future Scholarship

This study is a first step in the use of narrative criticism to better understand the significance of Jesus' resurrection in the Gospel of Matthew. A narrative-critical analysis of the remainder of Matthew (4:12—27:66), which is a necessary second step, could either strengthen or require modifications to the conclusions reached in this study.

One unanticipated result of this study was the development of lists of possible effects of characterization, setting, and plot on the implied audience. The development of these lists became necessary when no similar lists were discovered in the research for this study. One possible explanation for reader-response criticism's eclipse of narrative criticism is narrative criticism's relative failure to produce unique, objective conclusions.[8] The lists of possible effects developed for this study could restart a conversation about the ways in which narrative criticism can produce valuable results. This conversation should include contributions from the study of orality and performance criticism with the goal of clarifying or modifying these lists.[9] As the relationships between narrative elements and their effects on the implied audience are better understood, narrative criticism could fulfill its potential as a valuable methodology for NT studies.[10]

The ultimate goal of this study is to contribute to a better understanding of the significance of Jesus' resurrection so that it may be

---

Matthew, 684). Even in these works, Jesus' messianic identity and mission are not presented as the primary context in which his resurrection is understood.

8. This is my own inference based on the similarities between the conclusions of narrative critics and historical critics regarding the significance of Jesus' resurrection in Matthew, as well as the similarities between Kingsbury's redaction-critical (e.g., his *Matthew* in the Proclamation Commentaries series) and narrative-critical conclusions (e.g., *Matthew as Story*). Powell ("Reading Strategy," 22) and Malbon ("Characters," 46) note this shift in interest toward reader-response criticism. Perhaps some scholars would have resisted this shift if narrative criticism had produced more unique results.

9. Although NT scholars have not written much recently about the ways that aspects of narrative produce an effect on the implied audience, recent study of orality and performance have the potential to contribute to narrative criticism's goal of understanding a narrative's effect on the implied audience. See, for example, Iverson, *From Text to Performance*, and van Oyen, "Performance Criticism," 107–28.

10. Any list of possible effects on the implied audience used in NT narrative criticism could also be used for OT narrative criticism. In addition, the possibility of non-literal (i.e., figural/figurative or typological) interpretations of the OT provide additional possibilities for the ways that OT narrative can affect the implied audience. See the discussion in Noble, *Canonical Approach*, 307–27.

articulated more clearly in the church and in the academy. For this to happen, the results of this study must be combined with the results of other research—narrative-critical studies of the other three Gospels,[11] research on Jesus' resurrection in other NT works,[12] and related NT theological studies.[13] Narrative criticism should not be the only methodology that contributes to this more comprehensive work. Because, however, it provides a way to understand the significance of Jesus' resurrection in the literary context of each Gospel, this work would be incomplete without the contributions of narrative criticism.

Finally, an author-centered approach to narrative criticism—in which the effect on the implied audience is understood to reflect the historical author's intent—allows this study to contribute to historical-critical discussions. For example, we noted above that there are many verbal and conceptual similarities between Matthew's prologue and resurrection narrative. Several of these similarities result from Matthew's redaction of Mark 16:1–8.[14] In addition, much of Matthew 28 and nearly all of Matthew's prologue contain material not found in Mark.[15] A comparison of Matthew and Mark, therefore, suggests that the historical author-redactor of Matthew has added a prologue and modified the resurrection narrative in a way that strongly links the beginning and the end of that Gospel. Our narrative-critical analysis shows that one effect of this redactional work is that the implied audience is led to a particular point of view regarding the significance of Jesus' resurrection. By combining these redaction- and narrative-critical observations, we could argue that one original purpose of Matthew was to provide Matthew's

---

11. E.g., Boomershine, *Messiah of Peace*; Strauss, *Mark*; Matthews, "Fleshly Resurrection"; Prince, "Why Do You Seek"; Tidball, "Completing the Circle"; George, *Reading the Tapestry*; Moloney, *Resurrection*.

12. E.g., Wright, *Resurrection*; Matera, *Resurrection*; Bryan, *Resurrection of the Messiah*.

13. For example, Eskola's *Narrative Theology* contains a perspective found in this study (i.e., that Jesus came to restore Israel from exile) that may help determine the extent to which our conclusions regarding the significance of Jesus' resurrection may be applied to other NT writings.

14. E.g., "angel of the Lord" (Matt 28:2), "do not be afraid" (28:5), "great joy" (28:8). This statement, of course, assumes Markan Priority, as do most contemporary scholars.

15. Matthew 28:9–20 is not found in Mark (assuming that Mark ends at 16:8). Of the material in Matthew's prologue, only a shorter account of John's ministry (Mark 1:2–8), a shorter account of Jesus' baptism (1:9–11), and a two-verse reference to Jesus' temptation (1:12–13) appear in Mark. The balance of the prologue is unique to Matthew when compared to Mark.

community—a community that knew of Jesus' resurrection—a narrative that explained Jesus' resurrection in light of his messianic role and, for that matter, in light of the whole of Israel's history. It is our hope that the results of this study, as well as those of other narrative-critical studies, will contribute to a better understanding of the historical Jesus and of the early church that produced the NT.

Bibliography

Akin, Daniel L. "A Discourse Analysis of the Temptation of Jesus Christ as Recorded in Matthew 4:1-11." *Occasional Papers in Translation and Text Linguistics* 1 (1987) 78-86.
Alkier, Stefan. "From Text to Intertext: Intertextuality as a Paradigm for Reading Matthew." *HTS Theological Studies* 61 (2005) 1-18.
Allen, O. Wesley, Jr. *Matthew*. Fortress Biblical Preaching Commentaries. Minneapolis: Fortress, 2013.
Allison, Dale C. *The New Moses: A Matthean Typology*. Minneapolis: Fortress, 1993.
Anderson, Janice Capel. "Double and Triple Stories, the Implied Reader, and Redundancy in Matthew." *Semeia* 31 (1985) 71-89.
———. "The Implied Reader in Matthew." Unpublished paper, SBL Symposium on Literary Analysis of the Gospels and Acts, 1983.
———. *Matthew's Narrative Web: Over, and Over, and Over Again*. Journal for the Study of the New Testament Supplement Series 91. Sheffield: JSOT, 1994.
———. "Point of View in Matthew: Evidence." Unpublished paper, SBL Symposium on Literary Analysis of the Gospels and Acts, 1981.
Argyle, Aubrey W. *The Gospel According to Matthew*. Cambridge Bible Commentary. Cambridge: Cambridge University Press, 1963.
Ashton, John. *Studying John: Approaches to the Fourth Gospel*. Oxford: Clarendon, 1994.
Augustine. *Sermons on New-Testament Lessons II.I*. Nicene and Post-Nicene Fathers[1] 6. Edited by Philip Schaff. Grand Rapids: Eerdmans, 1956.
Bacon, Benjamin W. "The 'Five Books' of Matthew against the Jews." *Expositor* 15 (1918) 56-66.
Barth, Markus, and Verne H. Fletcher. *Acquittal by Resurrection*. New York: Holt, Rinehart & Winston, 1964.
Bauckham, Richard, ed. *The Gospels for All Christians: Rethinking the Gospel Audiences*. Grand Rapids: Eerdmans, 1998.
———. "Tamar's Ancestry and Rahab's Marriage: Two Problems in the Matthean Genealogy." *Novum Testamentum* 37 (1995) 313-29.
Bauer, David R. "The Kingship of Jesus in the Matthean Infancy Narrative: A Literary Analysis." *Catholic Biblical Quarterly* 57 (1995) 306-23.
———. "The Literary and Theological Function of the Genealogy in Matthew's Gospel." In *Treasures New and Old: Recent Contributions to Matthean Studies*, edited by David R. Bauer and Mark Allan Powell, 129-59. SBL Symposium Series 1. Atlanta: Scholars, 1996.

———. "The Major Characters of Matthew's Story: Their Function and Significance." *Interpretation* 46 (1992) 357–67.

———. "The Structure of Matthew's Gospel." PhD diss., Union Theological Seminary in Virginia, 1985.

Bauer, David R., and Mark Allan Powell, eds. *Treasures New and Old: Recent Contributions to Matthean Studies*. SBL Symposium Series 1. Atlanta: Scholars, 1996.

Bauer, Walter, et al. *Greek English Lexicon of the New Testament and Other Early Christian Literature*. 3rd ed. Chicago: University of Chicago Press, 2000.

Baumgärtel, Friedrich. "πνεῦμα, πνευματικός." In *Theological Dictionary of the New Testament*, edited by Gerhard Friedrich, 6:359–68. Translated by Geoffrey W. Bromiley. Grand Rapids: Eerdmans, 1969.

Baxter, Wayne S. "Mosaic Imagery in the Gospel of Matthew." *Trinity Journal* 20 (1999) 69–83.

Beardslee, William A. *Literary Criticism of the New Testament*. Guides to Biblical Scholarship. Philadelphia: Fortress, 1970.

Beare, Francis W. *The Gospel According to Matthew: Translation, Introduction and Commentary*. Peabody, MA: Hendrickson, 1981.

Bennema, Cornelis. "A Comprehensive Approach to Understanding Character in the Gospel of John." In *Characters and Characterization in the Gospel of John*, edited by Christopher W. Skinner, 37–58. Library of New Testament Studies 461. New York: Bloomsbury, 2013.

Bockmuehl, Markus. "Being Emmanuel: Matthew's Ever-Present Jesus?" *New Testament Studies* 68 (2022) 1–12.

———. "The Son of David and His Mother." *Journal of Theological Studies* 62 (2011) 476–93.

Bond, Helen K. *Caiaphas: Friend of Rome and Judge of Jesus?* Louisville: Westminster John Knox, 2004.

Bonnard, Pierre. *L'évangile selon Saint Matthieu*. 2nd ed. Commentaire du Nouveau Testament 1. Neuchâtel: Delachaux & Niestlé, 1970.

Boomershine, Thomas E. *The Messiah of Peace: A Performance-Criticism Commentary on Mark's Passion–Resurrection Narrative*. Biblical Performance Criticism 12. Eugene, OR: Cascade Books, 2015.

Boring, M. Eugene. "Matthew's Narrative Christology: Three Stories." *Interpretation* 64 (2010) 356–67.

Bornkamm, Günther. *Studien zum Matthäus-Evangelium*. Neukirchen-Vluyn: Neukirchener Verlag, 2009.

Boxall, Ian. *Discovering Matthew: Content, Interpretation, Reception*. Discovering Biblical Texts. Grand Rapids: Eerdmans, 2014.

Branden, Robert Charles. *Satanic Conflict and the Plot of Matthew*. Studies in Biblical Literature 89. New York: Lang, 2006.

Brossier, François. "Les évangiles de l'enfance." *Lumière et Vie* 55 (2006) 19–28.

Brown, Jeannine K. *The Disciples in Narrative Perspective*. Academia Biblica 9. Leiden: Brill, 2002.

———. *Matthew*. Teach the Text. Grand Rapids: Baker, 2015.

Brown, Raymond E. *The Birth of the Messiah: A Commentary on the Infancy Narratives in the Gospels of Matthew and Luke*. New York: Doubleday, 1993.

Bruner, Frederick Dale. *Matthew: A Commentary*. Vol. 1: *The Christbook, Matthew 1–12*. Rev. ed. Grand Rapids: Eerdmans, 2004.

———. *Matthew: A Commentary*. Vol. 2: *The Churchbook, Matthew 13–28*. Grand Rapids: Eerdmans, 1990.

Bryan, Christopher. *The Resurrection of the Messiah*. Oxford: Oxford University Press, 2011.

Burnett, Fred W. "Characterization and Christology in Matthew: Jesus in the Gospel of Matthew." In *Society of Biblical Literature 1989 Seminar Papers*, 588–603. Atlanta: Society of Biblical Literature, 1989.

———. "Exposing the Anti-Jewish Ideology of Matthew's Implied Author: The Characterization of God as Father." *Semeia* 59 (1992) 155–91.

Cabrido, John Aranda. *The Shepherd of Israel for All Nations: A Portrayal of Jesus in the Gospel of Matthew: A Narrative-Critical and Theological Study*. Rome: Pontificiae Universitas Gregoriana, 2008.

Caneday, Ardel B. "Christ's Baptism and Crucifixion: The Anointing and Enthronement of God's Son." *Southern Baptist Journal of Theology* 8 (2004) 70–85.

Carlson, Richard. "Reading and Interpreting Matthew from the Beginning." *Currents in Theology and Mission* 34 (2007) 434–43.

Carter, Warren. "Kernels and Narrative Blocks: The Structure of Matthew's Gospel." *Catholic Biblical Quarterly* 54 (1992) 463–81.

———. *Matthew and the Margins: A Sociopolitical and Religious Reading*. Bible & Liberation. Maryknoll, NY: Orbis, 2000.

———. *Matthew: Storyteller, Interpreter, Evangelist*. Peabody, MA: Hendrickson, 1996.

———. "Narrative/Literary Approaches to Matthean Theology: The 'Reign of the Heavens' as an Example (Mt. 4.17–5.12)." *Journal for the Study of the New Testament* 67 (1997) 3–27.

———. *Telling Tales about Jesus: An Introduction to the New Testament Gospels*. Minneapolis: Fortress, 2016.

———. "'To Save His People from Their Sins' (Matt 1:21): Rome's Empire and Matthew's Salvation as Sovereignty." In *Society of Biblical Literature 2000 Seminar Papers*, 379–401. Atlanta: Society of Biblical Literature, 2000.

———. "'To See the Tomb': Matthew's Women at the Tomb." *Expository Times* 107 (1996) 201–5.

Carter, Warren, and John Paul Heil. *Matthew's Parables: Audience-Oriented Perspectives*. Catholic Biblical Quarterly Monograph Series 30. Washington, DC: Catholic Biblical Association of America, 1998.

Case-Winters, Anna. *Matthew*. Belief: A Theological Commentary on the Bible. Louisville: Westminster John Knox, 2015.

Casey, Maurice. "Where Wright Is Wrong: A Critical Review of N. T. Wright's *Jesus and the Victory of God*." *Journal for the Study of the New Testament* 69 (1998) 95–103.

Charette, Blaine. *Restoring Presence: The Spirit in Matthew's Gospel*. Journal of Pentecostal Theology Supplement Series 18. Sheffield: Sheffield Academic, 2000.

Charlesworth, James H. "From Messianology to Christology: Problems and Prospects." In *The Messiah: Developments in Earliest Judaism and Christianity: The First Princeton Symposium on Judaism and Christian Origins*, edited by James H. Charlesworth, 3–35. Minneapolis: Fortress, 1992.

———. "Resurrection: The Dead Sea Scrolls and the New Testament." In *Resurrection: The Origin and Future of a Biblical Doctrine*, edited by James H. Charlesworth, 138–86. New York: T. & T. Clark, 2006.

Chatman, Seymour. *Coming to Terms: The Rhetoric of Narrative in Fiction and Film*. Ithaca, NY: Cornell University Press, 1990.

———. *Story and Discourse: Narrative Structure in Fiction and Film*. Ithaca, NY: Cornell University Press, 1978.

Collins, John J., ed. *Apocalypse: The Morphology of a Genre*. Semeia 14. Missoula, MT: Society of Biblical Literature, 1979.

Collins, Raymond F. *An Introduction to the New Testament*. Garden City, NY: Doubleday, 1983.

Conrad, Edgar W. "The Annunciation of Birth and the Birth of the Messiah." *Catholic Biblical Quarterly* 47 (1985) 656–63.

Crossan, John Dominic. "From Moses to Jesus: Parallel Themes." *Bible Review* 2 (1986) 18–27.

Culpepper, R. Alan. *Anatomy of the Fourth Gospel: A Study in Literary Design*. Philadelphia: Fortress, 1983.

———. "The Weave of the Tapestry: Character and Theme in John." In *Characters and Characterization in the Gospel of John*, edited by Christopher W. Skinner, 18–35. Library of New Testament Studies 461. New York: Bloomsbury, 2013.

Davies, Margaret. *Matthew*. Readings—A New Biblical Commentary. Sheffield: Sheffield Academic, 1993.

Davies, W. D., and Dale C. Allison. *A Critical and Exegetical Commentary on the Gospel According to Saint Matthew*. 3 vols. International Critical Commentary. Edinburgh: T. & T. Clark, 1988–1997.

Derickson, Gary W. "Matthew's Chiastic Structure and Its Dispensational Implications." *Bibliotheca Sacra* 163 (2006) 423–37.

Donaldson, Terrence. *Jesus on the Mountain: A Study in Matthean Theology*. Journal for the Study of the New Testament Supplement Series 8. Sheffield: JSOT Press, 1985.

———. "The Vindicated Son: A Narrative Approach to Matthean Christology." In *Contours of Christology in the New Testament*, edited by Richard N. Longenecker, 100–21. McMaster NT Studies 7. Grand Rapids: Eerdmans, 2005.

Dreyer, Yolanda. "Names of Jesus in Matthew and Luke—A Synchronic Perspective." *Acta Patristica et Byzantina* 12 (2001) 86–104.

Dunn, James D. G. *Did the First Christians Worship Jesus? The New Testament Evidence*. Louisville: Westminster John Knox, 2010.

Edwards, O. C., Jr. *Luke's Story of Jesus*. Philadelphia: Fortress, 1981.

Edwards, Richard A. *Matthew's Narrative Portrait of the Disciples: How the Text-Connoted Reader Is Informed*. Harrisburg, PA: Trinity, 1997.

———. *Matthew's Story of Jesus*. Philadelphia: Fortress, 1985.

———. Review of *Matthew as Story*, by Jack Dean Kingsbury. *Catholic Biblical Quarterly* 49 (1987) 505–6.

Ellis, I. P. "But Some Doubted." *New Testament Studies* 14 (1968) 574–80.

Ellis, Peter F. *Matthew: His Mind and His Message*. Collegeville, MN: Liturgical, 1985.

Eloff, Mervyn. "Exile, Restoration and Matthew's Genealogy of Jesus ὁ Χριστός." *Neotestamentica* 28 (2004) 75–87.

Erickson, Richard J. "Joseph and the Birth of Isaac in Matthew 1." *Bulletin for Biblical Research* 10 (2000) 35–51.

Eskola, Timo. *A Narrative Theology of the New Testament: Exploring the Metanarrative of Exile and Restoration*. Wissenschaftliche Untersuchungen zum Neuen Testament 350. Tübingen: Mohr Siebeck, 2015.
Evans, Craig. *Matthew*. New Cambridge Bible Commentary. Cambridge: Cambridge University Press, 2012.
Filson, Floyd V. *The Gospel According to St Matthew*. 2nd ed. Black's New Testament Commentary. London: Adam & Charles Black, 1971.
Fitzmyer, Joseph A. *A Wandering Aramean: Collected Aramaic Essays*. SBL Monograph Series 25. Missoula, MT: Scholars, 1979.
Forster, Edward Morgan. *Aspects of the Novel*. San Diego: Harcourt, Brace, Jovanovich, 1985.
Foster, Robert. "Why on Earth Use 'Kingdom of Heaven'?: Matthew's Terminology Revisited." *New Testament Studies* 48 (2002) 487–99.
Fowler, Robert. "Is 'What is?' Enough? One Reader's Response to Mark Allan Powell's *What Is Narrative Criticism?*" *Proceedings* 12 (1992) 171–75.
———. "Who Is 'the Reader' in Reader Response Criticism?" *Semeia* 31 (1985) 5–23.
France, R. T. *The Gospel of Matthew*. New International Commentary on the New Testament. Grand Rapids: Eerdmans, 2007.
Frei, Hans W. *The Eclipse of Biblical Narrative: A Study in Eighteenth and Nineteenth Century Hermeneutics*. New Haven: Yale University Press, 1974.
Freyne, Sean. *Galilee, Jesus, and the Gospels: Literary Approaches and Historical Investigations*. Philadelphia: Fortress, 1988.
Gaffin, Richard B., Jr. "Redemption and Resurrection: An Exercise in Biblical–Systematic Theology." *Themelios* 27 (2002) 16–31.
Garland, David E. *Reading Matthew: A Literary and Theological Commentary on the First Gospel*. Reading the New Testament. New York: Crossroad, 1983.
George, Larry Darnell. *Reading the Tapestry: A Literary-Rhetorical Analysis of the Johannine Resurrection Narrative (John 20–21)*. Studies in Biblical Literature 14. New York: Lang, 2000.
Gnilka, Joachim. *Das Matthäusevangelium*. Vol. 2. Herders theologischer Kommentar zum Neuen Testament 1. Freiburg: Herder, 1988.
Goldingay John. *A Critical and Exegetical Commentary on Isaiah 55–66*. International Critical Commentary. New York: Bloomsbury, 2014.
Goodacre, Mark. "Scripturalization in Mark's Crucifixion Narrative." In *The Trial and Death of Jesus: Essays on the Passion Narrative in Mark*, edited by Geert van Oyen and Tom Shepherd, 33–47. Contributions to Biblical Exegesis & Theology 45. Leuven: Peeters, 2006.
Gundry, Robert H. *Matthew: A Commentary on His Handbook for a Mixed Church under Persecution,* 2nd ed. Grand Rapids: Eerdmans, 1994.
Hagner, Donald A. *Matthew 1–13*. Word Biblical Commentary 33A. Dallas: Word, 1993.
———. *Matthew 14–28*. Word Biblical Commentary 33B.. Dallas: Word, 1995.
Hanson, John S. "Dreams and Visions in the Graeco–Roman World and Early Christianity." *Aufstieg und Niedergang der römischen Welt* 23.2 (1980) 1395–427.
Hare, Douglas R. A. *Matthew*. International Bible Commentary. Louisville: Westminster John Knox, 1993.
Hare, Douglas R. A. and Daniel J. Harrington. "Make Disciples of all the Gentiles (Mt 28:9)." *Catholic Biblical Quarterly* 37 (1975) 359–69.

Harrington, Daniel J., S.J. *The Gospel of Matthew*. Sacra Pagina 1. Collegeville, MN: Liturgical, 1991.

Hauerwas, Stanley. *Matthew*. Brazos Theological Commentary on the Bible. Grand Rapids: Brazos, 2006.

Hays, Richard B. *Echoes of Scripture in the Letters of Paul*. New Haven: Yale University Press, 1989.

Heil, John Paul. "The Blood of Jesus in Matthew: A Narrative-critical Perspective." *Perspectives in Religious Studies* 18 (1991) 117–24.

———. *The Death and Resurrection of Jesus: A Narrative-Critical Reading of Matthew 26–28*. Minneapolis: Fortress, 1991.

———. "The Double Meaning of the Narrative of Universal Judgment in Matthew 25:31–46." *Journal for the Study of the New Testament* 69 (1998) 3–14.

———. "Ezekiel 34 and the Narrative Strategy of the Shepherd and Sheep Metaphor in Matthew." *Catholic Biblical Quarterly* 55 (1993) 698–708.

———. *The Gospel of Matthew: Worship in the Kingdom of Heaven*. Eugene, OR: Cascade Books, 2017.

———. "The Narrative Roles of the Women in Matthew's Genealogy." *Biblica* 72 (1991) 538–45.

———. "The Narrative Structure of Matthew 27:55—28:20." *Journal of Biblical Literature* 110 (1991) 419–38.

Hieke, Thomas. "Frauen und Manner in Jesu Ahnengalerie." *Bibel und Kirche* 66 (2011) 4–8.

Hill, David. "The Figure of Jesus in Matthew's Story: A Response to Professor Kingsbury's Literary-Critical Probe." *Journal for the Study of the New Testament* 21 (1984) 37–52.

———. *The Gospel of Matthew*. New Century Bible. London: Oliphants, 1972.

Hooker, Morna D. "Beginnings and Endings." In *The Written Gospel*, edited by Markus Bockmuehl and Donald A. Hagner, 184–202. New York: Cambridge University Press, 2005.

Howell, David B. *Matthew's Inclusive Story: A Study in the Narrative Rhetoric of the First Gospel*. Journal for the Study of the New Testament Supplement Series 42. Sheffield: Sheffield Academic, 1990.

Huizenga, Leroy Andrew. "The Matthean Jesus and the Isaac of the Early Jewish Encyclopedia." In *Reading the Bible Intertextually*, edited by Richard B. Hays et al., 63–81. Waco, TX: Baylor University Press, 2008.

———. "Obedience unto Death: The Matthean Gethsemane and Arrest Sequence and the Aqedah." *Catholic Biblical Quarterly* 71 (2009) 507–26.

Hunsberger, George R. "Recovering the Resurrection of Jesus as Essential Gospel Core." *Missiology: An International Review* 52 (2024) 253–65.

Hurtado, Larry W. *Lord Jesus Christ: Devotion to Jesus in Earliest Christianity*. Grand Rapids: Eerdmans, 2003.

Isaksson, Abel. *Marriage and Ministry in the New Temple: A Study with Special Reference to Mt. 19.13–12 and 1 Cor. 11.3–16*. Translated by Neil Tomkinson with Jean Gray. Acta Seminarii Neotestamentici Upsaliensis 24. Lund: Gleerup, 1965.

Iser, Wofgang. *The Act of Reading: A Theory of Aesthetic Response*. Baltimore: Johns Hopkins University Press, 1978.

———. *The Implied Reader: Patterns of Communication in Prose Fiction from Bunyan to Beckett*. Baltimore: Johns Hopkins University Press, 1974.

Iverson, Kelly R., ed. *From Text to Performance: Narrative and Performance Criticisms in Dialogue and Debate*. Biblical Performance Criticism 10. Eugene, OR: Cascade Books, 2014.
Jerome. *Commentary on Matthew*. Translated by Thomas P. Scheck. The Fathers of the Church 117. Washington, DC: Catholic University of America Press, 2008.
Jones, Alexander. *The Gospel According to St Matthew: A Text and Commentary for Students*. New York: Sheed & Ward, 1965.
Jones, Ivor H. "Disputed Questions in Biblical Studies 4. Exile and Eschatology." *Expository Times* 112 (2001) 401–5.
Jones, John Mark. "Subverting the Textuality of Davidic Messianism: Matthew's Presentation of the Genealogy and the Davidic Title." *Catholic Biblical Quarterly* 56 (1994) 256–72.
Josephus. *Jewish Antiquities*. Translated by Henry St. John Thackeray et al. 7 vols. Loeb Classical Library. Cambridge: Harvard University Press, 1930–1965.
———. *Jewish War*. Translated by Henry St. John Thackeray et al. 3 vols. Loeb Classical Library. Cambridge: Harvard University Press, 1927–1928.
Justinian. *Digest*. 4 vols. Edited by Alan Watson. Philadelphia: University of Pennsylvania Press, 1998.
Kampen, John. *Matthew within Sectarian Judaism*. New Haven: Yale University Press, 2019.
Keener, Craig S. *A Commentary on the Gospel of Matthew*. Grand Rapids: Eerdmans, 1999.
———. "Matthew's Missiology: Making Disciples of the Nations (Matthew 28:19–20)." *Asian Journal of Pentecostal Studies* 12 (2009) 3–20.
Keerankeri, George. "The Birth of the Messiah and His Reception: Matthew's Infancy Story." *Vidyajyoti Journal* 71 (2007) 831–49.
Kelber, Werner H. *Mark's Story of Jesus*. Philadelphia: Fortress, 1979.
Kensky, Allan. "Moses and Jesus: The Birth of the Savior." *Judaism* 42 (1993) 43–49.
Kim, Hak Chol. "The Worship of Jesus in the Gospel of Matthew." *Biblica* 93 (2012) 227–41.
Kingsbury, Jack Dean. "The Birth Narrative of Matthew." In *The Gospel of Matthew in Current Study: Studies in Memory of William G. Thompson, S.J.*, edited by David E. Aune, 154–65. Grand Rapids: Eerdmans, 2001.
———. "The Developing Conflict between Jesus and Jewish Leaders in Matthew's Gospel: A Literary-Critical Study." *Catholic Biblical Quarterly* 49 (1987) 57–73.
———. "The Figure of Jesus in Matthew's Story: A Literary-Critical Probe." *Journal for the Study of the New Testament* 21 (1984) 3–36.
———. *Matthew*. 2nd ed. Proclamation Commentaries. Philadelphia: Fortress, 1986.
———. *Matthew as Story*. 2nd ed. Philadelphia: Fortress, 1988.
Kirk, J. R. Daniel. *A Man Attested by God: The Human Jesus of the Synoptic Gospels*. Grand Rapids: Eerdmans, 2016.
Kittel, Gerhard, and Gerhard Friedrich, eds. *Theological Dictionary of the New Testament*. 10 vols. Translated by Geoffrey W. Bromiley. Grand Rapids: Eerdmans, 1964–1976.
Knowles, Michael P. "Plotting Jesus: Characterization, Identity and the Voice of God in Matthew's Gospel." In *Biblical Interpretation in Early Christian Gospels. Vol. 2: The Gospel of Matthew*, edited by Thomas Hatina, 119–32. Library of New Testament Studies 310. London: T. & T. Clark, 2008.

Korthals Altes, Liesbeth. *Ethos and Narrative Interpretation: The Negotiation of Values in Fiction*. Frontiers of Narrative Series. Lincoln: University of Nebraska Press, 2014.

Krentz, Edgar. "Missionary Matthew: Matthew 28:16–20 as Summary of the Gospel." *Currents in Theology and Mission* 31 (2004) 24–31.

Kupp, David D. *Matthew's Emmanuel: Divine Presence and God's People in the First Gospel*. Society for New Testament Studies Monograph Series 90. New York: Cambridge University Press, 1996.

Kysar, Robert. *John's Story of Jesus*. Philadelphia: Fortress, 1984.

Lagrange, Marie-Joseph. *Évangile selon Saint Matthieu*. 3rd ed. Etudes bibliques. Paris: Lecoffre, 1927.

Lange, John Peter. *The Gospel According to Matthew, Together with a General Theological and Homiletical Introduction to the NT*. 5th ed. Translated by Philip Schaff. New York: Scribner, 1866.

Lee, Chee-Chiew. "Once Again: The Niphal and the Hithpael of ברך in the Abrahamic Blessing for the Nations." *Journal for the Study of the Old Testament* 36 (2012) 279–96.

Lee, Kukzin, and Francois P. Viljoen, "The Target Group of the Ultimate Commission (Matthew 28:19)." *HTS Theological Studies* 66 (2010) 91–95.

———. "The Ultimate Commission: The Key for the Gospel according to Matthew." *Acta Theologica* 30 (2010) 64–83.

Lehtipuu, Outi. "Characterization and Persuasion: The Rich Man and the Poor Man in Luke 16.19–31." In *Characterization in the Gospel: Reconceiving Narrative Criticism*, edited by David Rhoads and Kari Syreeni, 73–105. Journal for the Study of the New Testament Supplement Series 184. Sheffield: Sheffield Academic, 1999.

Léon-Dufour, Xavier, SJ. *L'évangile selon Saint Matthieu*. Lyon: Profac, 1972.

Levin, Yigal. "Jesus, 'Son of God' and 'Son of David': The 'Adoption' of Jesus into the Davidic Line." *Journal for the Study of the New Testament* 28 (2006) 415–42.

Longman, Tremper, III. *Literary Approaches to Biblical Interpretation*. Foundations of Contemporary Interpretation 3. Grand Rapids: Academie Books, 1987.

———. "The Messiah: Explorations in the Law and Writings." In *The Messiah in the Old and New Testaments*, edited by Stanley Porter, 13–34. Grand Rapids: Eerdmans, 2007.

Longstaff, Thomas R. W. "From the Birth of Jesus to the Resurrection: Women in the Gospel of Matthew." In *When Judaism and Christianity Began*. Vol. 1, *Christianity in the Beginning: Essays in Memory of Anthony J. Saldarini*, edited by Alan J. Avery-Peck et al, 147–78. Supplements to the Journal for the Study of Judaism 85. Leiden: Brill, 2004.

———. "The Women at the Tomb: Matthew 28:1 Re-examined." *New Testament Studies* 27 (1981) 277–82.

Luz, Ulrich. "The Disciples in the Gospel according to Matthew." In *The Interpretation of Matthew*, edited by Graham Stanton, 98–128. Issues in Religion and Theology 3. Philadelphia: Fortress, 1983.

———. *Matthew 1–7: A Commentary*. Translated by James E. Crouch. Hermeneia. Minneapolis: Fortress, 2007.

———. *Matthew 21–28: A Commentary*. Translated by James E. Crouch. Hermeneia. Minneapolis: Fortress, 2005.

———. *The Theology of the Gospel of Matthew.* New York: Cambridge University Press, 1995.
Malbon, Elizabeth Struthers. "Characters in Mark's Story: Changing Perspectives on the Narrative Process." In *Mark as Story: Retrospect and Prospect*, edited by Kelly R. Iverson and Christopher W. Skinner, 45–69. Resources for Biblical Study 65. Atlanta: SBL, 2011.
Marguerat, Daniel. "Le point de vue dans le récit: Matthieu, Jean et les autres." In *Studien zu Matthäus und Johannes: Festschrift für Jean Zumstein zu seinem 65. Geburtstag*, edited by Andreas Dettwiler and Uta Poplutz, 91–107. Abhandlungen zur Theologie des Alten und Neuen Testaments 97. Zurich: TVZ, 2009.
Marguerat, Daniel et al. *How to Read Bible Stories: An Introduction to Narrative Criticism.* Translated by John Bowden. London: SCM, 1999.
Mason, Steve. "N. T. Wright on Paul the Pharisee and Ancient Jews in Exile." *Scottish Journal of Theology* 69 (2016) 432–52.
Matera, Frank J. "The Plot of Matthew's Gospel." *Catholic Biblical Quarterly* 49 (1987) 233–53.
———. *Resurrection: The Origin and Goal of the Christian Life.* Collegeville, MN: Liturgical, 2015.
Matthews, Shelly. "Fleshly Resurrection, Authority Claims, and the Scriptural Practices of Lukan Christianity." *Journal of Biblical Literature* 136 (2017) 163–83.
McDonald, Patricia M. "I Am with You Always, to the End of the Age." *Proceedings of the Irish Biblical Association* 28 (2005) 66–86.
Meier, John P. *Matthew.* New Testament Message 3. Wilmington, DE: Glazier, 1980.
———. "Nations or Gentiles in Matthew 28:19?" *Catholic Biblical Quarterly* 39 (1977) 94–102.
———. *The Vision of Matthew: Christ, Church, and Morality in the First Gospel.* New York: Crossroad, 1991.
Mello, Alberto. *Évangile selon Saint Matthieu: Commentaire midrashique et narrative.* Translated by Aimée Chevillon. Lectio Divina 179. Paris: Cerf, 1999.
Merenlahti, Petri. "Characters in the Making: Individuality and Ideology in the Gospels." In *Characterization in the Gospel: Reconceiving Narrative Criticism*, edited by David Rhoads and Kari Syreeni, 49–72. Journal for the Study of the New Testament Supplement Series 184. Sheffield: Sheffield Academic, 1999.
Merenlahti, Petri, and Raimo Hakola. "Reconceiving Narrative Criticism." In *Characterization in the Gospel: Reconceiving Narrative Criticism*, edited by David Rhoads and Kari Syreeni, 13–48. Journal for the Study of the New Testament Supplement Series 184. Sheffield: Sheffield Academic, 1999.
Mitch, Curtis and Edward Sri. *The Gospel of Matthew.* Catholic Commentary on Sacred Scripture. Grand Rapids: Baker Academic, 2010.
Moloney, Francis J. *The Resurrection of the Messiah: A Narrative Commentary on the Resurrection Accounts in the Four Gospels.* New York: Paulist, 2013.
———. *The Shape of Matthew's Story.* New York: Paulist, 2023.
Moore, Stephen D. *Literary Criticism and the Gospels: The Theoretical Challenges.* New Haven: Yale University Press, 1989.
———. "Why There Are No Humans or Animals in the Gospel of Mark." In *Mark as Story: Retrospect and Prospect*, edited by Kelly R. Iverson and Christopher W. Skinner, 71–93. Resources for Biblical Study 65. Atlanta: SBL, 2011.

Morgan, James M. "Emplotment, Plot and Explotment: Refining Plot Analysis of Biblical Narratives from the Reader's Perspective." *Biblical Interpretation* 21 (2013) 64–98.

Morris, Leon. *The Gospel According to Matthew*. Grand Rapids: Eerdmans, 1992.

Mounce, Robert H. *Matthew*. New International Bible Commentary. Peabody, MA: Hendrickson, 1991.

Navarre, University of, Faculty of Theology. *The Navarre Bible: Saint Matthew's Gospel*. Dublin: Four Courts, 1988.

Nicklas, Tobias. "Resurrection: Some Biblical Perspectives." In "Resurrection", edited by Béatrice Faye et al. Translated by Francis McDonagh. *Concilium* 2 (2024) 17–26.

Noble, Paul R. *The Canonical Approach: A Critical Reconstruction of the Hermeneutics of Brevard S. Childs*. Biblical Interpretation Series 16. Leiden: Brill, 1995.

Nolland, John. "Genealogical Annotation in Genesis as Background for the Matthean Genealogy of Jesus." *Tyndale Bulletin* 47 (1996) 115–22.

Oepke, Albrecht. "ὄναρ." In *Theological Dictionary of the New Testament*, vol 5, edited by Gerhard Friedrich, 220–38. Translated by Geoffrey W. Bromiley. Grand Rapids: Eerdmans, 1968.

Osborne, Grant R. *Matthew*. Exegetical Commentary on the New Testament. Grand Rapids: Zondervan, 2010.

———. *The Resurrection Narratives: A Redactional Study*. Grand Rapids: Baker, 1984.

Patte, Daniel. *The Gospel According to Matthew: A Structural Commentary on Matthew's Faith*. Philadelphia: Fortress, 1987.

Pennington, Jonathan. *Reading the Gospels Wisely: A Narrative and Theological Introduction*. Grand Rapids: Baker Academic, 2012.

Perrin, Norman. "The Evangelist as Author: Reflections on Method in the Study and Interpretation of the Synoptic Gospels and Acts." *Biblical Research* 17 (1972) 5–18.

Peterson, Norman R. *Literary Criticism for New Testament Critics*. Guides to Biblical Scholarship. Philadelphia: Fortress, 1978.

Phelan, James, and Peter J. Rabinowitz, eds. *A Companion to Narrative Theory*. Blackwell Companions to Literature and Culture 33. Malden, MA: Blackwell, 2005.

Philo. *On Abraham. On Joseph. On Moses*. Translated by F. H. Colson. Loeb Classical Library. Cambridge: Harvard University Press, 1935.

Piotrowski, Nicholas G. "'After the Deportation': Observations in Matthew's Apocalyptic Genealogy." *Bulletin for Biblical Research* 25 (2015) 189–203.

Poe, Harry Lee. *The Gospel and Its Meaning: A Theology for Evangelism and Church Growth*. Grand Rapids: Zondervan, 1996.

Powell, Mark Allan. "Characterization on the Phraseological Plane in the Gospel of Matthew." In *Treasures New and Old: Recent Contributions to Matthean Studies*, edited by David R. Bauer and Mark Allan Powell, 161–78. SBL Symposium Series 1. Atlanta: Scholars, 1996.

———. *Chasing the Eastern Star: Adventures in Biblical Reader-Response Criticism*. Louisville: Westminster John Knox, 2001.

———. "The Magi as Kings: An Adventure in Reader-Response Criticism." *Catholic Biblical Quarterly* 62 (2000) 459–80.

———, ed. *Methods for Matthew*. Methods in Biblical Interpretation. New York: Cambridge University Press, 2009.

———. "Narrative Criticism: The Emergence of a Prominent Reading Strategy." In *Mark as Story: Retrospect and Prospect*, edited by Kelly R. Iverson and Christopher W. Skinner, 20–43. Resources for Biblical Study 65. Atlanta: SBL, 2011.

———. "The Plot and Subplots of Matthew's Gospel." *New Testament Studies* 38 (1992) 187–204.

———. "The Religious Leaders in Matthew's Gospel: A Literary-Critical Approach." PhD diss., Union Theological Seminary in Virginia, 1985.

———. *What Is Narrative Criticism?* Guides to Biblical Scholarship. Minneapolis: Fortress, 1990.

Pregeant, Russell. *Matthew*. Chalice Commentaries for Today. Saint Louis: Chalice, 2004.

Prince, Deborah T. "'Why Do You Seek the Living among the Dead?': Rhetorical Questions in the Lukan Resurrection Narrative." *Journal of Biblical Literature* 135 (2016) 123–39.

Quarles, Charles L. *Matthew*. Exegetical Guide for the Greek New Testament. Nashville: B&H, 2017.

Quesnel, Michel. "De quelques avatars du titre neotestamentaire Fils de Dieu et de leurs consequences en christologie." *Transversalites* 86 (2003) 53–70.

Reeves, Keith Howard. "The Resurrection Narrative in Matthew: A Literary-Critical Examination." PhD diss., Union Theological Seminary in Virginia, 1988.

———. *The Resurrection Narrative in Matthew: A Literary-Critical Examination*. Lewiston, NY: Mellen Biblical, 1993.

Reeves, Rodney. *Matthew*. The Story of God Bible Commentary. Grand Rapids: Zondervan Academic, 2017.

Repschinski, Boris. "'For He Will Save His People from Their Sins' (Matthew 1:21): A Christology for Christian Jews." *Catholic Biblical Quarterly* 68 (2006) 248–67.

Resseguie, James L. *Narrative Criticism of the New Testament: An Introduction*. Grand Rapids: Baker Academic, 2005.

Rhoads, David. "Narrative Criticism and the Gospel of Mark." *Journal of the American Academy of Religion* 50 (1982) 411–34.

Rhoads, David, and Donald Michie. *Mark as Story: An Introduction to the Narrative of the Gospel*. Philadelphia: Fortress, 1982.

Rhoads, David and Joanna Dewey. "Performance Criticism: A Paradigm Shift in New Testament Studies." In *From Text to Performance: Narrative and Performance Criticisms in Dialogue and Debate*, edited by Kelly R. Iverson, 1–26. Biblical Performance Criticism 10. Eugene, OR: Cascade Books, 2014.

Rhoads, David, et al. *Mark as Story: An Introduction to the Narrative of a Gospel*. 2nd ed. Minneapolis: Fortress, 1999.

———. *Mark as Story: An Introduction to the Narrative of a Gospel*. 3rd ed. Minneapolis: Fortress, 2012.

Richardson, Peter, and Amy Marie Fisher. *Herod: King of the Jews and Friend of the Romans*. 2nd ed. New York: Routledge, 2018.

Roberts, J. J. M. "The Old Testament's Contribution to Messianic Expectations." In *The Messiah: Developments in Earliest Judaism and Christianity: The First Princeton Symposium on Judaism and Christian Origins*, edited by James H. Charlesworth, 39–51. Minneapolis: Fortress, 1992.

Rogers, Cleon. "The Promises to David in Early Judaism." *Bibliotheca Sacra* 150 (1993) 285–302.

Rogers, Trent. "The Great Commission as the Climax of Matthew's Mountain Scenes." *Bulletin for Biblical Research* 22 (2012) 383–98.

Saint Athanasius Orthodox Academy. *Orthodox Study Bible*. Nashville: Nelson, 2008.

Saldarini, Anthony J. *Pharisees, Scribes and Sadducees in Palestinian Society*. Wilmington, DE: Glazier, 1988.

Sánchez Navarro, Luis A. "The Revealer of the Son: Narrative Function of the Father of Jesus in the Gospel of Saint Matthew." In *'Perché stessero con Lui': scritti in onore di Klemens Stock SJ, nel suo 75° compleanno*, edited by Lorenzo de Santos and Santi Grasso, 71–83. Translated by Paul S. Stevenson. Analecta Biblica 180. Rome: Gregorian & Biblical Press, 2010.

Scaer, David P. "The Relation of Matthew 28:16–20 to the Rest of the Gospel." *Catholic Theological Quarterly* 56 (1992) 245–66.

———. "Sadducees, the Resurrection, and an Early Date for Matthew." *Catholic Theological Quarterly* 88 (2024) 143–59.

Schneider, M. and Leroy Andrew Huizenga. "Das Matthäusevangelium in intertextueller Perspektive." *Zeitschrift für Neues Testament* 8 (2005) 20–29.

Schniewind, Julius. *Das Evangelium nach Matthäus*. Göttingen: Vandenhoech & Ruprecht, 1984.

Schreiner, Patrick. *Matthew, Disciple and Scribe: The First Gospel and Its Portrait of Jesus*. Grand Rapids: Baker Academic, 2019.

Schweizer, Eduard. *Das Evangelium nach Matthäus: Übersetzt und Erklärt*. Göttingen: Vandenhoeck & Ruprecht, 1981.

———. *Good News According to Matthew*. Translated by David E. Green. Atlanta: John Knox, 1975.

Senior, Donald. "Directions in Matthean Studies." In *The Gospel of Matthew in Current Study: Studies in Memory of William G. Thompson, S.J.*, edited by David E. Aune, 5–21. Grand Rapids: Eerdmans, 2001.

———. *The Gospel of Matthew*. Interpreting Biblical Texts. Nashville: Abingdon, 1997.

Shively, Elizabeth E. Review of *A Man Attested by God: The Human Jesus of the Synoptic Gospels*, by J. R. Daniel Kirk. *Journal of the Evangelical Theological Society* 60 (2017) 637–39.

Skinner, Christopher W. "Telling the Story: The Appearance and Impact of 'Mark as Story.'" In *Mark as Story: Retrospect and Prospect*, edited by Kelly R. Iverson and Christopher W. Skinner, 1–16. Resources for Biblical Study 65. Atlanta: SBL, 2011.

Skinner, Matthew L. *Locating Paul: Places of Custody as Narrative Settings in Acts 21–28*. Society of Biblical Literature Academia Biblica 13. Atlanta: SBL, 2003.

Soares-Prabhu, George M. "Jesus in Egypt: A Reflection on Mt 2:13–15,19–21 in the Light of the Old Testament." *Estudios Biblicos* 50 (1992) 225–49.

Sonnet, Jean-Pierre. "De la généalogie au 'faites disciples' (Mt 28.19): le livre de la génération de Jesus." In *Analyse narrative et Bible: deuxiéme colloque international de RRENAB, Louvain-la-Neuve, avril 2004*, edited by Camille Focant and André Wénin, 199–209. Bibliotheca Ephemeridum theologicarum Lovaniensium 191. Leuven: Leuven University Press, 2005.

Stock, Augustine. *The Method and Message of Matthew*. Collegeville, MN: Liturgical Press, 1994.

Strauss, Mark L. *Mark*. Exegetical Commentary on the New Testament. Grand Rapids: Zondervan, 2014.

Talbert, Charles H. *Matthew*. Paideia Commentaries on the New Testament. Grand Rapids: Baker Academic, 2010.
Tannehill, Robert C. *The Narrative Unity of Luke-Acts*. 2 vols. Philadelphia: Fortress, 1986–1990.
Tate, Marvin. *Psalms 51–100*. Word Biblical Commentary 20. Dallas: Word, 1990.
Thiselton, Anthony C. *New Horizons in Hermeneutics*. Grand Rapids: Zondervan, 1992.
Thompson, William G. *Matthew's Advice to a Divided Community (Mt 17,22—18,35)*. Analecta Biblica 44. Rome: Biblical Institute, 1970.
———. "Reflections on the Composition of Mt 8:1—9:34." *Catholic Biblical Quarterly* 33 (1971) 365–88.
Tidball, Derek. "Completing the Circle: The Resurrection according to John." *Evangelical Review of Theology* 30 (2006) 169–83.
Tomasulo, Frank P. Review of *Story and Discourse*, by Seymour Chatman. *Journal of the University Film Association* 32 (1980) 71–74.
Tsumura, David Toshio. *The First Book of Samuel*. New International Commentary on the Old Testament. Grand Rapids: Eerdmans, 2007.
Turner, David L. *Matthew*. Baker Exegetical Commentary on the New Testament. Grand Rapids: Baker Academic, 2008.
Van Aarde, Andries. "The Ideological/Theological Perspective in Matthew's Story." In *God-With-Us: The Dominant Perspective in Matthew's Story and Other Essays*, 34–43. Hervormde Teologiese Studies Supplementum 5. Pretoria: Hervormde Teologiese Studies, 1994.
———. "Plot Mediated through Point of View: Mt 22:1–14—A Case Study." In *A South African Perspective on the New Testament: Essays by South African New Testament Scholars Presented to Bruce Manning Metzger During His Visit*, edited by J. H. Hartin and P. J. Petzer, 62–75. Leiden: Brill, 1986.
Van Oyen, Geert. "No Performance Criticism without Narrative Criticism: Performance as a Test of Interpretation" In *Communication, Pedagogy, and the Gospel of Mark*, edited by Elizabeth E. Shively and Geert van Oyen, 107–28. Resources for Biblical Study 83. Atlanta: SBL, 2016.
Vermes, Geza. *The True Herod*. New York: Bloomsbury, 2014.
Viljoen, Francois P. "The characterisation of the Matthean Jesus by the angel of the Lord." *Verbum at Ecclesia* 41 (2020) 1–8.
———. "The Matthean Characterisation of Jesus by Angels." *HTS Theological Studies* 76 (2020) 1–7.
Vinson, Richard. "'King of the Jews': Kingship and Anti-Kingship Rhetoric in Matthew's Birth, Baptism, and Transfiguration Narratives." *Review and Expositor* 104 (2007) 243–68.
Viviano, Benedict Thomas. "God in the Gospel According to Matthew." *Interpretation* 64 (2010) 341–54.
Wallace, Daniel B. *Greek Grammar Beyond the Basics: An Exegetical Syntax of the New Testament*. Grand Rapids: Zondervan, 1996.
Weaver, Dorothy Jean. "Power and Powerlessness: Matthew's Use of Irony in the Portrayal of Political Leaders." In *Treasures New and Old: Recent Contributions to Matthean Studies*, edited by David R. Bauer and Mark Allan Powell, 179–96. SBL Symposium Series 1. Atlanta: Scholars, 1996.
———. "Rewriting the Messianic Script: Matthew's Account of the Birth of Jesus." *Interpretation* 54 (2000) 376–85.

Weren, Wim. "Children in Matthew: A Semantic Study." In *Little Children Suffer*, edited by Maureen Junker-Kenny and Norbert Mette, 53–63. London: SCM, 1996.

White, Stephen L. "Angel of the Lord: Messenger or Euphemism?" *Tyndale Bulletin* 50 (1999) 299–305.

Wilkins, Michael J. *Matthew*. New International Version Application Commentary. Grand Rapids: Zondervan, 2004.

Williams, Joel F. "The Characterization of Jesus as Lord in Mark's Gospel." In *Character Studies and the Gospel of Mark*, edited by Christopher W. Skinner and Matthew Ryan Hauge, 107–26. Library of New Testament Studies 483. New York: Bloomsbury, 2014.

Willis, Steve. "Matthew's Birth Stories: Prophecy and the Magi." *Expository Times* 105 (1993) 43–45.

Witherington, Ben, III. *New Testament Rhetoric: An Introductory Guide to the Art of Persuasion in and of the New Testament*. Eugene, OR: Cascade Books, 2009.

Witherup, Ronald D. "The Cross of Jesus: A Literary-Critical Study of Matthew 27." PhD diss., Union Theological Seminary in Virginia, 1985.

Woodley, Matt. *The Gospel of Matthew: God with Us*. Resonate Series. Downers Grove, IL: InterVarsity, 2011.

Wright, N. T. *Matthew for Everyone: Part 2, Chapters 16–28*. London: SPCK, 2002.

———. *The New Testament and the People of God*. Christian Origins and the Question of God 1. Minneapolis: Fortress, 1992.

———. *The Resurrection of the Son of God*. Christian Origins and the Question of God 3. Minneapolis: Fortress: 2003.

Yamasaki, Gary. *John the Baptist in Life and Death: Audience-oriented Criticism of Matthew's Narrative*. Journal for the Study of the New Testament Supplement Series 167. Sheffield: Sheffield Academic, 1998.

Zacharias, H. Daniel. *Matthew's Presentation of the Son of David: Davidic Tradition and Typology in the Gospel of Matthew*. T&T Clark Biblical Studies. London: Bloomsbury T. & T. Clark, 2017.

www.ingramcontent.com/pod-product-compliance
Lightning Source LLC
Chambersburg PA
CBHW070254230426
43664CB00014B/2526